When All the
World Was Young

When All the World Was Young

A Memoir

BARBARA HOLLAND

BLOOMSBURY

Published by Bloomsbury Publishing, New York and London
Distributed to the trade by Holtzbrinck Publishers

All papers used by Bloomsbury Publishing are natural, recyclable products made from wood grown in well-managed forests. The manufacturing processes conform to the environmental regulations of the country of origin.

Library of Congress Cataloging-in-Publication Data

Holland, Barbara.
   When all the world was young : a memoir / Barbara Holland.
      p. cm.
   ISBN 1–58234–525–2 (hardcover)
   1. Holland, Barbara—Childhood and youth. 2. Holland, Barbara—
Homes and haunts—Washington (D.C.). 3. Authors, American—20th century—
Biography. 4. Washington (D.C.)—Social life and customs. 5. Journalists—
United States—Biography. I. Title.

PS3558.O34789Z477 2005
813′.54—dc22

                                                      2004014826

ISBN-13 9781582345253

First U.S. Edition 2005

1 3 5 7 9 10 8 6 4 2

Typeset by Hewer Text Ltd, Edinburgh
Printed in the United States of America
by Quebecor World Fairfield

To my noble & tireless agent, Al Hart

Contents

IN WHICH THE CHAIRS & DOMESTIC HABITS OF FATHERS ARE EXPLORED, & NICK IS BORN

To begin with, there was the chair. Every household had the chair. It was the most comfortable and by far the largest in the house, usually covered in green or maroon leather, with the only adequate reading light and often a footstool or ottoman in front of it, and it was the Father's chair. Neither wife nor child sat there, even when the Father was out of town on business or off at the war. In his absence the chair represented him, stood *in loco parentis*, and imposed order on the room. Thus did Ulysses's chair wait for him, while Penelope and Telemachus perched on stools.

Oh, maybe for a brief dangerous joke. I can see in memory a small child of three or four clambering up into the chair and, giggling, leaning back and spreading his arms as if reading a newspaper, and then, frightened by his own miniature patricide, scrambling back down and scampering away. The child is not me. Possibly my next-younger brother; I was a girl, and a dismal coward.

When the Father came home from work he sat in his chair and opened his newspaper and was not to be bothered, not that anyone would dream of such a thing. He had had a hard day at work: all days at work were by definition hard days. Nobody had any clear idea what fathers did by day; we might have asked and been given a job title like lawyer or superintendent or bureau chief, but we knew nothing about what this entailed except that it was hard, and beyond our comprehension. Fathers never discussed it, any more than the Delphic oracles would have babbled about their mysteries around the house.

When I went to Cynthia's house to play, we played quietly,

like all proper children, in her bedroom. Her mother, like all mothers except my own, would have made up her bed as soon as she got out of it, all sealed up tight and wrinkle-free and the pillow centered, so we weren't allowed to sit on it or even touch it. We played on the small, chilly square of linoleum floor space, jacks or board games or Pick-Up-Sticks, until her father came home. Her mother would put her head around the bedroom door to signal his coming, and I slipped quickly and silently, like the shadow of a child, out the kitchen door as Cynthia's father came up the front walk. I never saw his face.

Fathers used the front door, always. There was no actual rule, at least in my circles, against other people using it, and Mothers rarely went out anyway, but basically it was the Father's door. He came through it, and sat in his chair, and unfurled his newspaper.

Magazine ads sometimes showed fathers among their children. Ads for station wagons showed a father proudly displaying his acquisition to a romping boy, girl, and Dalmatian; ads for the *Encyclopedia Britannica* showed him in his big leather chair with his leather slippers on, reading aloud from a volume to a boy and girl crouched beside him and a Mother leaning over his shoulder, the whole family laughing with glee. My friends and I had never seen fathers acting like that, but somewhere, perhaps; who knew?

The other Father's chair stood at the head of the dinner table, which is why round dinner tables will never sell and King Arthur's dream of equality faded. The Father chair at the table—pompous manufacturers call it the captain's chair—had, and has, and always will have, arms, the mark of striking power, while the lesser chairs have only legs, or fleeing power. No one but the Father sits in the Father chair. Here he presides over the food and parcels it out, and sometimes stands to dismember a roast or a

4

turkey, and glances around the table, and dispenses it judiciously while the family waits, always with the understanding that, if he chooses, he can withhold it, or eat it all himself.

At the family dinner table then, just as now by the barbecue grill, men commanded the meat, they were the priests of meat, they subdued it and dispensed it. Vegetables and other secondary matters, being female, may be passed around by mothers or the maid, but meat is male and needs a man's hand.

In some houses the Father also had a closed-off space of his own, called a den or study or office, where not even the cleaning woman was allowed, and when a child of the family was called in there for conference it was serious indeed, meaning a truly awful transgression, some life-shaking change, or the obligatory lecture on sex to a son. Sometimes, my friends said, a mother would be called into the study, usually about money matters, while children waited anxiously and tried to eavesdrop.

Basically, of course, the whole house and everything in it belonged to the Father, and he often said things like, "Not in *my* house, you don't, young man." My friends and I were all deathly afraid of our fathers, which was right and proper and even biblically ordained. Fathers were angry; it was their job. The language is rich with contempt for an angry woman, an unnatural creature—termagant, scold, shrew, fishwife, virago, harridan—but an angry man is awesome. Anger is his badge of manhood. If here and there some child had a Father who was kindly and mild, that child would lie about him and invent terrible beatings, since who would admit being sired by such a limp excuse for a man?

Fathers were the necessary antidote to Mothers, who by their very nature were fond and foolish and lacking in the firmness of character needed to put their foot down. Mothers could never say "no," Fathers rarely said anything else. With girls, it didn't much matter, but a boy who grew up fatherless would be a poor useless specimen, lazy and timid, with fat, soft hands. In some times and places motherly care was considered so toxic to boys that they were sent away very young, to British boarding schools or, in feudal times, to grow up in the household of a neighboring baron, where they could cry themselves to sleep alone until the toughening process took hold.

I see by the newspaper that today, as then and always, the experts agree that children raised without a resident Father do badly in school, suffer emotional and behavioral problems, and often end up in jail. Nobody spells out the essential ingredient, but it would seem to be fear, pure and simple, necessary nourishment for the growing child.

I was probably more afraid than most, and with reason. Mine was not what was called my "real father." The transition from real to unreal remains shrouded in mystery. My mother, always morbidly reticent on personal matters, explained nothing. At some point when I was perhaps four my real father faded from the picture, and then Mother and I were in Hot Springs, Arkansas, where divorces, I found out later, could be had after three months' residence. (She would never have gone to rowdy six-week Reno, code word for irresponsible women.)

Then somehow we were back in Washington, living in a vast old house near Dupont Circle that my new stepfather shared with some law school or Labor Department cronies. Nothing was explained. I suppose there'd been a wedding of some sort, but I don't remember hearing about it and certainly I wasn't invited. I suppose I must have been introduced to the man before we moved in with him, but that too is a blank.

In our new life I was to stay as much as possible out of sight, eating supper in the kitchen with a housekeeper, who complained about the extra work, and climbing the back stairs from the kitchen to my back bedroom, where I waited and waited for Mother to come tuck me in and say goodnight. Then we moved to a little row house in Georgetown.

I was to call the man by his first name. Not call him, exactly, since I wasn't encouraged to address him directly, but refer to him. At the time, a handful of militant progressives were in favor of children calling their parents by their first names, first names being more democratic than the hierarchical Mother and Father, but democracy can hardly have been the point here. No doubt the man recoiled at the thought of this cuckoo's child in his nest, this dependent trailing-behind leftover embarrassment of his new wife's, calling him Father.

Even now, and he's long dead, I'm afraid to write his name out, invoking bad luck, reprisals, ill winds. Just thinking his name brings him back too vividly and I can even remember his smell, not noxious but sharp and distinct like a whiff of danger in the forest. I will call him, instead, maybe "Carl," since that wasn't his name.

As might have been foreseen, this was a problem as his own children came along, since how to explain that they were to call him Dad while I called him Carl? All the children, five of us eventually, called him Carl, and never was there a man less suited to irreverence. Not that we felt it as such: like Jehovah, he was a force to be reckoned with under any name. In fact, "Dad" would have implied an unseemly chumminess, a kind of back-

7

slapping familiarity. Early on, in moments of affection, my mother called him "Sir." Perhaps we should have too.

Carl might have liked me better if I'd been more winsome and sunny, but in my mother's Brownie snapshots of the time I was a stolid, frightened-looking child with round cheeks, straight yellow hair, and round dark anxious eyes. Apparently I never smiled. Under the lax previous regime of my mother, her sisters, my grandparents, and perhaps my real father as well, I had been allowed, even encouraged, to talk, and I did. The only child on the premises for those first years, I developed a phenomenal vocabulary and often, they say, made clever and perceptive comments; in short, a real pain in the neck, classic precocious child of the times. Carl, as he himself said, put his foot down. I was often allowed to eat dinner with them, but I was not to talk at the table. Nursery school had taught me to raise my hand to be called on to speak, so I tried that, and Carl snapped, "Stop giving us that Nazi salute." I dropped my hand and closed my mouth.

This was the Father of the dinner table, the Father whose words and silences ruled the discourse or lack of it. A Father might, at table, ask his children what they'd learned in school today, but he was not bound to listen to the answers, if any. Sometimes he would speak on the issues of the day, but his words were addressed to an abstract audience, not a specific listener, and called for no comment. Later, I had a friend with a jolly father who told jokes at the table, and his family laughed, but it would have been impertinent for them to offer jokes of their own, and unthinkable for a Mother to tell one, anywhere.

Sometimes, to relieve the tension, Mother gave me a sandwich in the kitchen and put me to bed very early, before Carl came home, and I lay for hours watching the sunlight on the tree in the back yard, my arms held rigidly at my sides because of the wolves under the bed lurking in wait for exposed flesh.

On weekends, at an unusual expense, I was put in a taxi and sent far uptown to stay with my grandparents, to be returned only at bedtime Sunday. My grandfather died, leaving in memory only a sweet whiff of pipe smoke and the smoke rings he blew for me to poke my finger through, but my grandmother was always kind to me, and asked me what I'd like for breakfast, and let me follow her around talking.

Another figure comes and goes in memory, my aunt Lois, Mother's middle sister, still unmarried, working in a bookstore and living at home. Understandably, she wasn't much interested in me, but sometimes she gave me bits of costume jewelry she was tired of, or paused in her busy life to tell me odd facts about adulthood, and once she tried to teach me to dance, me with my bare feet on top of her shoes, moving me back and forth, but I couldn't make sense of it and never did learn properly. Sometimes beaux of hers came by, maybe dressed in shorts and sneakers and carrying tennis rackets, maybe down in the basement playing Ping-Pong, which sent wonderfully pleasant pockety-pocking sounds up through the floor.

But it was Grandmother who took care of me. She was a brisk, no-nonsense little woman, made brisker by forty years of teaching history in public high school, and capable domestically as Mother never was. She chopped onions, stuffed chickens, slapped raw food into cooked obedience. In the grocery store she argued with the produce manager about his choice of apples and spoke slightingly of "cold-storage eggs," so long removed from their mother that they needed refrigeration.

In the summer I squatted in the grass to watch her enforcing

9

discipline among the cabbages and fruit trees. She told me the names of the flowers, and I remembered them always: "tradescantia," she would say, and thirty years later a flower hundreds of miles away would say "tradescantia" in my head. In summer, I slept on the second-floor screened porch and apples thumped down on the roof. In winter she built a fire in the fireplace that always burned perfectly, and I sat and stared all evening at the coals until my eyes were scalded.

I suppose she saved my life. Without her, I might have committed suicide as soon as I grasped the possibility, but I could never repay her with the unconditional love she deserved. She was undemonstrative, unsentimental, and she was neither Mother nor Father, only a parent-once-removed, so her attention somehow slid off me as not quite the real thing, not nourishing enough. She couldn't affect my life at home and her kindness drifted away like feathers during the long dark taxi ride back, where I was alone with my new life.

Carl, always frugal, was mindful of heat and electric bills, and coming home from Grandmother's warm, lighted house struck a blow of reality. Carl grew up in Michigan and I think he felt that darkness and chill were the stuff of moral fiber. He was a lapsed Irish Catholic and proud atheist, but he would have been perfectly cast as a Lutheran minister in an Ingmar Bergman film, a tall, long-jawed man with long, bony hands and feet, eyes like small blue pebbles, and a voice that dropped decisively at the end of a sentence, closing the subject.

It was during this transition period that I did one of the most shameful things I have ever done, something that even now, a lifetime later, makes me squirm with disgust. I have never confessed this to anyone; perhaps writing it down will draw out some of the sting. Confessions are said to be healing.

Here it is. Carl sat in the Father chair in the living room. I walked straight over to him, propelled by God knows what alien demons, certainly not of my own volition, and I said, "Can I sit in your lap?"

I don't even know why "lap" occurred to me, since laps, except for convenience when pulling on my shoes and socks, weren't featured anywhere in the family. This was clearly not me, not my words. Not my thought.

No, it doesn't feel healing to admit it. It feels almost as humiliating as it did at the time.

He didn't answer, of course, and he glanced down at me only briefly, but I can still feel the withering contempt of his look and how richly I deserved it, and somehow still do. It was an act of purest toadying. Abject, groveling, dishonest. A worm's whine for mercy.

I don't even remember how I got myself out of the room afterwards. Certainly Mother wouldn't have helped, since any help would have been disloyal to Carl, but perhaps she didn't notice; she had a wonderful talent for not noticing and avoided confrontation always.

In all the decades since, I have never been able to ask any man, however well disposed, for affection. My shame stays green. It extends to other people, and when a friend asks her husband for a kiss, I wince and cringe for her.

How would matters have gone if I'd been a boy instead of a girl, trailing into the marriage behind my mother's ankles; maybe a boy with my real father's straight black hair and aristocratic nose? Not a happy thought. I've read that children are roughly a hundred times more likely to be killed by their stepfathers than by their biological fathers, which may be ungracious but makes good genetic sense: when a lion takes over a previously married lioness, his first act is to kill her cubs by the former mate. Girls, being of less consequence and no territorial threat, are always safer; who would bother to kill a girl, except perhaps in time of famine to save on food?

A few weeks after I turned five, I was sent to Grandmother's in the middle of the week, and when I was sent back home, Mother had brought a new baby into the house, my brother Nick. I was horrified. How could she have been so reckless and irresponsible? She must have known what would happen, seen how it would be. I at least understood what was expected and worked mightily to please; I'd cried terribly over *The Story of Ferdinand* because he didn't do what he was expected to do and I was worried and ashamed for him. But the baby didn't know a word of English and everything he did called down doom on his downy head. He howled when Carl was trying to read his paper; he howled at night when Carl needed his sleep. He fouled his diapers and made outrageous demands on Mother's time and attention, even during dinner. He was totally ignorant of the danger he was in; how could he know? He just got here.

Apparently Mother didn't understand the danger either. She had, as I said, a great capacity for refusing to notice. Apparently only I realized that any minute now, probably in the night, Carl would put his foot down and bundle both of us, me and the baby, out of his house onto the sidewalk and slam the door.

What would I do? Launching myself into a ten-year bout of insomnia, I wrestled with my coming responsibility. I had no illusions; I knew I couldn't take care of myself on my own, even without a baby. Somehow I would have to get us to Grandmother's house. A cockier five-year-old might have imagined walking, but I knew it was too far, too strange and fierce, and Nick was a heavy armful; I could barely stagger across the room carrying him. A stranger would have to help. I pinned my hopes on strangers who, not knowing me, might be more inclined to kindness. I imagined strangers passing the busy corner, down at M Street, on their way home from work, in their topcoats. I would tug at their sleeves and coattails, explaining, until one of them smiled and flagged down a taxi. Once in the taxi, we'd be safe. Somehow the taxi would find Grandmother's house, and she would open the door and take us in, and build a fire in the fireplace.

I fidgeted with this scenario far into the nights. When Nick woke up and cried in the dark, I stiffened and wondered whether Carl would give me time to dress, or would I be out in the street in my pajamas, lugging the baby, and the strangers all gone home to their houses. If anyone had told me it was illegal for respectable fathers to thrust their small children out of the house, I wouldn't have believed it; what child would? Impossible to imagine even armies of policemen outranking or intimidating a Father, not in his own house.

Months passed. Nick's manners slowly improved, and he slept through the night. Propped up, he gaped like a baby bird while I spooned in his cereal and scraped the overflow from his chin. I ran my finger down the wrinkled, unused skin of his foot and he clenched his toes. He writhed and gurgled when I blew into his fat stomach. I helped wash and dry and dress him, and the feel of his skin was new and strangely pleasing; flesh other than my own, all warm and rubbery and elastic.

Families like ours, the middle class of northern European stock, didn't touch each other back then. The current practice of hugging, now considered indispensable in family groups and even in politics, would have seemed vulgar and slightly indecent; emotional; *Mediterranean.*

Freud was in full swing, and it was best to touch children as rarely and coolly as possible to avoid sexualizing them; even infants were a seething cauldron of latent sexuality which, if awakened, would lead straight to neurosis. I got my first non-romantic hug in the early 1980s, at a street fair in Philadelphia, from an ample black lady working a church booth. No strings attached. Just free hugs. She clasped me briefly to her big warm bosom and then moved on to the next applicant. It was quite wonderful. I was dazzled.

I don't remember Carl ever holding Nick, or taking an interest in him. Surely the man must have been gratified, his firstborn being a male? It's the fashion now to pretend it doesn't matter, but people were franker then and "It's a boy!" was a shout of triumph in the delivery room and later, in the office, with cigars handed out and congratulations, as if the new father had created a son with his bare hands. Often, to underline his success, he addressed the product as "Son" for the rest of his life; daughters were never called "Daughter." "It's a girl" was a setback to be dealt with, at least on the first try. If the second was another girl, relatives urged the Mother to keep trying until she got it right. (Modern medical science has stolen the surprise, but at least the parents have months now to reconcile themselves to the outcome.) Most people, consciously or unconsciously, agreed with Aristotle that a girl was simply a defective boy, a common developmental failure in utero.

Oddly, once the father of a series of girls adjusted to his fate, he often learned to enjoy it, and swaggered like a sultan when he came home, and called his womenfolk to come kiss him. The master of a happy harem has it easier than the father of sons.

Daughters incubate no secret threats or future rivalry; his main responsibility is fending off unsuitable suitors, which is nothing compared to shaping satisfactory boys, manly and ambitious yet deferring always to the sire.

Girls, being simpler organisms with only a single destiny, couldn't help growing up to be women, but boys had to be taught to be men. Sonless fathers may choose a daughter to be an honorary son, and teach her to throw overhand and play golf, and enjoy her in peace, since she's never a hierarchical threat. For the sheer ego of it, though, a son is the thing to have, living proof that one's seed was forceful enough to conquer the egg's natural inclination to be a girl.

Nick was a boy, the right move to start with, and he'd survived, but I knew better than to drop my guard, since anything or nothing might set Carl in a rage, and by this time I'd lost the habit of sleeping.

Grandmother had a small house built for herself out in the woods beyond Bethesda, and moved to it, and we moved into her old familiar house where her gardens still grew, and her several kinds of apple trees—you didn't eat the pie apples or make pies out of the eating apples, and applesauce was made only from windfalls, with the wasps shooed away and the bruises cut out—and the sour-cherry tree that could be climbed from the vantage point of the garage roof. It wasn't Carl's house—we were only renting it, or maybe borrowing it—and I felt safer there, still under Grandmother's leftover wing. On weekends I was sent to her new house in the woods and watched her dig her new gardens.

Mother went to the hospital and came home with another baby, Judith, but I couldn't see that we really needed another one. Nick was on his feet now, which he found hugely funny, and gripped my finger and staggered around on his fat legs roaring with laughter.

I was allowed out. Here in this gentle old suburb, the doors opened and a person could haul her tricycle down the porch steps and look around at the outside world. There were other children out there. For a while I lurked in my own front yard and inspected them from a safe distance, but then some of them came over and interrogated me, and I merged with them, a bit diffidently, but accepted.

Claire was my age and lived at the corner of Upland Terrace. We played. I don't remember Claire coming to my house, but I went to hers, and examined it closely to see what the world was like, since other people's lives always feel more valid than one's own.

Her house was formal and spotless, full of polished dark furniture, and we weren't to touch anything in the downstairs rooms. In the dining room tall white candles stood in ranks in their silvery candlesticks, and I asked Claire's mother when she was going to light them. Oh, no, she said, you mustn't light them because it makes them ugly, the wicks turn black. Unlit, they stay pretty. I filed this curious fact away. Once or twice I was invited to stay for lunch, and we had to keep our left hands on the table, palm down flat, beside our plates. When Claire let hers drop into her lap, her mother smiled and shook her head and picked it up by the wrist and laid it back where it belonged. This too I filed away.

Claire's mother never read to her, being too busy with her house, and this gave me an edge. Mother was reading me *Peter Pan*, and I decided to try out this flying business on Claire before I risked it myself. I explained how a pinch of fairy dust and a little faith would let her soar through the air like a bird, and I found some suitable-looking dust and rubbed it on her arms and led her up the back steps. "You can fly," I told her. "Jump! Jump!"

Luckily she wasn't badly hurt and didn't tell her mother. Wrong kind of dust, I decided.

One sunny day we found the garage door open and looked inside, sniffing concrete and engine oil. Claire's father, like her mother, was orderly, and all his manly tools and implements were neatly arranged. A set of tire chains hung from hooks on the wall, though here in the mild and well-kept suburbs he can't have needed them often, and they looked to me like horse-harness.

We unhooked them and I fastened them onto Claire and drove her around the yard at a gallop, clicking my tongue and flapping the chains up and down. Cold and heavy and serious, they made a satisfying change from toys. We circled the house several times, but Claire kept complaining that they hurt her neck, so we put them back and wandered off to do something else.

That evening Claire's mother called my mother. Claire's father, she said, was very, very angry. Apparently we hadn't hung them back the way he'd had them, and even in full summer he must have checked them daily when he came home from work, or just run an eye around his domain of rakes and shovels and such, and the disorder of the chains sprang out at him, and Claire was sent to her room in disgrace.

I was not, Claire's mother said, to play with Claire for a week, and I must promise never, never to touch her father's things again, but only to play with Claire's nice toys. She extracted a proxy apology from my mother, who hung up the phone and sniffed, "*Tire* chains. It's not as if you could have *hurt* them."

She didn't understand. It wasn't damage, it was desecration, and I knew it and had known it before I touched them. If Carl

17

had had tire chains, I wouldn't have gone within twenty feet of them, any more than I would have used his bathroom, but he disliked anything to do with cars and when he needed a ride Mother drove him. But this was Claire's father and not mine, and I gloated in my immunity. That was the joy of leaving the house: Fathers were everywhere, but out there they were spread thin, diluted and defanged. Someone else's worry.

Children played outside with their sleds or roller skates. Suburbs then were alive all day. All day there were people at home in their houses or sitting on their porches and delivery trucks in the street, bringing them their dry-cleaning or medicine from the drugstore or socks and underwear from the downtown department stores. Weekly or so, a square green truck with gold lettering that said KNIVES & SAWS SHARPENED clanged slowly down the street, pausing for housewives to run out with their sewing scissors and carving knives. In the spring a colored man in overalls strode down the sidewalk balancing a loaded tray on high and calling out "STRAAW-berries! STRAAW-berries!"

At dusk the Fathers came home from the bus stop down at Tennyson Street, wearing their hats, carrying their evening newspapers. As the streetlights blinked on, Mothers stepped out onto the front porches and blew the police whistles that called us, two longs and a short for Audrey, three shorts for Claire, long-short-long for Johnny, and then the street was empty. The Fathers took off their hats, lifting them with one hand cupped gently around the crown, and placed them on the shelf in the coat closet that was sacred to Fathers' hats. They sat down in their Father's chairs, producing a leathery sigh from the cushions, and opened their papers while a child set the table, forks on the left.

18

IN WHICH MOTHERS & THEIR DUTIES ARE
CONSIDERED & CONTRASTED WITH THE
PECULIARITIES OF MY OWN

There were no Mother chairs. Mothers didn't need chairs. They were always on their feet, in my friends' houses and in pictures on soap and cereal boxes and in books and ads in magazines. Mothers pacing the supermarket aisles for their favorite brands, hanging out their laundry and gloating over its whiteness, gladly mopping their floors and gaily washing their dishes, pouring milk for their children and stirring pots on the stove. Maybe rarely an ancient couple appeared in twin rocking chairs on either side of a fireplace, but they had aged themselves out of the real world and no longer mattered. Never was a woman between eighteen and eighty seen in a chair.

According to the common wisdom I absorbed through my pores, Mothers also fussed endlessly over their children, making them wash their hands and eat their spinach, sewing on their buttons, fretting over their stomachaches. They gave out candy as rewards for virtue and taped crayon drawings to the refrigerator. They wore aprons. In literature, they were Tom Kitten's mother, Mrs. Tabitha Twitchett, who was expecting friends for tea and washed and brushed her kittens and dressed them in their best, then sent them outside while she made hot buttered toast. They were Roo's mother Kanga in the Christopher Robin stories, dosing her child with strengthening medicine, and Peter Rabbit's mother dosing him with camomile tea. Even females who weren't already Mothers, like the insufferable Wendy, pretended to be, and fussed.

It had to be true. It was the same in all the stories and seemed to be true in all houses but mine. Since no part of the picture could possibly be applied to my own mother, I moved her to one side in my mind and made room for two categories, Mothers and my mother.

Carl needed no explaining. He was an archetypal father, even a bit larger than life. Mother could not be explained to anyone.

We had a maid named Hallelujah.

"Maids" was what people called the household hired help, not servants, which would have sounded British and elitist. There were no nannies or cleaning services, but there were maids all over, or perhaps "hired girls" in the West. They were cheap and plentiful and for the most part cheerful and friendly. Households with children hired them principally as baby-sitters, with a bit of dusting and ironing on the side. It's fashionable now to see them as ruthlessly exploited, but their lives were not onerous; any modern working mother would envy their work days. The job required no expensive education or training, only good-nature and the simplest domestic skills.

In the South and much of the East they were black; in New England, Irish; in the Western Plains they were Scandinavian; and in the Southwest, Mexican; while California sometimes sported a Japanese houseboy. For the children of the white middle class, they offered a window into a different world that broadened our view.

As secondary mothers, they were calmer and more objective than the real mothers, and with one of these installed, no real mother had to drag all three children whining to the supermarket and the dry cleaner and the obstetrician's office. When she got home, she had another grownup to talk to. They were a blessing and have been a great loss.

22

Hallelujah and my mother were kindred spirits in that neither of them cared a rap for housekeeping or cooking. Mother had a secret fear that hired help might ask her how she wanted things done around the house—however would she know?—but Hallelujah never asked. When the spirit moved her she ran the vacuum cleaner, miraculously singing hymns with a cigarette balanced on her lower lip. While I watched, the ash grew longer and longer, bent low, and then fell on the rug, whence she vacuumed it up, still singing. Mother brought home groceries—ground beef, green beans, potatoes, a pot roast or a chicken—and Hallelujah cooked them up and brought them to the table, shuffling in men's leather slippers with the toes cut out for her corns, called "Dinner!" and went back to the kitchen.

I gathered that her private life, on weekends, was wild and free, and sometimes Carl had to journey to unfamiliar precincts on Monday mornings to post bail for her. She could be alarming and unpredictable and liked to hide behind doors and jump out at me whooping, but I envied her spirit. She was quite unimpressed by Carl; no doubt she'd known worse in her day and lived to tell the tale. Every Friday he counted out her salary, slowly, from his wallet into her hand, reciting the numbers aloud just as he did with Mother's grocery money, but she never said "thank you." She poked the bills into her pocketbook and swooped out the door to her real life.

Mother curled up at the far end of the couch and read murder mysteries. She had never owned an apron and dressed in blue jeans, sweatshirts, and sneakers, all from the boys' department at Sears because she was small and boys' clothes were cheaper. When a child of hers came into the room and spoke to her, she struggled to take her eyes from the page, and finally wrenched them away and looked up and smiled dimly, as if she'd been asleep. Sometimes she didn't seem to know quite who we were or how we'd gotten into the house and sometimes, as our numbers increased, she had trouble with our names and ran down the whole roster before hitting on the right one. I adored her, but from a respectful distance.

Through four pregnancies and post-partums and God knows how many head colds and menstrual cycles, I never saw her in bed by day, never saw her take an aspirin. Like the wounded General "Chinese" Gordon saying it only hurt him when he laughed, she felt that the right sort of people didn't whimper. Relentlessly healthy, she disapproved of sickness in others and held the vaguely Freudian view that all maladies were a whine for attention, and the less attention she paid them, the sooner they would give up and leave. Sick children were sent to their rooms, to come back when they were well. Minor ailments, she felt, were self-induced or at least self-perpetuated and talking about headaches and stomachaches always made them worse. Ignore them and they go away. As for purely emotional distress and tears, they were self-indulgent. Vulgar.

How did a woman so temperamentally unmaternal come to have so many children? I suppose she couldn't decide what else to do.

She was one of an elite handful of women that sprang up after the Great War and stormed into the best colleges clamoring for higher education. She was pretty as a peach and brilliant, back in an innocent age that still believed that intelligence mattered, and talented, darling of her art and English teachers, blazing star of her high school and college stage productions, even tagged by a Broadway talent scout, though given her native austerity, the raucous theater world must have seemed out of the question. Phi Beta Kappa and summa cum laude in history at Swarthmore, a ground-breaking honors paper on judicial reform in the reign of Richard III, followed by a year at Columbia Law School, she blazed forth into the world and then vanished, suburban mother of five, of all possible lives the least suitable.

She gave me her Phi Beta Kappa key to play with and I lost it in the sandbox. I don't know whether she minded or not.

Maybe, after the girlhood successes, she was afraid of not living up to herself. Perhaps we were her substitute offerings to the world. Certainly she inspected us for talents. She set a vase of flowers in front of me and gave me a pencil and paper and told me to draw it. Anxious, I gripped the pencil and made a hard, uncertain line. She explained about sketching, about making many light experimental lines in search of the true one, but my lines yielded no truths. She shook her head and took the paper away; I think I heard her say, "Well, *that's* not it." She was right.

When Nick poked a screwdriver into a light socket and got knocked across the room, and then went back and put the same screwdriver into the same light socket, instead of assuming he wasn't quite right in the head, she was delighted and said he'd be a scientist, doggedly repeating the experiment in case the first time was a fluke. She was right.

She read to us. Last flicker of the promising actress, her readings were fine theater. She loved doing dialects; Kipling's *Soldiers Three* was a perennial, with its rich lode of Irish, Cockney, and Yorkshire, and I was fully twelve the last time she sat me down to listen to *Pickwick Papers*, for the joy of doing Sam Weller. Sometimes, in the car, she recited Goethe's *Erlkönig* in German, with such a passion of terror and grief as death rides closer and the

25

father flogs his horse and then the boy dies anyway, that it gave me chills. No need to understand the words.

As each of us mastered the necessary arithmetic, she taught us gin rummy and blackjack, and she played hard. Other mothers, when they smiled and sat down to play with their children, did it self-consciously, only playing at playing, but Mother cursed when she lost and gloated when she won, and she could shuffle the deck like a professional, its two halves springing together in midair and devouring each other.

There were the Mothers of hugs and kisses, housework and fussing, and then there was mine, of card games and Kipling. Judith, I think, would have given an arm for the former, but Nick and I were content. Mother was odd, but she was us. Every day for lunch she warmed up a can of Campbell's chicken-noodle soup, and if the soup ran out she made peanut butter sandwiches. Left to her own devices, she lived entirely on corn flakes and boiled eggs.

She never played cards with other women. She knew no other women, except the neighbors to nod hello to over the hedge she was clipping. She used the telephone only in emergencies and she never drank coffee in other people's kitchens, as Mothers were said to do, but what would she have talked about with them? What did they talk about in their kitchens: husbands, children, recipes, clothes? The small change of women's friendships, complaints and anecdotes and confessions, weddings and funerals, housework? Mother would have frozen with outrage and boredom. She had no talent for the vernacular. Forced into a setting that called for generic women's chat, she slid out of focus and took on what I thought of as her blind-baby look, with a small fixed smile and bemused blink.

There was no bend in her; if she couldn't be with her own kind and speak her own language, she would stay alone and silent. To try to communicate and fail would have made things worse. If, after making a dentist appointment, she said, "How sharper than a serpent's child / It is to have a thankless tooth" and people looked baffled or, worse, said, "That's from *King Lear* but you've got it all wrong," she would have been even lonelier.

How lonely was she, after the merry years in college and that brief frolic in Greenwich Village and law school? As was the custom everywhere, when guests came to dinner, they were couples of which the man was a colleague of the Father's. At our dinner table, the talk was of labor arbitration and Supreme Court skirmishes. The Taft-Hartley Act. Since men's and women's lives had nothing in common, the women at table were purely ornamental. They weren't expected to contribute; what could they know?

There sits Mother at the end of the couch, one hand buried in her short curly hair, knees cocked, sneakers kicked off, flexing her small bare toes, reading Agatha Christie. In my struggle to understand the world, she was useless. I turned to study the real Mothers, the ones who wore aprons and never sat down.

I understood from the Laura Ingalls Wilder books that Mothers once had serious work, skilled jobs that kept the family from freezing and starving. Interesting work, like making cheese and sausage and candles, and maybe in the evenings something pretty as well as useful, like piecing scraps together for a quilt. Now in the twentieth century, commerce had stolen all the good jobs and left Mothers with nothing but keeping the hosue clean. Not *cleaning* the house, which could maybe be satisfying, if it was dirty enough, but maintaining its cleanliness. Wiping up dust before dust could settle. Shining the shiny furniture. This must have been tricky work, since who could tell which shelf had been dusted or which table polished? And never the moment of triumph when you stand back and admire the fruits of your labor, since all would look the same as before.

In my friends' houses, dishes were not just washed immediately after every meal, they had to be dried too, and put away in cupboards. Leaving them dirty for even an hour was unthinkable, and "dishes in the sink" was code for either repulsive slovenry or a catastrophe, such as the Mother whisked to the hospital with appendicitis, with the dishes awaiting her return. Almost as bad as ignoring them was leaving them to dry themselves in the rack, in plain sight of any passerby peeking in the kitchen window. The rack was where the washer, usually the Mother, stacked them until the dryer, usually a daughter, could snatch them up and scour them top and bottom with a dish towel and stow them in their proper places. Except during actual meals, dishes had to be as invisible as underwear, which was why the domestic dishwashing machine came as such a blessing, not for washing but for hiding them.

Girls helped their mothers. Boys couldn't help their fathers, who were away having a hard day at the office, and their chores were strictly limited: any boy who helped with the dishes or the laundry was doomed to become what was delicately termed a "sissy." Girlish chores led inevitably down the dreaded path to homosexuality. Boys could only cut the lawn, shovel the snow, carry out the garbage, and lift or move anything too heavy for girls. In many households even harvesting their own dirty clothes from the floor and tossing them into the laundry hamper would undermine their future manhoods, and mothers and sisters did it for them.

The Mother, if she was a proper Mother, wore an apron to keep from spattering her cotton housedress, and when all was tidy she untied the strings at its waist, lifted the neckpiece over her head carefully, so as not to rumple her hair, and hung it to dry beside the dish towels. At least in the ads, she was happy, because cleanliness was her daily joy.

The itchy question nobody answered was: Where did they come from, these Mothers? Where were they before? Did they have a larval form or spring full-blown and aproned into the family?

My own house took in only the *New Yorker* and the *Atlantic Monthly*, but other people's coffee tables were rich with *McCall's* and *Redbook* and the *Saturday Evening Post*. Ads for the married, selling floor wax that sparkled like diamonds, stood face-to-face with ads for the unmarried, selling blond hair, sweet-smelling breath and flesh, and colorings for the face. Apparently they were linked, the lipstick leading to the floor wax as inevitably as day to night.

The *Washington Post* had a section segregated from the real paper called "For and About Women." I studied the pictures. Here was the demure young thing newly engaged, followed by the radiant bride at the triumphant pinnacle of her life, and that was the end of her. She was never seen again. Her wedding was the end of the story, the wand that transformed the girl with red lips and fingernails into the happy Mother with the mop, invisible within her walls. All those hours of choosing dresses and scenting the flesh, traded overnight for furniture polish. It seemed a steep price, but it must be fair, since every woman longed and planned and schemed to be an unpaid live-in housekeeper.

The cartoons in the *New Yorker* showed a darker side of the story. There, married women were stout and overbearing, and their husbands seized every chance to slip away from them and be with other men, usually in a bar: "If my wife calls, I'm not here." In the comics, wives were tyrants with rolling pins. In Thurber's drawings, husbands cringed and hid from their monstrous mates; in Peter Arno's, the unmarried women were all breasts and lips bursting with invitation, the married were armor-plated dragons with lorgnettes.

Men, then, simply didn't like their wives very much. Women wanted nothing except marriage, but men hated marriage. They'd been tricked into it somehow.

The next piece in the puzzle was a long time falling into place. I knew about reproduction, of course, with graphic help from unspayed female cats in the household, but sex was more complicated. Gradually I absorbed the message: men lusted after the pretty girls in pretty dresses, but no sensible girl would gratify their lust without the promise of a house to clean, in trade. So they married. Unfortunately, men are so constructed that once is enough as far as lust is concerned. The women got what they wanted, floors to sweep and dishes and sheets to wash, and the men were locked up with what they no longer wanted, wives. The Mothers.

I stared into my own future. The hair curlers and the mop were equally unappealing, and the whole complicated laying of the marriage trap, followed by the victim's dismay and loathing, too awful to think about. The only option mentioned was to become what was called a "career girl," lonely and bitter, who spent her days in an office typing letters for men too proud or too lazy to do it themselves.

I decided never to grow up.

MY EDUCATION BEGINS INAUSPICIOUSLY, & WE TRAVEL TO FLORIDA

Firstborn in the family, early talker, by rights I should have stormed triumphant through school like my mother. Instead, I slogged as through a swamp. We simply never connected, school and I. I was there under false pretenses from the start anyway, though I didn't know it until I applied for my first passport.

Divorce by then was accepted as regrettable though not disreputable, but apparently Mother felt it was a blot, or more likely she didn't feel like explaining, so she simply turned me over to the school system under Carl's surname, somehow getting me registered without birth certificate or adoption papers. Apparently they took her word for me, and so did I until the passport crisis, when I had to root around in shoe boxes full of papers for my original birth certificate and sail off to Europe dressed as someone I'd never heard of.

School was seven blocks away, and I remember it as a looming fortress on a hill, but there aren't any hills in that neighborhood and it was a perfectly typical, square, red-brick building. Mother walked me there on the first day of kindergarten. I'd been to nursery schools, but somehow they'd seemed, well, smaller. They seemed to make sense. Though I was silent there and solitary, I wasn't frightened. I understood what was happening. It would be years and years before I knew what was happening in real school.

Things went wrong early. The kindergarten had a piano, and we carried our chairs to form a semicircle around it, and the teacher read us the words to the songs, and then played them on the piano, and we sang. My one accomplishment, my parlor trick, was remembering words. If the words rhymed, I couldn't help but remember them. Over the years this has resulted in a mind so deep in accumulated litter—Said Aristotle unto Plato / "Have another sweet potato." / Said Plato unto Aristotle / "Thank you, I prefer the bottle"—that it's hard to move around in it. I remembered all the words to the songs, and I sang forth proudly while the other children mumbled and faked it.

Presently the teacher stopped playing and came over and laid a hand on my shoulder. I was singing off-key, she said, not unkindly, and I couldn't carry a tune, and this was throwing the others into confusion. From now on, at music time, I was to bring my chair to the circle with the others but sit in silence.

The others stared at me and some of them giggled. The information worked its way through me in a series of shock waves. The only currency I'd brought to the table was worthless. Words didn't matter. Something else mattered, and I was the only person in the room, possibly in the world, who didn't understand. All the other children knew that a key wasn't something to open a door with and a tune meant more than just making it go higher or lower. When had they learned? Did their mothers teach them, or did they just naturally know it, like knowing how to taste and smell? What else did they know that I didn't? Suddenly my fellow five-year-olds looked infinitely wise and sophisticated, and I couldn't tell how they got that way or how to follow them. As instructed, I shut up.

Useless to try to figure things out. At lunch time, the other children lined up in the back to be led to something called the lunchroom. I didn't know where or what it was. Even marching there in a column of children, I might get separated from them and grope forever through the maze of hallways, never to find my way out. Instead, every day I slipped from the room and out the front door, always relieved to remember how to find it, and walked the seven blocks home, where Mother fed me a bowl of chicken-noodle soup before I walked back. Alone.

Why was I alone? Where were the children of my neighborhood, Claire and Johnny and Audrey? I walked to school, and home for lunch, and back again and home again alone. At recess, I hid in whatever cranny seemed safest from the swarming mob. My neighbors must have gone to the same school, since there was no other; why did I never see them in the halls or on the playground? Maybe they just merged with the general darkness and confusion and I didn't recognize them. I was afraid of everyone in the building. I was afraid of the building itself and had nightmares about its menacing halls. I was stupefied with cowardice and hated myself for it.

I must have reeked of it, and nothing excites the blood lust in children more than the smell of fear. Groups of girls jeered at me; boys threw mud and snowballs and stuck out their feet to trip me. One boy swooped past me and snatched off my knit cap and threw it in a puddle and stomped on it while the others laughed.

Mother frowned at the cap. I explained, and she said, "I expect that means he likes you." I stared. "That's how little boys show they like you," she said, and went back to her book. There was no way to tell her how things were; her memory of school and my reality were too far apart. Best not to tell her anything. She'd expected me to be a success, took it for granted that I'd be as admired and happy as she'd been. I was already disappointing her and I'd barely started.

In the years to come, illness was to be my only ally, and it came to my rescue shortly after I started first grade. I came down with whooping cough. Whooping cough was one of what were called, when filling out forms in later life, the "usual childhood diseases," diseases every child had to go through as part of the childhood process, like shedding your baby-teeth, and milder if contracted early; if by age ten or eleven you hadn't had whooping cough, chickenpox, mumps, and both kinds of measles, you might be sent to visit a sick friend to absorb the germs and get it over with.

On the whole, these provided a lovely respite for the child if not for the Mother. Measles, not German measles but "regular" measles, was good for at least two weeks—the school nurse wouldn't let you back till your spots faded. It sometimes affected the eyes, so you lay in a darkened room, roller-shades pulled down clear to the windowsills, forbidden to read, and might have the family radio brought upstairs and lie there in the gloom trying to unravel the mysteries of afternoon soap operas.

Whooping cough, however, laid me low and I've been coughing ever since. I must have been very sick indeed—children did die of whooping cough—because even Mother noticed, and the doctor came. By day, after Carl left for work, I was moved from the back bedroom into the big sunny master bedroom and lay coughing and staring out the window. The bed was covered with a weightless down comforter in bright red satin so slippery it escaped onto the floor unless you kept a grip on it. (A red satin comforter, on Mother and Carl's spartan bed? It seems indecent. Was there something I missed? Perhaps it was a wedding present from a friend with a sense of humor, and since it was there they might as well use it. When it fell apart, it was replaced by sturdy, practical Hudson Bay blankets.)

The school days passed by without me and the cough lingered on and on. Winter loomed, and apparently the doctor recommended getting me out of damp, raw Washington and into the sun. We went to Florida.

Carl had an eccentric widowed aunt who dealt in real estate in Fort Lauderdale, and for a wedding present she'd given him and Mother a cottage far north of town, out on the deserted end of the beach, provided he could get rid of the current inhabitants. Their name was pronounced "Soo-cup"; I don't know how it was spelled, if indeed it was ever spelled, and they threw their trash and garbage out the windows and refused to pay the rent. When Aunt Mary went in person to collect it, she was chased and bitten by their attack goose, a vicious bird named Baby.

Peculiar as it seems now, long stretches of Florida's east coast were sparsely settled then by shadowy people said to have drifted down from Georgia after Georgia required them to fence in their pigs and cattle instead of foraging them on public land. "Crackers," they were called, Mother said, because they drove their bony livestock in front of them cracking stock-whips. Their names were often corruptions of the Huguenot. They lived along the beach, not to play in the sand and surf but because the mosquitoes were less bloodthirsty there, and they earned their livings mysteriously in the mangrove swamps and waterways and palmetto scrub inland, with rifles and flat-bottomed boats, fishing, trapping alligators, making whisky; whatever private enterprise fell to hand.

Carl being, among other things, a lawyer, he had managed to get rid of the Soocups somehow, goose and all, and the house was scrubbed and the garbage hauled away.

At home, we packed. Carl would stay, of course, but Hallelujah was to come with us, to give a hand with Nick and Judith. She rolled her eyes, dubious. Washington born and raised, she'd heard stories about life in the South. "Down there," she said, "I hear you got to call even the white *horses* 'mister.' " I believed her.

We rolled down old Route 1, Main Street of the East, stopping often to feed the baby, creeping through dusty speed-trap towns, dawdling behind trucks full of calves or cabbages, through Raleigh, Savannah, Jacksonville, past faded red barns with painted signs advertising Mail Pouch tobacco, sleeping in tiny tourist cabins smelling of mold. Giddy with freedom, Mother sang "Mairzy-Doates" and "Casey Jones" and "Button up your overcoat / Be in bed by three / Take good care of yourself / You belong to me!" We had three flat tires.

The car was a dignified old black Plymouth sedan. For Mother, a car's most important attribute, after longevity, was modesty; the last car of her life was a custard-colored Ford Escort, hard-gaited and hard-bitted but so modest it was impossible to find anywhere, even in the driveway. The Plymouth smelled of past car-sickness, and Hallelujah and I sat in the back with the baby between us. Cows and horses grazed on either side of the road, and when we spotted a white horse we wound down our windows and leaned far out and bellowed "*Mister* White Horse!" I threw up by the roadside over and over, especially in Brunswick and Savannah, which reeked of paper mills. It was a lovely journey.

In Florida the sun was always shining. Mother filled the cabin with boards and paint cans and sawhorses and threw herself unchecked into her secret passion, carpentry. She built book-cases into every wall, and bunk-bed couches and cupboards and molding, all of it built for the ages and long ago knocked down by bulldozers to make room for the pastel hotels that would line the shore and screen off the sea to all but paying customers. From the stepladder, she mumbled down with her mouth full of finishing nails, and I handed her things. She tried to teach me to cut along a straight pencil line with a carpenter's handsaw, but I disappointed her again; in later life I got pretty fair with a chain saw but I never could cut a straight line. She tried to show me how to paint window mullions without slopping over onto the glass, but I was clumsy at that too.

Just recently, in this house she built for herself on the mountain long later, where I live now, I mentioned to the youngest of us, Andrew, that, on top of painting the place inside and out, she'd done all the carpentry here and built the bookshelves herself.

Andrew laughed. "Look at this," he said, caressing the shelves. "Look at the finishing. These were built by a *professional*. Mr. Martz must have done it."

"Mr. Martz was a general contractor," I retorted. "Not a carpenter. Mother would never have let him build a bookcase. And she did all the interior carpentry in the house you grew up in, too."

"Don't be silly," he said. "*Mother?* No way."

She was older when he came along. Time passes. Each sibling has a different mother.

In Florida, the baby slept in her car bed under the softly rattling fronds of the coconut palm. The road between our house and the beach was made of chalk, or something like it, all white dust in dry weather and, after a storm, all potholes filled with chalky-white water to stomp in. We trekked to the ocean through the beachgrass and seagrape bushes, along a pathway of warped, bleached, splintery boards, Mother leading the way with the big umbrella held high like a flag. Sometimes I wore a bathing suit, but when the crotch filled with sand I took it off. The only other person who ever came by was a beachcomber, flotsam of the Great Depression, a well-spoken fellow who lived in a shack made of driftwood and ate fish. He collected the oddments that washed ashore, shells, glass floats from fishing nets, fan-shaped seaweeds, twisted bits of driftwood artistic in flower arrangements, and sold them to the tourist shop in town.

My teacher had given Mother mimeographed arithmetic assignments and she took them to the damp sand below the tide line and scratched out the sums with a sharp stick, 2 + 3 = , and I followed behind her and wrote in the answers with my finger. I didn't understand the concept, and still don't, but I memorized the numbers as words, thinking "Two plus three equals five." I was often wrong. (To this day, in order to punch in a telephone number, I have to recite it aloud, listening to the words, and then dial quickly before the sound fades.)

In the sun-bleached snapshots, the stolid five-year-old me had lengthened and turned all ribs and elbows and my bobbed hair was now short, wet pigtails curled like the letter C. I was still coughing but apparently out of danger; Mother had lost interest. Nick, continuing his scientific experiments, ate handfuls of sand and howled dismally at the effects, but persevered.

Mother made a long, flat racing dive out through the breakers to where the water quieted, and swam. She swam as efficiently as a shark, with the geometrically neat Australian crawl she never could teach me—she'd been the star of her college swimming team—and headed out to sea as if she heard Portugal calling.

Nick and I sat watching her at the water's edge, where the waves came foaming in over our laps and then receded, sucking the sand out from under our rumps and legs until we were sitting in watery holes. When she came back she shook herself like a dog and covered our noses with thick white zinc oxide against the sun. Hallelujah sat majestically on a blanket under the striped umbrella gazing out to sea like an African queen on the lookout for slave ships.

After swimming, Mother walked away up the beach, toward the faraway curve at the Pompano lighthouse. From time to time she'd bend to pick up a shell and inspect it, then pitch it or pocket it. She got smaller and smaller, fastened to us only by the trail of her footprints, heel and ball disconnected.

She was always scornful of personal vanity, caring nothing for clothes and untouched by cosmetics, but she was pleased by her small, high-arched feet, and I was relieved that my own feet left the same two-part prints instead of a vulgar wedge.

Mother was deeply snobbish about the flesh, especially its bones. She felt that it meant something, and connected genetically to personal worth. The shape of the jaw, spacing of the eyes, length of toes and fingers were the marks of good protoplasm, well put together, and woe to the politician or boyfriend or even relative with cramped forehead, receding chin, short neck, weak mouth, fat fingers. Little in the way of intelligence or moral character could be expected of such a one. The right sort of people had long legs and broad foreheads and small ears set close to the head.

It occurs to me only now, as I write this, that her mother, my grandmother, Welsh by ancestry, was built like a tree stump, with a short nose and stubby hands, while my grandfather was everything she admired, long-boned and tall, with an elegantly sculpted skull, the very model of an English aristocrat at a shooting party. I'm sure he had narrow, high-arched feet. My own father too, in the old photographs, was tall and long-jawed and narrow; was that why she chose him?

I don't know how she reconciled this snobbery with her liberal politics, but no doubt she didn't bother. In the main, she hadn't much use for the poor, a lazy feckless lot, but the rich were worse, shallow and vulgar and wasting their time on golf and dinner parties and shopping. Money, in Mother's view, didn't much matter one way or the other. Brains and breeding mattered. Decades later, she was disgusted when Grace Kelly threw herself away on that stumpy greasy little Prince Rainier: Prince forsooth, his grandmother was a washerwoman. She had no use for the British royal house of Windsor either, Johnny-come-latelies with scarcely a drop of English blood.

She walked away up the beach.

One of these days, just possibly, she would keep on walking until she disappeared, and the waves would wash out her trail. She may well have been thinking the same thing as she walked, feeling the footprints between us stretching thin like elastic ready to snap.

In Mother, the impulse to flee always struggled with the grip of duty. After I was grown, she told me that when she couldn't sleep, she'd get in the car and drive, west into Virginia, north up through Maryland, east toward the Bay. Her adored father had taught her to drive, in a time when many nice girls considered it unladylike, and perhaps the steering wheel and clutch and brake still connected her with his ghost.

I think of her out there, alone except for her own headlights on the dark two-lane roads, empty at night in those days. Maybe she sang to herself. There was no radio. While heaters and radios were still optional in cars, she rejected them as even more decadent than automatic transmissions and wore extra socks in winter and carried blankets for passengers, and her last car, the Ford Escort, was chosen partly because it had no radio, though heaters were by then compulsory. So were the headrests on poles, designed to prevent whiplash; she drove straight to a machine shop and had them sawed off. She refused to use the seat belt either and in her last years her travels were accompanied by its warning howl of impending doom. The physical restraint was galling and besides, fussing about safety was, like worrying about health, ungentlemanly. Undignified.

During the diciest of the nuclear threat for Washingtonians, when I mentioned it, she said sternly that if you learned that the bomb was about to fall on your neighborhood, the only proper thing, the only thing nice people would do, was to go right on with whatever you were doing, reading the paper or frying the pork chops or pruning the hedge, not even glancing at the fiery cloud.

Back then, out there, she would drive and drive until she'd worn down the urge to run away and turned for home, undressed, and got back in bed beside the sleeping Carl.

Receding down the beach, separated from us, she looked less like a mother and more like a person, and like all children I flinched from seeing her as a person, since persons were subject to whims, willful impulses, misgivings, and secrets that could tear the world to shreds, like the way Carl came into our life. Mothers

43

should be the nonpersonal eternal, everywhere and nowhere in particular and pretty much invisible; mothers should be pure concept, like the modern gods. Persons were like the old gods, not to be trusted.

Waiting, I let dry sand dribble through my fingers onto the sunburned tops of my feet and stared after her till my eyes watered. The tide would already be nibbling at her trail when she doubled back on it and came to reclaim us and spread her finds out on a towel, turkey-wings and angel-shells and Turks'-caps. Then she would lie down and stretch her legs into the sun, turning from time to time. She hated wearing stockings and a dark, even tan could be worn instead.

Coconuts ripened and fell from our tree and Mother and I learned to smash our way into them without losing all the juice. During a cold snap, she buttoned me into the red wool sweater Grandmother made and sent me out to collect driftwood in the thickets of beach grass. Marinated in seawater and bleached in the sun, it burned in our little fireplace with fierce chemical colors.

Roaches as big as mice scurried around the kitchen—Mother called them palmetto bugs and ignored them—and snakes, some venomous and some benign, lived under the bushes and in the crawlspace below the house; once I came within an inch of planting my bare foot on a small, bright, deadly coral snake. Mother was casual about snakes too. Whatever else she may have failed to do, she did raise three daughters blessedly free of those terrors that plague so many grown women, violent shaking irrational fears of spiders, snakes, mice, bats, bumblebees, roaches, all learned early from mothers and impossible to shake off by means of college degrees and professional careers.

Long after I was grown, Mother confessed that she was afraid in thunderstorms, and I was stunned. We'd never known. We thought she enjoyed the bangs and flashes. Courage, of course, like high arches, was a mark of breeding.

Sometimes jellyfish washed ashore and I collected them in a bucket and tried to keep them as pets, but they died and stank. Once a screech owl flew in the open door and perched for a long time on the mantle, looking cross, and then left again. Small scorpions hid in our shoes.

The Depression still lay over the land and refrigerators weren't considered, certainly not by Mother, a necessary expense; the iceman came with a truck full of big, glittering squares of ice and hoisted one up in his tongs and carried it into the back entryway and slid it into the icebox, over the drip pan we kept forgetting to empty, where it shrank interestingly over the days. We ate at a splintery picnic table, on benches, with no chair for Fathers. If you sat down hard on the end of an empty bench, it reared up and dumped you on the floor. Nick sat on telephone books.

At night he and I were bedded on the screened porch to the distant boom and hiss and cold-metal smell of the Atlantic. It was very much like heaven, but there was even more to come.

Up the beach road half a mile or so lived a family named Robinson, in a cottage like our own, and they had a daughter named Betsy. In the extrasensory way children learn these things, she sniffed out my presence and came to find me, much pleased, since there were no other children for miles, or at least no others not totally feral, and in those primitive times children had only each other for entertainment.

She came most days after we got back from our afternoon

swim, after the school bus dropped her off, in her school clothes. Sometimes I went to her house, and we climbed the big rubber tree in her back yard, with its flesh-like smooth gray branches. When you broke off the leaves and twigs, they leaked a white gooey fluid, rubber in its primal state, that stuck to your arms and legs and turned black and was hard to scrub off. We played jacks, at which she beat me so quickly and easily it's a wonder we kept on playing. We set up housekeeping under a sea-grape bush that we shared with assorted snakes, and furnished the sand with the poisonous beans from the wild castor plants out back.

She was a year older and far ahead in school, and one day she brought her reading workbook to show me.

I can still see its creased red paper cover. The pages were full of words with spaces to fill in where letters were missing. This was a book for children, ordinary children like me, and I stared and stared at it. Somehow I'd never made the connection, that reading was something I too could do. Mother read to me at bedtime, and then put the book down on the table and went away, and the book that sang stories to Mother lay dumb as a stone for me. I could look at the pictures and try to remember the words but it hadn't occurred to me to make them speak. Certainly it didn't occur to Mother, with her blind faith in public schooling, to teach me.

I sat staring at Betsy's workbook until, like a sudden infusion of grace, it came to me. It simply sprang off the page and into my head, full grown. The letters arranged themselves and spoke to me. I could read. It wasn't a process so much as an event: I could read nothing, and then I could read anything. It was a gift, unearned, no strings attached, a blessing, a fairy godmother.

46

I don't remember that Mother was pleased or even much interested that I'd learned to read, any more than if I'd skinned my knee or caught a butterfly, but after I'd read all the books we'd brought with us she took me to the library in town and we came back with our arms full, not the easy readers that came along later to bridge the gap after Dick and Jane but the solid eight-to-twelve-year-old fare, full of meat and muscle, pioneers and princesses, trolls, poetry, and plucky orphans. In the dark cave of me, a stone door creaked and swung open and let in the blazing landscape of the other.

Drunk with literature, I dictated a novel to Mother, who printed it in colored crayon so I could read my own works, and I illustrated it lavishly. "The Happy Mouse Family Holland," it was called. The mice, as I recall, had a butler, and Mother Mouse said, "We are very lucky to have a butler. Not so many people have butlers," but Father Mouse said, "Enough people have butlers that we are not so lucky as to talk about it." Their oldest son was named Meitel, and when the time came for him to arise and go, he put on his arising-and-going dress and, after an elaborate party, went. Many fine adventures were had. I know Mother saved it, and I suppose it must still be in one of the many boxes, if the real mice haven't eaten it.

In time we had to leave the sunlight and the lovely days and drive back home to Fathers and school, but nothing could ever be quite so bleak again. I could slip through a hundred doors and out to anywhere, free and safe, free to worry or weep about somebody else's danger or grief.

I inspected books. Such small things they were, to so magically unfold and rise up and blot out the known world. How were they born? I knew about the first two names on the cover, but what were those mysterious third names, Macmillan, Dutton, Viking? Mother explained that it was publishers who took the stories and pictures and made them into books, and I was mightily impressed. Anyone could write stories and draw pictures, but to turn them into books for stores and libraries seemed God-like. When I grew up, then, I would be a publisher, and rain books down over the world like a shower of gold.

These days, from time to time, the public libraries launch an effort to get children together with books, and signs bloom on their walls saying Read to Succeed! This seems singularly wrong-headed, since few seven-year-olds care about their future job categories, or at least no seven-year-old you'd want to know. The signs ought to say Books: The Way Out.

These days, when I read, I'm conscious of reading. It's a physical act, eyes moving from left to right, pages turned, maybe glancing up at the bird feeder beyond the window. Sometimes a line reminds me of something else and my mind wanders and I have to go back and reread the paragraph. Sometimes I get up to open a beer or make a cup of tea. Back in those early years, there was nothing deliberate about reading. It was wholly unconscious: I simply tipped forward and fell in and disappeared. "Losing oneself in a book" is a fatuous old phrase, but I did, shucking the self gladly like a shirt full of fleas. When called for dinner, putting it back on again was misery. Presently I hardly needed the physical books at all and read myself into them at night in the dark or at school, sitting at my desk, eyes glazed, embroidering scenes and adding chapters. I began to narrate my own life to myself in the third person—"She started up the stairs to bed"—which scared me; I might separate into two of me, and then the first-person me would fade and disappear and the third-person, the one in the narrative, take over. With effort, I managed to stop it.

Because I'd missed most of the semester, I was put back into a different first grade, with different children, to start over. When the teacher noticed I could read, she sent me away to advanced first grade, whose teacher promptly unloaded me into second. Every night I woke up twisted in my sheets from dreams of wandering the enormous halls looking for the right room, and then opening the wrong door to the wrong class, and the teacher and all the children laughing and pointing.

I developed peculiar hiccups that struck without warning, startling me as much as the bystanders. Wrenched out of deep visceral spasms, they were louder than anyone else's, much louder, and drowned out the teacher, and I couldn't swallow or mute them. They sounded faked, and everyone assumed they were; I was sent to the principal's office for creating a disturbance, I was sent to stand in the hall, I was sent to the school nurse and soundly scolded. After experiment, Grandmother came up with a cure: I was to hold both ears pressed firmly shut with my fingers, hold my breath, and take many small sips from a glass of water. It always worked, but unfortunately it called for three hands, one to hold the water, and since nobody at school believed they were real, nobody would help. Like the crocodile in *Peter Pan* who swallowed the clock, or perhaps more like the lepers' bell-ringer crying "Unclean," I ticked my way around for years until, in high school, they tapered off and finally stopped as mysteriously as they'd begun.

The educational authorities didn't notice or care that I could barely count my fingers. This was before math and science rose up as the keystone of education and reading slid back to a mere tool for deciphering the owner's manual. This was so long ago that mathematical talent was considered unbecoming in a girl, while boys who took to reading might be closet sissies. Later, in my high school, one lone girl insisted on taking physics, but her teacher and classmates teased her until she dropped it; if the concept had been commoner then, the word "lesbian" would have murmured down the halls.

Under the current guidelines I'd never have made it as far as high school but would still be wedged into my fourth-grade desk, gray hair and all, wrestling with fractions. Back then, education made some benign allowances for individual strengths and weaknesses that couldn't be tolerated now, now that we need a huge uniform work force uniformly trained in uniform math and technology. At mid-century, employers expected to train the young on the job and education was expected to be its own reward.

Reading shoved me ahead until I was younger and smaller than everyone else, socially miles behind, baffled by the simplest arithmetic, and more bewildered than ever. Being the star reader made me something of a freak and my vocabulary, already unwieldy, got downright grotesque. I couldn't control it. Reaching for words, I couldn't remember which were in daily use and which were peculiar; I might find myself saying "seek" instead of "look for." Even the teachers couldn't help laughing at me. Plainly my kindergarten teacher was right and silence was best; when called on, I dropped my eyes and shook my head. Sometimes, daydreaming, I hadn't heard the question, and sometimes the answer seemed so obvious it had to be a trick, and the real answer something quite different that, like singing, everyone understood but me.

Over the years I fell in love, silently, with a succession of bad boys, the ones who steadfastly refused to learn to read, who sassed the teachers, threw erasers, and got sent to the office. Coming from a sandy-haired family and neighborhood, I was drawn to the dark ones; they looked dangerous, with their opaque dark eyes. They were unimaginably brave. I knew that if I could, just once, throw an eraser, my whole world would be brighter. I couldn't, of course.

I stayed mute for years. This has hung over me all my life so that now, when I acquire an odd fact, I squirrel it away hoping that some day a teacher, or maybe a quiz-show host, will ask, and I will finally raise my hand and answer loud and strong, "Oxygen and hydrogen" or "In Avignon, in 1309" or "Sir Isaac Newton." Nobody ever asks.

They said school was where you went to learn things, but it hadn't taught me anything yet, or at least not anything pleasant, and now that I could read there was nothing more I needed. Long years later I collected a smattering of Latin, an odd slant on the Civil War (the teacher was from Georgia), hundreds of songs and quite a bit of French, but that was about it.

SCHOOL & I STRUGGLE WITH EACH OTHER,
PLUS HARD TIMES WITH THE OLD TESTAMENT

We moved. We moved out of Grandmother's friendly rooms, leaving the sleeping porch and the windfall apples in the grass all noisy with wasps and smelling sweetly of rot, and into our own house, or, rather, Carl's own house. It was only a few miles away, over the line in Maryland, a similar sleepy suburb with clipped hedges and children on bicycles.

Mother again brought in stepladders and sawhorses and built bookcases and cupboards in every room. Rasp of saw and bang of nail filled the air, and newspapers lay spread to catch the sawdust. She painted everything. The smell of Kem-Tone haunted the rooms and she always had paint flecks in her hair and paint speckles on her little rimless glasses. She made curtains, her one domesticated adventure, heavy linen curtains in dark green with a gold vertical stripe, and attached them to wooden rings and hung them over the French doors in the living room, where they stayed for fifty years, fading in streaks from the sun.

My insomnia tightened its grip and, since it was forbidden to turn on a light and read, I wandered the dark house. The second step down from the upstairs hall squeaked unless you stepped on its far-right edge. Streetlights made bright patches on certain areas, in certain rooms, and in between a person could run her hand over the furniture for guidance, prowling around and around on cold bare feet, staring at the glow of the pilot light in the kitchen stove, thinking about nothing at all.

The house sat beside a grassy traffic circle planted with fir trees, and my new school sprawled on the other side. I could see it from my bedroom window. It was no less daunting than any other school, but being so close made it feel safer: escape, if necessary, would be a short run. On PTA nights, shadowy couples moved along all the sidewalks to converge on the lighted school, and sometimes even Carl, benevolent with hat and cane, walked over with Mother. Morning and afternoon, Patrol Boys guarded our corner, and on mornings when my pleas of sickness were convincing enough and I was allowed to stay home, I burrowed back into my bed and, just after nine, heard their sweet cries of "Off!" "Off!" "Off!" relayed like owls from corner to corner and knew I was safe for the day: Carl had left for work; school had started without me.

Patrol Boys were the crown princes of elementary school, chosen from the sixth graders for their manliness and character. They swaggered into the classroom late and swaggered out early as duty called. Even if you knew their names, you didn't speak to them while they were on duty in their white Sam Browne belts, and I think that if you had, like the guards at Buckingham Palace, they weren't allowed to answer: dignity forbade.

White belts gleaming, staring straight ahead, they held their arms out rigidly to keep the schoolchildren out of the street, then stepped manfully into the intersection and held their arms out to keep cars at bay while the children crossed. As far as I know, not even the wickedest renegade ever challenged or disobeyed them, nor did any Patrol Boy lapse into chat and frivolity on the job.

I don't know just when they disappeared, to be replaced by matrons in orange vests called crossing guards. I suppose they were a casualty of the women's movement of the seventies, when the schools were under mandate to treat boys and girls as if they were the same. Nobody could imagine a Patrol Girl: how could you evaluate her manliness and character? And however manly, she wouldn't have the moral authority to stop children from running into traffic: who so spineless, even today, as to stop when a girl says "Stop," belt or no belt? Doomed by gender, the Patrol Boys were disbanded and swagger no more.

Because of some structural discrepancy between the school systems, I was put in third grade instead of second. The teacher, Mrs. Cope, warned us not to act up while she was writing on the blackboard because she had eyes in the back of her head. I believed her—who disbelieved a teacher?—but I didn't know how she could see through her thick pepper-and-salt hair, worn in the ordained style of teachers, in a bun or twist, for respectability. Short hair would have been frivolous, like the flappers of yore, and loose hair lascivious. Teachers, being role models, were the very essence of sexlessness and solemnity, and their clothes were shapeless and somber, their faces innocent of lipstick, and their breasts welded into a single, indivisible bulge.

Mrs. Cope believed in handwriting. Cursive, she called it. The only decoration in the room was a frieze of spidery cursive letters. Daily she wrestled with our clumsy hands and pencils, patrolling the aisles, seizing a wrist here, fingers there, correcting our grip and the slant of our paper. She was a true believer and kept urging us on to fresh efforts, because our futures depended on it. Everything depended on the curly elegance of our job applications, marriage proposals, apologies, invitations, and requests for bank loans. I have an etiquette book published in 1873 and it quite agrees, showing examples exactly like Mrs. Cope's.

The greater our efforts, the more tightly we choked the pencil and the clumsier our capitals grew, to be rubbed out with erasers that tore holes in the paper. My own writing was among the worst in the class but secretly—Carl was afraid I'd break it—I was learning to use Mother's typewriter and felt my future lay in its keys. My handwriting remains to this day the script of an awkward third-grader with emotional problems and embarrasses me in Christmas-card season.

My mind wandered. I slid helplessly into daydreaming. The desk-tops had been scribbled and carved, and I traced the messages of former third-graders and made up names to go with the initials gouged in the wood and filled with ink. One memorably awful day Mrs. Cope passed back the half-sheets of coarse paper used for exams. I took mine and handed the rest over my shoulder to the person behind me, and the smell of the cheap paper reminded me of newsprint, which reminded me of the comic strips in the *Post*, where I struggled to understand the world through the lens of Hal Foster's languorously elegant *Prince Valiant*, Milt Caniff's violent China of *Terry and the Pirates*, and the innocent loonies of Dogpatch. I fell to wondering about their structure. How did the author tell a story in only four panels, with no room to fill in the transitions? Sometimes a banner at the top of a box said LATER THAT DAY or IN ANOTHER PART OF THE WOODS, but usually not; how much could the author assume that the reader would figure out? If the people are beside the road and a truck is coming, and then they are inside the truck, we know they got into it, but we don't see them getting in. We know what happened, but how do we know? And if the story is just a conversation, you can't keep showing the same picture or it would be boring; the artist varies the angle, the distance, the background, or leaps to an eavesdropper behind a bush, and the reader has to bridge the gap. The same was true of a written story in a book: gaps were left, and the reader jumped over them rather than plod through connecting details.

I drew a long box and divided it into four. In the first I drew two clumsy people (I can still see them, one with a hand raised to deliver a slap) with dialogue balloons. What could I skip between the first and second panels without leaving the reader bewildered in the gap?

"Pass your papers to the front of the room," said Mrs. Cope.

I didn't even know if it had been a spelling test or an arithmetic quiz. I sat staring in helpless horror at what I'd been doing to my paper while the teacher was asking a string of questions I'd never heard. I was out of control. My unmanageable self was leading me into danger. I made fresh efforts to get a grip, to pay attention, to understand, but it was no use. My school days and I were as ships that pass in the night.

I was luckier in the neighborhood. The houses and yards were arranged in the friendliest possible manner, and from both Tracy's and Lucille's houses our hedge and lawn were the shortest connection to school for them and their little brothers. (Mother was vain of both hedge and lawn, tending them obsessively, but she held her tongue in the interest of peace.) Our street was the kind in which weary hound-dogs slept at noonday—the Flemings' Wags in particular could not be dislodged by the loudest car-horn—and we roamed. Children were turned out of the house after school. Children with better-organized mothers than mine had to change from school clothes into play clothes, but I had no alternate wardrobe: to Mother, clothes were clothes, and lost buttons were lost forever. Out we went, younger and older together, with the big ones in brutally casual charge of the small. I played in other people's yards and houses until their fathers came home, when I slipped away through the kitchen door or the gap in the hedge. We played across the lines of age and gender. When no one else was available, I even played with Peter.

Poor Peter. An only child whose parents had been killed in a car accident, he was being raised, three houses up the street, by his loving grandparents. Having no parents was, by itself, oddity enough, and children are suspicious of the odd, but his toys were even stranger, if "toys" is the right word for his dazzling possessions. His bedroom would have shamed King Tut. Peter had miles of electric trains with their attendant buildings and scenery and an Erector set with a motor. He had an English bike, a Raleigh I think, with a shining chrome headlight and gears, the first gears any of us had seen, though he didn't ride it often; I expect his grandparents were afraid it might get hurt, out in our rude world. He had a mechanical horse that jiggled up and down, almost life-sized and covered in real pony skin. He had costume sets and props for dressing up and the super-deluxe master chemistry set, with which a person could make evil smells and sometimes even whiffs of smoke, and toy guns of every size and capability. All of it, he told us, was the fanciest and most expensive to be had. He had everything a well-stocked Fifth-Avenue toy store would have had, if any of us had ever been to such a thing, or even to a toy store at all.

I suppose the neighborhood should have envied him his loot, but for some reason we laughed at it. We didn't want to play with his toys. We made do with the essentials of hand-me-down sled and roller skates, a few dolls and balls, and we took a puritanical pride in their sparseness. I suppose we absorbed this from our parents, who were puritans by today's standards and thought it was vulgar to have fancier possessions than one's neighbors. It was impossible to know, for instance, whose father made more money, since all the cars were black and modest, the clothes and food the same, and everyone listened to the Washington Nationals'—later the Senators'—games on the same brown celluloid radios.

During the Depression, it had been embarrassing to have more things, and during the war, not having things rather mysteriously helped what was called the "war effort." The best advertising minds in the country worked in reverse: "Use it up, wear it out, make it do, or do without." After the war, when we creaked back into consumer mode, someone—General Electric? General Motors?—came up with the slogan, "How American it is to want something better," and I was shocked. Surely if you always wanted something better, you were always unhappy with what you had? Jealous of your neighbors? It sounded nasty.

Naturally we all had certain essentials. Boys were supposed to play with balls and girls with dolls. I had dolls; I remember having dolls; they lived on the floor in a corner of the room, some of their heads flopping down on their chests, but I never knew quite how to play with them. Dressing them was a bore and pretending to mother them was silly when you had real babies available. I made up a language for them, called Doytle-Doah, and tried to hold conversations, but it was all pretty self-conscious.

The best children's toys were projects. Unharnessed by organized sports programs, we threw our energy into private accomplishment, and practiced in private, honing our expertise until it was ready for public display. Boys worked in secret on their yo-yo repertoire, perfecting each dazzling maneuver before they brought it forth to whistles of admiration. Girls worked on their roller-skating; an effortless wheeling stop, performed in the shortest space while casually chatting, required trial and error and many skinned knees. Jump-rope choreography was elaborately traditional and the skill levels were sharply marked. Slingshots had to be made by hand, needing a short, tough forked stick and a length of stout elastic, and then the target practice began, often involving the family cat and then, as one's aim improved, small birds.

Deep cultural factors swam under the surface, and no girl was allowed to play marbles or even watch too closely, as no boy would have been caught dead playing jacks: jacks resemble marbles in the skills and control involved, but the gender gap between them was sacred. Girls would throw balls, but they rarely worked at throwing them any faster or more accurately. Boys worked ceaselessly, since they were all going to be major-league pitchers someday. Basketball, back then, was what you had to play when the snow was too deep for baseball. Football was for colleges. Baseball was king. When not busy pitching at a mark on the garage wall, boys collected baseball cards and memorized World Series statistics with which to bore the grown-ups.

Peter's toys were anti-project: nobody ever got any better at starting and stopping an electric train. There was nothing to *do* with them. Even the Erector and chemistry sets required only a set of instructions to follow. In any case, Peter's grandfather took a dim view of strangers in his grandson's room possibly breaking his elegant stuff.

Outdoors, the only thing Peter wanted to play was Buck

Rogers, intergalactic space hero of comic books, for which he had a fancy costume and assorted ray-guns. I had to be his girlfriend, Dale, whose role was strictly supporting, and after a while I'd go home and read.

At some point Peter was at our house, and horsing around took place. I don't think I was involved, but maybe Nick was. The big metal garbage cans were somehow savaged and over-turned, and the mess spread far and wide. It was such an epic mess, blocking the driveway, that Mother called Peter's grand-father to suggest that Peter come back down and help clean up.

Peter's grandfather said, "Picking up garbage is no job for my grandson. Hire a blackamoor to do it." She swears that's exactly what he said, and I don't think even she could have made it up; she told it at dinner parties for years. The neighborhood children got wind of it, and when requests were made, such as "Hey, toss that ball over the hedge to me, will ya?" the answer was, "Hire a blackamoor to do it," and shrieks of laughter. It was pretty much the end of Peter socially. I think they moved away soon after, taking the English bike and the mechanical horse. Poor Peter. I suppose he was an unhappy child, but we had no sympathy. Children sympathize only with animals.

In the winter we dragged our sleds far afield in search of good sled runs. The best was a couple of blocks below the school, on Meadow Lane; it was quite amazingly steep for the area, zigzagging through woods, and at the bottom a slight rise kept most of us from shooting out into the street, at least most of the time. As winter wore on the run turned to ice, so that nothing controlled your progress but the frozen snow on either side, like an ungroomed bobsled run. Clumps of tree-roots stuck up and we sailed over them and landed with a teeth-rattling thud and flew on. One day Marshall Gibson landed with an exceptionally fine thud and ruptured his spleen and had to be rushed to the hospital. He himself reported later that he'd almost died. We were impressed. Not that we wished Marshall ill, but it certainly proved what we'd hoped all along: this was a gloriously dangerous run. We dubbed it Suicide Hill, and its fame spread until we had to stand in line waiting at the top, crowded by children we'd never seen before.

Our Mothers, even the most traditionally motherly, never had the slightest idea what we were doing. We didn't tell them. They didn't ask.

Fourth grade. The teacher, Miss Dobbins, hated us all equally and demographically and told us so on the first day of school, immediately after the Lord's Prayer. She hated us for being over-privileged and never even thinking about children who didn't have our advantages. Who didn't even have warm coats. Didn't have *shoes*. At her last teaching job, the children were so poor that they trudged long miles through the snow with their feet wrapped up in rags. (Somehow I got them confused with George Washington's army at Valley Forge, their feet also in bloody rags, and struggled for years not to see the Continental forces as fourth-graders with pigtails and freckles and three-ring binders.) We never found out where this school was and she may have made it up; I suppose she was slightly insane. Our school system, as Mother kept reminding me, was one of the finest in the country, but I had several teachers so interesting that they can't have been tested for mental stability; perhaps they still aren't. Or, again, Miss Dobbins might have been telling the truth, of Appalachia, at the tail of the Depression.

Geography was on the curriculum and she rolled down a map

of the United States and told us strange new things. The state where Mother and I had gone for her divorce, once AR-kn-saw, now turned out to be called Ar-KAN-zss, and we got yelled at for saying it wrong, and for neglecting the *s* in Illinois. Most geography was more local, and because we were in Maryland, we were given tracing paper and forced to reproduce its outline over and over. O fortunate children of the square midwestern states, of Kansas and South Dakota! Maryland's shoreline is a lacework of bays, rivers, and inlets of the Chesapeake, and our tracing paper was a tattered smudge full of eraser holes where the Potomac should have meandered.

Those were parochial days. We sang the Maryland state anthem, written rather a long time previously to the tune of "O Tannenbaum" and now inscrutable. Our childish trebles belted out,

The despot's heel is on thy shore, Maryland!
The torch is at thy temple door, Maryland!
Avenge the patriotic gore
That flecked the streets of Baltimore
And be the battle queen of yore, Maryland, my Maryland!

Most of us had been to Baltimore without noticing the bloody streets; many had even been to Ocean City without noticing the despot's heel. Nobody explained. After the War began, we sang the anthems of the armed forces and fierce ad-hoc ditties calling for victory over Germany and Japan and interspersed them loyally with the Maryland song urging our fair state to secede from the Union and join the Confederacy.

Miss Dobbins ad-libbed much of our education. I was impressed to learn that while all other life forms personally reproduced their kind, flies sprang spontaneously from dirt, filth, and evil, rising up without parentage like a Biblical plague to punish the unclean, and if we had flies around our house, it was a Sign. (I ran this past Mother, who said she rather thought flies laid eggs in the usual way, and went back to Agatha Christie.) I paid better attention to Miss Dobbins than to most of my teachers, because she was more interesting and had blood-curdling tantrums when her face turned purple and she threatened to shake our teeth out, but little that she told us—always dig your well uphill from your outhouse; cold water, not hot, for chronic chilblains; slashes and sucking for snakebite—was useful in later life.

The higher school authorities, whoever they were, had proclaimed that the overall theme of elementary school in that time and place was something called "community living." I can't imagine why nobody has written a hilarious novel about school authorities. Anyway, they decided that the perfect example of community living was goldfish. The goldfish lived in a bowl with plants, and the plants produced oxygen, or maybe nitrogen, and the goldfish shat in the bottom, and somehow photosynthesis was involved—I don't remember—and it all added up to co-operative community living, which children were supposed to apply to their future civic life somehow. As directed, Miss Dobbins had a goldfish bowl, and the fish kept floating to the surface with their white undersides showing, and I suppose this was instructive too. Anyway, for the few hours that I remembered the lessons, I went home and told Nick.

He wasn't in school yet, and sometimes he wasn't even in nursery school; there were sweet, understanding teachers in the local Nursery Cooperative but Nick was beyond the pale and kept getting thrown out for assault and biting. Unemployed, he waited for me to come home with revealed truths. I laid out the oxygen/nitrogen/plant/fish equation as I remembered it, and somehow, since nobody was teaching him anything else at the time, he noticed. It burrowed into him like a tropical worm, as these things do, all unnoticed, in children, and fish tanks appeared and multiplied, and he is now a world-famous marine biologist, so Miss Dobbins and the educational authorities did not live in vain, though as far as I can see he has never applied his knowledge to community living; he speaks only to his colleagues and post-docs and avoids his neighbors like cholera, but then, the goldfish never seemed much interested in their neighbors either.

Another idea struck the educational authorities, and word came down that a selected pupil was to read the Bible daily to the class. We already recited the Lord's Prayer and the Pledge of Allegiance before getting down to work, and now this too; Miss Dobbins rolled her eyes, scanned the class for possible readers, and said, "Barbara, from now on you will read the Bible to the class every morning. Now get out your notebooks."

It was a Friday, and I spent a bad weekend. For starters, the educational authorities assumed that every child would have a Bible, so none had been provided; our house must have included several million books, stowed in the attic, stuffed in the base-ment, lining the walls, but somehow no Bible. I knew Cynthia and her family went to church, so I went to Cynthia's mother. She was plainly shocked at my need—she may never before have met a person without a Bible—but of course she would give me one, poor child, they had half a dozen or more, all inscribed as rewards for religious accomplishments. I took it home, big and black and solid, and carried it up to my room.

"Read the Bible," Miss Dobbins had said. Well, even the educational authorities must know that I couldn't read the whole book aloud every morning, so the idea must be to pick something from it. What? Was it really up to me to decide, and if I guessed wrong, would Miss Dobbins have one of her tantrums? I couldn't ask Mother's advice, since in our family anything to do with religion was, like health and money, a non-subject.

An orderly reader, I started at the beginning. Genesis was vaguely familiar; I'd heard about the snake and the apple, though I didn't understand why God would plant a fruit tree right there in plain sight and then tell His new people not to touch it; why was He teasing them and why did He bother to make fruit nobody could eat? And the sacrifices. Why was the Lord so happy with Abel for killing and burning innocent baby lambs and so cross with Cain for burning a bunch of stupid vegetables? And when Cain killed Abel, He didn't seem half as upset as He'd been with Eve for stealing fruit. It was all very strange.

If I'd been of a churchly family, I could have asked someone and received the orthodox gloss on it, but as it was I was on my own.

The story petered out in a list of unpronounceable names and was getting pretty long for the start of a school day, so I looked elsewhere, skipping desperately around through the strangeness, until with great good luck I stumbled on the psalms. These I could read. They were recognizable poetry, and mercifully self-contained. I read my classmates a psalm a day, looking for the more rousing ones to hold my audience. ("Thou hast also given me the necks of mine enemies, that I might destroy them that hate me. They cried, but there was none to save them: even unto the Lord, but he answered them not. Then did I beat them small as dust before the wind. I did cast them out as dirt in the streets." Psalm 18, perfect for the playground.)

Bible-reading turned out to be a permanent post, and I stood up every morning and read a psalm for the rest of that school year and the two years following. In the meantime, I still had Cynthia's mother's Bible ready to hand, and I meandered through it, more and more baffled and dismayed. I cried at the Flood, and all the newborn babies, surely sinless, washed away, and all the kittens and puppies and lambs that weren't chosen to come aboard, innocently waiting to drown. How could Noah's family possibly live happily ever after, climbing over the bodies of their former friends and neighbors and the skeletons of all those helpless animals? No wonder Noah got drunk.

I cried clear through Job, but I was crying with rage at the sheer meanness of God, teasing and torturing him in order to win a bet. I cried hardest at Lot's wife; I could hardly think of her without tears, poor woman; she was good, she was doing what she was told, she took her husband's hand and walked away from her home, and just once she turned around, probably in tears, for a last quick look at it, and He turned her into a pillar of salt. I had never seen such a thing, but it was smooth and white in my mind's eye and when the sun shone just right maybe you could see her trapped inside, dead. Struck down for a moment's homesickness.

Cynthia had told me that all proper people referred to this as the Good Book, so surely it must be some lack of character or insight in me, that everyone else saw only good and I saw only murder and misery. It was twenty years before I moved on into the book's second section—which may have been what the educational authorities were talking about to start with.

I wanted no more of God. He was Carl on a cosmic scale. When He put His foot down, everyone died.

IN WHICH THE BEHAVIOR OF FATHERS IS
FURTHER ELUCIDATED, & A SISTER JOINS US

Finally owner of his own house, his monarchy, Carl multiplied his rules and put his foot down harder. When he came home from work, Nick and I, if we fell under his eye, were likely to get taken upstairs and walloped. I hesitate to say "beaten," since that implies some extra appliance like a stick or a belt or the cat-o'-nine-tails, and Carl used only his hand, but "spanking" has taken on a cute and almost playful meaning, and there was nothing playful about Carl's. He was a big, strong man with big, long hands made entirely of bone except for the leaping black hairs on their backs. Carl's hand was in no way inferior to a stick, or a plank. As I got older, and prideful, I tried not to cry, but that was a mistake, since he kept hitting until I did, and he was stronger than I was. Nick and I both cried, every time, and hated ourselves for it.

Carl rarely gave a reason. Fathers didn't explain; it would have been undignified. We accepted it like weather. Sydney Smith, the nineteenth-century wit and Canon of St. Paul's Cathedral, wrote, "I found . . . many grandchildren, all of whom I whipt immediately—never give any reason; it increases their idea of power and makes them more obedient." Smith may have been joking. Carl wasn't.

After he was dead, my aunt Lois told me that in his last year he'd said to her, "I've been a terrible father. All my children hate me."

I was surprised. "Was he bragging or complaining?" I asked cautiously.

"Oh, bragging," said Lois. "Definitely bragging."

Carl was born in 1900, and I think, at the time, if a man's children grew up fond of him, it meant he'd been lax in his duties.

Carl disliked eating at other people's houses, never went to restaurants or movies or took vacations, and traveled only when called away on labor arbitration cases. I think he avoided places where he couldn't put his foot down, places where he'd have to sit where he was told to sit. At home, he wore his four walls like a spiny carapace and his leather chair like a bulletproof skin.

Much later, after I was away in the world, some of his laws fell into disuse, but these years were his legislative heyday. The thermostat stayed at sixty-two and the bedroom radiators must never be turned on, even during measles. Lightbulbs must be no more than forty watts and turned off if you leave the room, however briefly. Nobody may be excused from the table until Carl has finished eating or, if he's talking, finished talking. No child may question his statements, even or especially in self-defense: to be accused by Carl was to be convicted. No cat may remain in the house while Carl is eating or spend the night in the house, even in the basement, for any reason including blizzards.

One January morning I opened the door to leave for school and our cat du jour was huddled on the porch tiles, curled around a litter of kittens born that bitter night. Three were already dead of the cold; two had survived and Mother put them in a shoebox by a radiator, but they died before I got home from school.

A later cat was seen in the hall as Carl was about to eat dinner; he grabbed it up by the neck and carried it out the back door, where he drop-kicked it down the six or eight steps to the concrete below. We never saw it again. Mother said it probably found another home, though it seems just as likely to have died under a bush of internal bleeding. Under Carl's law, no money was wasted on store-bought cat food, no cat was taken to a vet for shots, no cat was spayed or neutered, and no cat lasted long. Even I never mourned them for more than a few days. For years, until Carl began to mellow, they were too temporary: Chippie, Ike, Mrs. Patterson, George the First, George the Second, Violet Muriel, what happened to them all? They came and they vanished, perhaps while we were at school; perhaps they died and were quickly buried or perhaps they got driven to the shelter when they showed signs of pregnancy. Mother wasn't equipped to face our possible grief or reproaches, and she never explained.

I developed an invisible, rainbow-colored cat of my own named Bun-Eye who lived safe from Carl because he never heard of her. Mother did, and declared a jihad against her, and often claimed to have drowned her, but she sprang up like the phoenix. Told she couldn't come with us to Florida, she ran along behind the car, trailing some of her hundreds of rainbow-colored kittens, and refused to perish in the big Atlantic waves Mother called Bun-Eye-drowners. Bun-Eye alone survived life at Carl's.

In our respectable middle-class neighborhood where most of the fathers had strings of graduate degrees, Carl was a bit more autocratic than most, but only a bit. Next door, for instance, Margie's father, a power in the government and the foremost authority on something-or-other, wielded money. Margie, her older sister, and her younger brother were each given a small weekly allowance and had to write down every penny of its spending for the Friday accounting. She and I cooked the books in a last-minute rush, inventing the small but respectable outlays she might have made from the vanished cash. When her father came home, he assembled the children and went over their accounts. If all was in order he reached into his pants pocket and brought forth a handful of change and threw it into the air. The children, even Mary, who was twelve and ladylike, had to scramble together on the floor and under the furniture for the bonus pennies and dimes while the father stood watching.

Without knowing why, I found this disgusting. I was almost proud of Carl, that he would never do such a thing. Carl didn't believe in allowances. Though he was deeply involved in Roosevelt's administration and a stalwart supporter of the New Deal's generous programs, he drew the line at letting children feel entitled to money, which would make them ungrateful and lazy and give them delusions of independence. In theory, if we needed money for something we were to come to him and ask, but it seemed unlikely he'd say yes and we never did. I stole instead, pocketing loose change whenever I found it, and felt this infinitely nobler than begging from Carl. Later I took up shoplifting.

Not asking for things was my first and fiercest lesson, and it's been a dreadful nuisance. I sit by the phone telling myself, over and over, that the drywall man doesn't *mind* me calling, that's what his job is, I'm going to *pay* him, he doesn't *expect* me to patch my own drywall, he'll be *glad* I called.

I fill out the order blank and mail it rather than calling the toll-free customer service number, because the lady on the phone might say, "Give me one good reason why I should send you the green cotton shirt, catalog number 0377-B6, page 28, size small? Make your own damned shirt."

I only hope that, when my house catches fire, I can summon up the nerve to call 911 and ask them please to come put it out.

As each new child rises up from prostrate infancy and springs into the stew, it alters the family flavor. Judith, who had fished her genes from a different pool, learned to walk and talk and joined us. She had perfectly round blue eyes, yellow curls, and a sunny smile that she flashed on strangers in public. She was the little friend of all the world and came trotting back to us beaming, "I hi'ed that man!" Nick would cringe and hiss, "Mother, she's talking to those people and *we don't even know them*. Make her stop." Our reclusive Mother, who must have been as bewildered as we were, always made a special effort to favor Judith, trying to welcome this extroverted ray of sunshine into such an alien family. Judith never felt quite part of us, though, and when Mother read her *Madeline* she wept with envy because she couldn't live in an orphanage, where everyone did things together.

Nick and I tried hard not to do things with Judith. She was different. She didn't even get carsick, and bounced cheerfully in her seat while Nick or I, green-faced, groped in the roadside bushes for a place to throw up. After she started school, her teachers hugged her and said they simply couldn't believe she was Nick's—or Barbara's—sister, so neat, so cheerful, so co-operative, so friendly, such a pleasure to have in class.

We couldn't have put it in words, but the problem was that Judith was normal, and normal, back in psychiatry's glory days, was the ultimate goal in human achievement, often pursued fruitlessly for years on the couch, relentlessly sanding down the splinters in the psyche. Maybe Nick and I, maybe Mother too, wedged into our crooked corners, were jealous. Judith made it look easy.

Siblings in those days saw much more of each other than they do now, saw each other inescapably, and Judith tagged along as we went about our neighborhood business. Whatever we did, she tried to do, and as an extra irritant, whatever we said, she parroted.

"Mother," Nick roared, "She's copy-catting me!" Mother would explain that imitation was a compliment. Nick would give Judith a surreptitious kick, and she would shriek and run to the nearest grownup for comfort and vengeance. She kept a close eye on our doings and reported them to the authorities, who never doubted her word: who could doubt such round blue eyes? She was the mole among us, and if I'd buried a dead doll in the daylily bed or Nick strayed out of bounds up to Bradley Lane, all was known as fast as her short legs could carry her.

She had subtle ways of taunting Nick, invisible to the grown-up eye. She made faces at him when no one was looking until he howled with rage and threw his fork at her and got hauled to his room and walloped. When I defended him, I too got walloped. For weeks on end he was banished from the table and his plate carried up to his bedroom and set on his little blue work table and the door latched on his solitude. This was supposed to lighten the atmosphere at the family dinner but I'm not sure it did, though of course Judith was pleased.

Having trouble with *th*, he hissed Joo-DISS, and if I'd gotten any further in the Bible I would have heard it as Judas. He felt helpless against her. He *was* helpless against her. He was dyslexic, though there was no such thing at the time, and clumsy, and spilled his milk, and his mind worked faster than his tongue.

She was cute and quick and tidy and in all ways foreign to him. Even now they're scarcely civil, even at funerals.

In a modern home the conflict would have been diluted, Nick dosed with pharmaceuticals yet to be invented, each child with a separate television set and perhaps a separate computer, a separate pizza for dinner, and each off to separate after-school and weekend sports and lessons and programs, but this was then. Families were inextricably together. Many siblings grew deeply, even morbidly, attached to each other, and many others became lifelong mortal enemies. Nick and Judith couldn't avoid each other until their teens and the strife between them stained the air. I can't remember what tactics came into play, why Nick got punished so often and so fiercely and spent so much time locked in his room, or what Judith did to antagonize him, and often me too.

She looks back at her childhood with bitterness and remembers herself as a misunderstood child who only wanted to be liked, and the rest of us as hateful, but she was never punished. Carl was indulgent with her; her friendliness and curls must have made her a more suitable, childlike kind of child to have around.

"I was the nicest person in the whole family," she says. "I was the *only* nice person in the family." She doesn't remember spying and tattling, and it may be she didn't realize it was a violation of code; she had a natural respect for authority and felt it should be kept informed.

Chaos settled upon us. Mother, dismayed by any conflict, even among the cats, never punished, never raised her voice, but she did take to wandering around the house with a dazed look and a small glass of whiskey in her hand.

I took to hiding out in my bedroom, reading with a blanket

over my shoulders and sitting on alternate hands for warmth. I'd hiked illegally into Bethesda and shoplifted a notebook from the five-and-ten, and I started writing poems. My subject matter was just as vapid as might be expected but my rhymes and meters were impeccable and often elaborate, and small wonder, with all the verse packed into my head. I was pleased with myself that I had the mechanical part down cold—here, finally, was something I could do—and firmly believed that someday I'd find the stuff to put inside it. In the meantime, I practiced.

I didn't mention it to Mother. She judged all her children's works by professional standards; they were either good or not, never pretty good for a nine-year-old. She might not have insisted on Shakespearean quality, but certainly A. E. Housman or John Masefield at the very least. Wordsworth in his dotage, which was what my efforts most resembled, would never have made the grade.

On weekends, I retreated to Grandmother's.

I don't know what other children's grandmothers talked to them about. Did they tell them old folk tales? Bible stories? Reminisce about girlhoods long ago? Mine taught me the words to "Solidarity Forever."

> In our hands is placed a power greater than their hordes of gold
> Greater than the strength of armies multiplied a thousand-fold
> We shall bring to birth a new world from the ashes of the old
> For union makes us strong!

Daughter of nineteenth-century Colorado mining country, she spoke joyfully of labor unions and Mother Jones and furiously of scabs and Pinkertons. I rarely see strikers these days, but when

I do I can feel her watching me from the great beyond, eyebrow cocked, in case I should even dream of straying, and buying clothes I still feel I should look for the ILGWU label.

Several years ago a well-heeled friend said to me, "I was brought up to believe you must never, ever dip into capital. Weren't you?" "No," I said, "I was brought up to believe you must never, ever cross a picket line," and we gazed at each other in dismay across the chasm.

Grandmother lectured me on Hitler, Poland, Neville Chamberlain, and the weakness of France's Maginot Line. She raged over the shame of our foot-dragging neutrality. I listened, happy with the attention, and pretended to understand, and hung around the kitchen watching her cook the gentle, unsurprising meals of the time, the creamed chicken spooned over boiled rice, the upside-down cake made with slices of Dole canned pineapple on the bottom that, in the triumphant decanting, turned up on top, so sweet they made your head hurt.

The white-bread American cuisine of the day was disgusting and a disgrace to a civilized nation, but at its grassroots it provided long peaceful gaps in the day when even the most industrious woman sat down in a kitchen chair beside a bag of peas or beans, with a little girl beside her, and the two of them snapped the beans, stem and stern, peeled off the strings and broke them in half, or thumbed open the fat crisp pea-pods and scooped out the peas inside, round as a baby's toes. With a dish towel around my waist, I pounded flour into a tough steak with the edge of a heavy plate. This was called, for some reason, Swiss steak, and you pounded flour in ridges, first one way and then the other, the more flour and pounding, the tenderer. Holding the paring knife aslant, Grandmother could undress an apple of its peel in a swift, unbroken, long, red ringlet, which I ate. In this, at least, she was a proper Grandmother.

She'd never quite transplanted to the East. When she played poker, she insisted on cutting the deck, twice, even among family, and she played only five-card draw or seven-card stud, with nothing wild, no Eastern folderol, and nobody who hadn't paid to see them ever saw her cards; she showed her openers and stuffed the rest back in the deck and shuffled.

She also explained that the secret of cooking a trout is to have your fire burning well and your pan hot before you catch and clean it. Sometimes she used language brought from beyond the establishment world: "Who has the smallest pecker in the baseball industry?" she asked me. "Ted Williams, he just knocked up a fly."

I flinched. The rules governing Grandmothers were even narrower than those on Mothers, leaving no leeway at all, and with a mother who went barefoot and built bookshelves and a Socialist grandmother who played poker and said "pecker" and longed for war, how would I ever find my way in the world? Peculiar relatives make good stories in later life, but to a child they're a wobbly rudder.

Still, her house was a haven. With only two of us sharing the bathroom, I took long, long baths, adding more hot with my toes when the water cooled, and sometimes the edge of a book dipped under; red bindings bled copiously. At night, I slept. It was a lovely respite, but home always waited to reclaim me and the struggle between Nick and Judith raged unchecked.

I have a pair of heavy old Russian brass candlesticks that perhaps would be valuable by now, but Nick threw one at Judith. He missed and it hit the wall and warped into a permanent tilt so that candles drip down its back.

Not that I was innocent. Sometimes Nick and I joined forces and worked her over with psychological tortures. She was deliciously gullible, and I made up spells and incantations, and we marched around her chanting and gesturing until she howled and we got punished. It was worth it, though. I embroidered gruesomely on the evil spirits that would come in through her bedroom window while she slept, and for years she shrieked if anyone tried to open it.

To be fair, the retributions weren't always her fault. One evening as we began dinner, she kept kicking Nick secretly under the table until he bellowed, "Cut it out, you dumbhead little kike!" It was awesome. Carl rose up and flung his napkin on the floor, his face more terrible than we had ever seen it. *"Not in my house, you don't!"* he shouted, and grabbed Nick's arm, knocking his chair over, and dragged him limp and thumping up the stairs. The beating that ensued was epic; Carl's blows echoed like rifle shots through Nick's howls, until finally his door was slammed with a crash that rattled the plates. Carl came back to the table, huffing audibly. Nobody said a word.

Afterwards, with the grownups settled in the living room, I slipped into the kitchen and collected some bits of food and smuggled them upstairs. Nick's door was fitted with a heavy farm-gate latch for moments like this, and his furious tuggings at it regularly ripped off the molding, which Mother regularly replaced and painted. I unlatched it and eased in. Nick sat in the tangled mess of his bedding, still hiccuping and tear-stained, but curious. "Listen," he said, "what does it *mean*? Kike? Billy said it, but he didn't know either."

"I don't know," I said. "I never heard it. I'll try to find out, and tell you."

How to find out, though? This was clearly the most momentous curse word of them all, since our previous efforts had been greeted only by a raised eyebrow that meant "People like us don't use words like that." ("People like us" was Mother's disciplinary yardstick: people like us didn't chew gum, argue in public, drink sodas, brag, whine, call underpants "panties" or say "between you and I.") How could I ask a friend about so thunderously awful a word, and would the friend, horrified, stop speaking to me? Report me to the police? I tried the dictionary, but it wasn't there.

It took us months to find out and when we did, we still didn't understand, since most of the family friends were Jews, drawn to town by Roosevelt, and we couldn't see why they were entitled to a special nickname, rude or not. Carl would have had Hitler in mind when he yanked Nick out of his chair, but how were we to know?

We found out. War came—"Well, it's *about time*," said Grandmother—and the neighborhood children rose up and joined in, rejoicing.

OF WAR & OTHER MERRY PASTIMES

If there had been one thing lacking in our green and pleasant neighborhood, with its variety of children, its quiet streets and sleeping dogs, its vacant lots for building forts and digging tunnels, its trees for climbing and floppy forsythia bushes for hide-and-seek, its gloriously ordinary lives, that lack was purpose. We went out and played, first one thing and then another, and came home for dinner with nothing accomplished. No larger cause had been served.

War united us and gave point to our lives. It became our only game. Energy galvanized the neighborhood.

We took great pride in living in Washington, where we would be first to be bombed, first to be invaded, primary target in the world. In the decades since then I have met a number of people who were deluded as children into thinking themselves the primary target, by reason of living in Detroit, or Atlanta, or Seattle, or some such out-of-the-way whistle-stop, but they were fools. We would be first. We lay on our backs in the grass and searched the skies for enemy bombers, holding cards with silhouettes showing which were theirs and which were ours, and a phone number to call when we saw the first Heinkel 111 or Junkers 88 cruising over Connecticut Avenue. We dug tiger-traps in the vacant lots to trip invading infantry. We combed the neighborhood for spies, eavesdropping under people's windows to catch them in a telltale "*achtung.*"

At school, music class was the high point. It was a big class, so my voice didn't bother anyone, and when the bulk of your oeuvre is "The Marines' Hymn" and "When the Caissons Go Rolling Along," tonal quality matters less than energy; teachers from nearby classrooms came in to complain. Mrs. Holcombe, our music teacher, was a big motherly lady who'd sung grand opera, and she led us in martial roars from every country and every war since the Norsemen plundered the Britons and, in passing, we picked up more solid history than the schools would ever again offer.

From time to time, by fiat I suppose, she made us stand up and sing "The Star-Spangled Banner" as best we could, and I always flinched at "*Thuh* bombs bursting in air." Surely, with a moment's thought, he could have replaced it with something that scanned, like "The cannon's bright flare," but maybe he thought it was so silly there was no use fiddling with it. (We pledged allegiance to "one nation, indivisible," and I would have been outraged at poking in "under God" to spoil the sayable rhythm.)

We sang the praises of our fighting men. However flawed they may have been in civilian clothes, once in uniform they were covered by a national blanket of love and admiration, and I was jealous. I wanted to be a soldier, loved and important, accepted among comrades, and learn to shoot guns and save the world. On the other hand, though it was unpatriotic to think so, soldiers might possibly be shot at instead of doing all the shooting themselves. They might get killed. Apparently they did get killed. It was part of being a man. Nobody killed women, not on purpose; who would bother?

There were advantages to being female. Girls were required only to be mannerly, clean, and obedient, and our rules weren't as binding; if we did run and shout and dirty our clothes, as in certain girls' books, we would be scolded and punished and then forgiven.

Boys' rules were harder, and involved always being brave, never crying, and never refusing a fight or a dare, however dangerous. Mothers sometimes begged them to act like gentlemen, but Fathers told them to act like men, which was quite different, and if a boy broke the code of boyhood with tears or cowardice, he slid far down in the world and might never recover face with his peers or his father. A father whose son fell from grace might struggle forever with the cold misgivings in his heart.

I didn't have all this spelled out at the time, but I did see that it was safer to be female, simply because we didn't much matter. You could tell just listening: the very word "man" had a weight and solidity to it, an echo like the resonant clang of an anvil struck with a hammer, a bronze finality. The word "woman" was a wisp of a sound, like an apron on a clothesline. You could blow the whole word away with a breath, like a dandelion puffball. An elusive target, which was safer.

On the home front we all found work to do. Our teachers wanted us to ring doorbells to sell War Bonds and collect scrap metal, but we were busy brewing poison from laundry soap and cigarette butts, in case German officers stopped by for breakfast on their way to the Capitol. Mother spaded up the front yard and planted vegetables. This was called a Victory Garden—for a while there, everything was a Victory-something—and some of the neighbors complained, saying vegetables were traditionally planted out of sight, behind the house, but Mother said the back was too shady. Happy and dirty, she grew a lot of quite nasty stuff like Swiss chard and made us eat it because of the war, but that wasn't *our* idea of war. We made bows and arrows out of illicit tree-prunings, poisoned the arrow tips, and practiced marksmanship.

*   *   *

Not that all in the neighborhood was joyful. For instance, Lucille, whose back yard marched with ours and who cut through our hedge on her way to and from school, had a falling out with me. Harsh words were exchanged and she flounced home. That evening, as it unraveled later, when her father came home she told him that I'd chased her all the way to school that morning with a heavy iron rake, frightening her most dreadfully.

Etiquette would have had her father call on mine for satisfaction, but instead he went to the school principal, Miss Anna P. Rose, and said it was a damned shame that the school authorities couldn't protect a sweet child like his Lucille from hooligans like me, trying to kill her virtually on the school grounds. Miss Rose sent a messenger to my classroom; Miss Dobbins cast me a look of loathing and sent me with the messenger to the office. On the way, I tried a small anxious smile on the messenger and she scowled back.

On the wall behind Miss Rose was a dark steel engraving of a house half-buried in snow: *Snowbound*, it said underneath in elaborate script. I kept my eyes on it while she told me what I'd done. I was scared but somehow not surprised, and I denied it, which made things worse. She was outraged: I was saying, then, that Lucille's father, a pillar of the community (I'd never heard the phrase before and was briefly fascinated by the image), owner of his own advertising agency, had told her a *lie*? Of course not, I sputtered, but Lucille was mad at me, maybe she'd made it up?

This was worse. Lucille, a sweet little girl like Lucille, lie to her father? Violence was bad enough, attacking a helpless smaller child was worse, but accusations like that, defamation of the innocent . . . I forget the rest. I think she explained that if she received any more complaints about me, from anyone, ever, I'd be expelled from school immediately and all other schools warned against admitting me. And she'd be keeping an eye on me.

I went blank as stone. It seemed fitting, somehow, that all authority should be as cold, deaf, and dangerous as God Himself, poised to smite. No use arguing with God, nothing to do but cringe and try to flee.

Looking at it now, Miss Rose seems more reasonable. I must have been visibly a ruffian, unkempt and haphazardly dressed. Lucille was indeed smaller than I was, and pretty, and dainty, and her winter coat had a fur collar and her yellow curls were even more endearing than Judith's, being longer and professionally washed and set every week at Head's beauty salon. And of course she had blue eyes. Even now, a blue-eyed blonde can say almost anything and even the sternest authorities believe. Juries believe; hardened traffic cops believe; college admissions boards believe. Blue eyes seem transparent, with no place to hide deceit; blue as the Virgin Mary's gown, innocent as the vault of heaven itself.

Besides, it was rare then for a woman to be principal of a school, even a suburban elementary school, and she must have needed to watch her step with pillars of the community.

I never told Mother about it. There was a chance, just a chance, that she too would believe Lucille instead of me, which would mean the end of the world. I couldn't risk it.

Presently Lucille's family traded up to a fancier suburb, one with no Jews or hooligans admitted, and I didn't see her again for forty years.

She was hosting a television show and I'd been invited to talk about a book I'd written. She introduced herself, and I said, "But of course I know you, for heaven's sake, you lived on Bradley

Lane, we lived on Rosemary Circle, we shared a back hedge. We played together for years. Our brothers played together."

She said I was mistaken. She remembered everything about that house, those years; she remembered Tracy and Johnny next door, but she was firm that there were no children in my house, the house beyond the hedge. I described her dolls; I knew her brother's name (Courtland) and her mother's favorite piano music ("The Blue Danube") and her father's agency's big account, High's ice cream, and the slogan he gave it (Don't Look Now, But There's a High's Store Near You) and the gallons of the stuff he brought home.

She looked more than suspicious. She seemed angry, as if I'd been stalking her, hiring private detectives to winkle out her past, and our interview went badly.

I could have added, and I remember what was in your garage. As the war knuckled down for the long slog, her father had called in contractors to fill their enormous garage with shelves, and stocked those shelves—shamelessly leaving the doors open for all to see—with everything scarce or rationed; sugar, coffee, rows and rows of canned goods, imported whiskey, tires, cigarettes, gasoline, supplies enough to ride out the Hundred Years' War.

In those more secular days, civic virtue took the place of church and the whole virtuous neighborhood was shocked to the bone and the knowledge of that garage spread over our blocks like the smell of burning flesh. Hoarding was a sin, the major sin of the day, and such booty could only have come from the black market, a mysterious place so awful it was mentioned only in whispers. I always thought of it as a real market, a shadowy walled compound where all the sellers and buyers wore black, hooded, furtive, slinking, reaching into their robes to pull out money that was also, of course, black.

I'm sure nobody spoke to Lucille's parents after that, but I don't suppose they minded; they were trading up. Funny about her forgetting me, though. Maybe even the Lucilles of the world have conscience enough to blot out their sins. What have I blotted, I wonder?

At some point Hallelujah vanished. She simply disappeared, without saying goodbye; nobody seemed to say goodbye to children, or explain; it had taken me six months to learn that my grandfather had died. When I pinned Mother down, she said vaguely that Hallelujah was frightening Judith with her wild whoops and pounces. She was replaced by Viola Chase, which was fine, and Viola was in every way an improvement; as an assistant mother, Hallelujah had been quite useless, more like a raucous big sibling. Still, people shouldn't just disappear.

Viola settled into the basement room where all was quiet, far from Carl and the running battle between Nick and Judith, and I spent a lot of time there. I helped her with her Dream Book. We sat at the centerpiece of the room, an immensely ugly mahogany table, legacy from Carl's eccentric aunt, built like a bunker, under which we all crouched during air-raid drills. Viola was a practicing Catholic and every Sunday morning a handsome, well-dressed man came to the door to drive her to mass, and when troubles threatened our family she made a novena, but she did play the numbers, which was against the law and quite possibly disapproved by the Church. Once a week she got a phone call from a man who seemed to be calling from deep inside a metal barrel, and when Nick or I answered the phone and heard him we ran to the top of the stairs and hollered, "Viola! It's your numbers man!" and she would hurry up the steps with a slip of paper. She played a quarter on each number, and often hit for a few dollars. The numbers came from the Dream Book, a limp, fat, tattered volume in which you looked up key words from your dreams. The dreams were analyzed, for publishing legitimacy, I suppose, and then assigned a number to play.

I always insisted on reading the whole explanation, rather more astrological than Freudian, while Viola kept saying, "Just the number, we just need the number." Once she dreamed that Carl was dead and laid out on the dining room table, under a sheet, with four candles, one at each corner. It was a clear and vivid dream, obviously useful, so we puzzled over it and finally picked the key words "death," "candles," "funeral," and "table," for a quarter each. The number that hit, and it hit big, was for the key word "employer." We both felt terrible, and I blamed myself for sloppy research.

Aside from her gambling, Viola was level-headed and clear-eyed. In the little black town of Hughesville, down in Maryland's tobacco country, she had raised eleven children of her own and learned a thing or two; if her grown children who sometimes came to visit were a sample, she was good at it. I never saw her calm crack. She was our rod and our staff, though not always to comfort us. She considered, and she judged, and when necessary she untied her apron and went up through the back yards to the kitchens of our friends and consulted there with the maids of our friends, and together they worked out judgments based on close daily knowledge of the children involved, knowledge that might have astonished our parents. In the underworld of the young, the maids' word was law, in a way the parents' word never could be, because we all knew that our parents, frankly, hadn't a clue what was happening. When parents intervened they usually made things worse and sometimes started blood feuds.

In the mornings, Viola tidied up, avoiding children's rooms in an inaccessible state of mess, which was all of them all of the time, and in the afternoons she sat at the kitchen table with ashtray and newspaper, free to dispense advice.

Viola believed that character was destiny. "Barbara," she said, "you is bullheaded. Just bullheaded. It's going to bring you great grief and sadness in life." Sometimes she said, "Born to trouble as the sparks fly upward." She shook her head with genuine regret, but I was made happy. It was a description, not a reproach. Everyone's mothers and fathers believed in perfectibility. They truly believed that if we all tried just a little harder, really worked on it, we could overcome every character flaw and become the perfect people they fully expected us to be. When we fell short, it was because our efforts weren't valiant enough; we should try harder. Viola felt we weren't going to change the way we were born to be. It was an immense relief.

In the spring, Viola paid us to pick dandelions, which she took down home for the annual making of dandelion wine. *Dandelion wine* seemed to me the most beautiful words in the language and still echo in my head with spring, and sweetness, and community, and love. I—and Nick till he got bored—pronged up the flowers between two fingers and stuffed them into their bag full of gold.

Mother was pleased. Every dandelion picked was a dandelion not left to mature into a puffball to be blown away, by child or wind, to make more dandelions.

On sunny afternoons Mother dug them out of the lawn, carefully, with a table knife, spiraling it as deftly as a surgeon so as not to break off the long pointy taproot and leave a scrap to engender a clutch of offspring. The same knife served for crabgrass, pried up with its massed white worms of roots. It was brainless, stressless, satisfying work that left the mind free to wander and left the lawn looking rather moth-eaten where she'd been over it.

Lawns now are strictly disciplined. Consisting of nothing but lawn grass, each blade engineered to grow like every other blade, they look quite splendid from a distance, through a window, calling to mind the stately homes of England, but up close they're as boring as rugs. The lawns of former days were broad, low-lying flowerbeds of uninvited guests, dandelions vivid yellow in the sunshine, violets blue and white in the shade. Up close they were a miniature ecosystem, and children could lie on their stomachs and watch the very smallest of nameless bugs laboriously climbing to the top of a grass blade, swaying for a moment, and then climbing back down, having accomplished nothing discernible.

Lawns then were full of clover, and the clover bloomed in small pink-and-white explosions, and honeybees came to them, and barefoot children stepped on the bees, over and over, all summer, and the bees stung them. With my bitten fingernails I couldn't pull the stinger out myself and had to hobble into the kitchen for Viola, who extracted it deftly and covered the wound with a paste of baking soda and water. Baking soda was the treatment of choice for all bites, burns, and itches, but I developed a taste for it and peeled it off and ate it, flake by flake, before it finished its therapy.

Sometimes there were four-leaf clovers. Not the proper Irish shamrock, too sturdy a growth for lawns, just the occasional genetic sport of the usual clover, and its leaves were good luck. We spent a lot of time looking for them and never found them. My aunt Peggy found them. Peggy could hardly walk six paces across a lawn, her own or someone else's, without bending over to pluck a lucky leaf. That was Peggy, though, that was just what you'd expect from Peggy, who walked always in a kind of grace and favor with the gods. Four-leaf clovers followed her. When you opened a book in Peggy's house, dried four-leaf-clover leaves pressed in its pages fell out and shattered on the floor.

In shady places, lawns then were full of sourgrass, which we ate for its wild bitterness, and chickweed with its tiny blue flowers like stars, and ground-ivy, and ant-hills of soft reddish-brown dirt, round as saucers, with their population endlessly marching around on the serious business of ants, sometimes over our bare legs because nothing sidetracks an ant bent on business. The red ants would sting you on their way by, but black ants kept their minds on their work.

After a rain there were earthworms, and we chopped them in half to see if, as we'd heard, each half went off on its own. If you cupped your hand and moved slowly and then pounced, you could catch a grasshopper, but they were jointy and twitchy and their feet scrabbled and you were glad to let them go. Cats couldn't resist them. Cats caught them and then felt duty bound to eat them, and afterward threw up on the porch.

Down below the grownup eye level, even the best-kept suburb seethed with action.

War brought new people to Washington and shook up our population. At school, one hot day in June, a girl who'd transferred in from San Diego came to class wearing Bermuda shorts—*pants*—and had to be sent home to change. The family who moved in next door came from Boston and brought a housekeeper named Lillian who was white; Carol's family moved in from southern California and brought a Japanese houseboy who chased children out of the kitchen with a broom and terrible strange words. (They must both have been dreadfully lonely, but I doubt if they made common cause.)

Strangest of all, four houses up, we got a family of Republicans. The son of the house, young Edward, Nick's age, went up and down the block ringing doorbells and telling us they were Republicans.

I'd asked Mother once what Republicans were, and she'd said, "They're people who give very dull parties where the men all stand around together talking about money and the women all stand around together complaining about the servants." Edward's family, however, gave wildly jolly parties, to which I was invited as a baby-sitter.

One night, after they'd been to a late party, the Republicans came home and he went to bed and instead of sending me home she invited me into the kitchen to talk to her while she disemboweled a goose. The following day was probably Thanksgiving or Christmas, and this daughter of Texas had found herself somewhere a whole goose, a goose in a state of nature, barely dead, and in her party dress, laughing, with her sleeves rolled up, she reached into it and extracted miles of brightly colored guts and peculiar organs and flung them down, and whacked off its head, still laughing and chatting in the midnight kitchen. Perhaps Mother was wrong about Republicans.

Nick fell helplessly, guiltily, in love with their daughter, Sally

Ann. They were Texans, and Texas women, even at age five, even Republicans, have a certain something.

Wartime rationing and shortages fell on the grownups, not the children. We had other things to do. Grownups had to fiddle with ration stamps of different colors, in limp little books, and construct a dinner out of them. Mother, who felt that every minute spent thinking about food was a minute thrown away, hated figuring out stamps for canned goods or meat or whatever, and it's a wonder she didn't just make us eat grass and trees. Viola, a good plain southern cook whose chicken dumplings were like clouds, learned to make messes out of boiled dried soybeans. We ate them. Children ate what was put in front of them, without comment, and barely noticed.

Not that we would have complained anyway; even before the war, no child was allowed to speak harshly of food. You didn't have to like it, but you did have to eat it. Legacy of the Depression, I suppose. By the same token, my generation was raised to feel that, while wasting money might be silly, wasting food was wicked, shameful, a sin, and to this day all of us still put unwanted bits of dinner in the refrigerator and wait patiently until they grow green fur so we can throw them away with a clear conscience.

The Federal government made no distinction, in clothing stamps, between children who outgrew their shoes four times a year and grownups who didn't, so Nick and I walked our way through all the shoe stamps in the extended family. Judith was pillaged of every stamp she was issued.

Cigarettes were sent off to our brave boys in uniform. Civilians stood in line for them, and except for my aunt Peggy, who was wicked and had contacts, often came away without. Viola brought tobacco from down home and Mother bought a rolling machine, a wobbly little device in red tin, and she and Viola toiled over it at the kitchen table. Viola, of course, didn't need a machine and could roll a smooth, professional cigarette and lick and seal it one-handed, without looking, like a cowboy. Mother's best efforts looked like a bundle of dirty socks and, if held at an angle, leaked flaming crumbs onto the table. Viola despaired of teaching her, as she despaired of making her hang up her coat.

Scarcities were for grownups to worry about. Imports were cut off, metal and rubber had gone to war, plastic hadn't yet come to town, and the only toys available for Christmas were makeshifts. New dolls were made of pink pressed celluloid that dented permanently under the thumb and squashed flat when stepped on in the dark. New toy cars and trucks were printed on sheets of stiff paper, to be punched out and stuck together by tabs in slots, and expected to roll around on punched-out paper wheels.

We didn't care. Christmas was an event, the great event of our year. At school, the Army Air Corps song yielded to carols. There was no Frosty, no Rudolph, just the old politically incorrect ones, and we sang all the verses of all of them. Our childish trebles rang out with

> Myrrh is mine, its bitter perfume
> Breathes a life of gathering gloom,
> Sorrowing, sighing, bleeding, dying,
> Sealed in a stone-cold tomb.

All unchurched as I was, it gave me goosebumps.

At home, Christmas, with or without loot, and aside from some sparklers on the Fourth, was our only event. Since Mother disdained food, Thanksgiving was a muted and slightly grudging affair; we were forbidden even to mention Mother's Day, mercenary trick concocted by florists and candy shops; and only Andrew, the last and youngest of us, with his passion for dates, ever discovered Mother's birthday. Christmas, though, she did properly, starting with the tree, which she selected and set up and trimmed herself, a long deliberate ritual with each light and ornament and strand of tinsel in its one perfect place. No child under ten was allowed even to hand things up to her on her stepladder.

It was a work of art, and neighbor children dropped by to admire it. One little boy spent most of an afternoon on the living room floor, gazing in wonder as if at the babe himself. Finally his sister came to haul him home for dinner.

"Why can't we have a Christmas tree?" he mourned.

"Because we're Jewish," she snapped, and dragged him away. He gazed over his shoulder like Lot's wife, clearly feeling that Jewishness was small compensation.

We understood that the presents this year would be thin, in honor of the war effort. Strangely, though, Nick got a big solid dump-truck and I got a bike, both made of what came to be called, wistfully, pre-war steel. We didn't ask where they came from—Christmas presents didn't "come from" anywhere, they simply were. Mother had read us "The Night Before Christmas," of course—though she rather spoiled the effect by adding, after "Tore open the shutters and threw up the sash," "Shouldn't have eaten the sash in the first place"—but she made it clear that Santa was a myth, or perhaps the author was dreaming, and while I sometimes wrote down my Christmas hopes and burned them in the fireplace, I knew it was pure superstition.

We told all our friends there was no Santa Claus and their mothers complained. Nick, larval scientist, also told them there was no God and how cats came to have kittens. It's a wonder anyone was allowed to play with us. Nick was a proselytizing atheist, and I once saw him out in the street, surrounded by his neighborhood pals, dancing up and down and shaking his fist at the dark sky, crying "God! God! If you're really up there, prove it! Hit me with lightning! Hit me with lightning!" Prudently, his friends ran for their homes, jackets pulled over their heads.

Years later, Mother confessed to the Christmas bike and truck. Over in Bethesda, by the Farm Women's Market, where fresh eggs and bread could be bought on Wednesdays and Saturdays, a sort of corral had been set aside for donations of scrap metal and rubber to aid the war effort. I don't know whether any of this junk actually made it as far as the war. It may have been a scam to keep the civilians feeling busy and useful.

Mother cased the collection and wrestled with her conscience. She'd recently wangled a pair of retread tires for the old Plymouth, stashing the bald retirees in the trunk. Under cover of darkness she went back to the corral and solemnly tipped her tires over the fence and liberated, in exchange, a rusty toy dumptruck and a battered girls' bike. These she hid away somewhere in the basement and worked on after bedtime. The truck was scoured with steel wool and repainted in bright yellow and its wobbly wheels tightened and its axles straightened. The bike got its inner tubes patched and inflated, its chrome polished, and its dented fenders banged out, sanded down, and painted red. In the meantime, Grandmother was recycling dinner napkins and dish towels and buttons to sew a magnificent wardrobe for Judith's doll. It was a fine, resourceful Christmas.

I don't know whether Mother ever confessed her trade to Carl, whose patriotic virtue was iron-clad, but probably she didn't need to, certainly he didn't ask. Christmas presents weren't his concern, though every year he did renew Mother's subscription to the *New Yorker* and make a ritual trip to the bank to buy a silver dollar for Viola. One year he gave me one too. I didn't know why, and it made me nervous. I hid it away in my sock drawer and eventually it disappeared—I expect Becky, the magpie sister, made off with it. Spending it might have been risky, like eating the gingerbread from the witch's house.

Except during courtship, men didn't give presents. One Christmas my long-lost father sent a deluxe, boxed, illustrated edition of *Peter Pan*, which I'd thoroughly outgrown, so we took it to a bookstore and traded it in. The next year he sent another, identical *Peter Pan*, and I was hurt: didn't he remember? Mother said he was a busy man—he was managing a chain of New York bookstores—and had probably told his secretary to pick out something and mail it, and besides, books could be exchanged for other books, so it was just as good as money, or better, since nice people didn't send money.

After that I didn't hear from him again. When I was twenty I looked him up and went to New York to see him, and we got drunk together at the Brevoort, drinking warm Scotch from the tooth glasses while he offered me tales of the Village in its golden days. My aunts had told me he was handsome, dashing, arrogant, and brilliant, but by this time he'd gone a bit seedy. I didn't mention Peter Pan. Back then, ex-parents didn't hang around; the children of divorce were expected to forget them as quickly as possible, like a bad dream. Come to think of it, forgetting was the therapy of choice for most wounds.

Though it was a size too small for me, the Christmas bike weighed a ton and wrestled with its rider at every turn and when it fell over on you, it gouged flesh. I loved it dearly. It was wheels, glorious wheels, and my horizons rolled out into the wild blue yonder, or at least as far as the public library, which was the same thing. If Carl evicted me, I could even ride it clear to Grandmother's house, now that I knew the way. I could find it even by night, clinging to the sides of the roads, and Carl, who didn't drive, couldn't give chase.

The war did have one horrible side effect, filtered down from the nation's draft boards. Inspecting the crop of young men called up for service, they found them a weedy lot, scarcely able to chin themselves on a bar or do more than a handful of push-ups before collapsing on their chests. Apparently they'd spent their childhoods pitching baseballs instead of chinning themselves, and how could we lick the Nazis if we couldn't even pull our chins up over a bar? The draft boards complained to the education authorities, and the education authorities handed down their mandate. All children in school, even the smallest, must give up their casual recess and spend part of each day in strenuous organized games to fit themselves for war.

I had worked out a fragile adjustment to school, and by never raising my hand or answering questions I was passed over as possibly feebleminded and left free to daydream my way through the hours. The dream was over. Hillcrest Place was closed to traffic and volleyball nets set up and teachers stood by with police whistles. The point of volleyball is to knock a large hard ball into the face of a classmate. If the target were quick she could punch it away with her fist, but it was safer just to cover your face and duck. Apparently it had rules, at least I was often yelled at for breaking them and everyone else already knew them, but I never even tried to figure them out. I was busy protecting myself.

I wore glasses, nasty little round glasses with wire rims that gave me a marsupial look, and they were made of glass. When they fell on the bathroom floor, they broke. When I got hit in the face with a ball, they broke. Mother always frowned anxiously at the cost of replacement. Also I thought about broken glass in my eyes. I thought about it a lot. Volleyball alternated with softball, which was better because you could spend some of the time out of harm's way, and when I was up at bat I held the bat with both hands squarely in front of my face, hoping to ward off the blow.

Always an outsider, now I became a pariah, and classmates who had never noticed me before came to know and hate me. When team captains chose up sides, they argued loudly over which team got me. (The opposing team should have received a stiff handicap, but that never occurred to anyone.)

Going to school escalated into torture. Fridays were lovely, Saturdays were all right, but Sundays were shadowed all day long by Monday. Countless children have come to sturdy grips with far worse, generations of British schoolboys survived, all the better for it, to write their memoirs, but I was made of flimsier stuff and simply folded.

The sports mandate stayed in place clear through my high school years and I devoted most of my attention to avoiding gym class, anything short of shooting my own foot off, while wily gym teachers grew skilled at rooting me out of my hiding places. I suppose I could have made an effort, worked at learning the rules of the games and somehow taken part in them, but I never tried: like carrying a tune, if you couldn't, you couldn't. At home, on my own turf, with neighbors, I chalked out hopscotch patterns on the sidewalk; I played swinging statues and freeze-tag and giant step and Mother may I; I knew all the jump-rope rhymes; we even played improvised baseball with a headless broom and a dead tennis ball and a tree for a base. But as soon as it moved across the street to school, any game snarled and bared its teeth.

I don't remember being sickly—Mother wouldn't have allowed it—but I did cough all winter. The whooping cough had damaged my pipes and tubes, and I coughed and coughed in the night, until she came in and stood over my bed in the dark and told me to control it. "The more you cough," she explained, "the more you're going to cough, because it irritates your throat. Just tell yourself you're going to stop, and you will."

Carl must have sent her, since Mother was a famously solid sleeper. I did try, clenching my jaws over the hacking and pressing them shut with both hands, and choked and gagged. As soon as I relaxed, I coughed harder than ever. Weekends, when I went to her house, Grandmother brewed her special cough medicine, equal parts of whiskey, honey, and lemon juice, stir and sip as needed. It was delicious, though I don't remember that it did much for the cough.

We went to Florida again. Viola declined to come with us, so Mother enlisted my aunt Peggy, always the merriest company, to join us and bring her little girl, Karen, aged just between Nick and Judith. They drove down; we took the train. It was wonderful, the train ride, even better than the car trip, especially when Nick insisted on going to the men's room, alone, and locked himself in the toilet and roared and banged in there until quite a crowd gathered. Mother persuaded a passing man to help. The man squatted down in front of the toilet door, at Nick-level, and patiently called out instructions to him until finally the latch moved and the prisoner emerged, tear-stained and quite enraged by the humiliation.

How did Peggy and Karen drive down? Impossible to stay out at the beach cottage without a car, but where did the gas come from? Had Peggy committed the ultimate crime, or did she and Mother save up and pool their ration stamps, which as I remember were good for only three gallons a week? Another mystery.

We made a fine, noisy houseful. Nick enticed the gullible little girls into acts of rebellion and then slipped hastily off the scene, leaving them to be caught alone in flagrante, but Carl was a thousand miles away and no punishments ever befell us. I worked my long-division problems in the wet sand. On days when the ocean lay flat, Mother struggled to improve my flutter kick, but I couldn't keep my knees straight, and I still can't. Other days, we all slopped around in battered old inner-tubes that Mother kept alive with a bicycle pump and many square pink patches. There was no school. No volleyball. I wallowed in a daze of bliss.

Nick and I tied threads to the back legs of palmetto bugs and raced them. After dozens of failed tries, we cornered a sand crab away from home by covering its holes. Knowing it was doomed, it stood its ground gallantly and waved its fighting claw at us, goggling with bright black eyes on stalks. Nick snatched it up and got a nasty pinch while wrapping it in his shirt. We brought it home and put it in a box under his bed, where its hopeless scritchings troubled the night.

In the morning we were going to take it back to the beach, but it was dead.

It was this time, on this trip, that Mother had a pretty dress. I don't remember the occasion—perhaps visitors down from the North? The dress, with a narrow waist and full skirt, was made of something called, I think, piqué, a heavy cotton fabric dimpled with tiny indentations, and it was white with big splashy purple-blue petunias all over, Georgia O'Keefe petunias. Mother looked dazzlingly, peculiarly beautiful, like someone else entirely. I stared and stared, alarmed.

Where did it come from, the dress? Did Peggy take her to a store and make her buy it, or was it maybe Peggy's, and Mother borrowed it for the occasion, whatever the occasion was? Perhaps so. I don't remember seeing it again.

In Washington the war, though great fun, was largely imaginary; on Florida's east coast it was actually happening. We were under full blackout every night, with Mother's dyed black curtains tacked to the window edges, and we hurried back from town before dark because the top halves of the headlights were painted black, seriously restricting vision and likely to send you wallowing into deep sand at the road's edge, so hard to tell from the shallow sand drifted across the road itself. The lighthouse up at the faraway point was dark now at night, inviting Germans and local fishermen to run aground. Weather forecasts were military secrets, lest they aid the enemy, and all the road signs had been taken away to confuse invaders. Every morning and evening the Coast Guard plane flew down the beach, low, checking for landing parties, and dipped its wings to greet our little red-tile roof, and we waved.

German submarines prowled under the smooth blue waters and sank our tankers on their way to Port Everglades. Great globs of crude washed up on the beach and stuck to our feet, to be scrubbed off in a bucket of turpentine kept on the doorstep. Fighter planes practiced just off our shores, peeling one by one out of formation to swoop down and strafe sleeve-targets towed by a slower plane. The highest point for miles around was an Australian pine tree at the edge of our chalk road, and I spent hours swaying in its thin top branches tracking the convoys that crawled along the horizon but never, alas, exploded in flames, or anyway not while I was watching.

Leona came days to help. She got a ride up the beach with the milkman in the morning, and in the afternoon Mother drove her back to Colored Town. Nick and I sometimes went along. Leona insisted on sitting in the back seat, and I felt silly sitting in front with a grownup in back, but Mother said it was the custom here.

We loved Colored Town. You could see right away how it got its name. Landscaping along a beach is harsh and monotone, limited to what grows in deep sand, but back inland, west of the train station in the land nobody else wanted, the dirt was black and rich and Colored Town simply bellowed with color. The little frame or cinder-block houses were painted pink or yellow or green, but you could hardly tell for the great flowering jasmine and bougainvillea vines that smothered them. Their front porches were draped with bright vines on strings and festooned with hanging baskets of red and purple fuchsias, and their yards were so thick with blooming crape myrtle and camellias and hibiscus there was no room to walk. The sky was blue over all. Everything smelled of flowers and frying fish.

The roads were smooth dirt. The only two-story building was

a pink cinder-block store on the corner with a Budweiser sign in the window and a bleached Coca-Cola poster on the wall. The Paradise Store, it was called. Once Leona took us in and bought us licorice whips.

Mother hauled the gallon thermos jug out of the car and carried it in to fill with Leona's water; the water out at the beach came from a shallow well under the house and tasted much like the ocean itself. Mother said she didn't mind it straight, but made into coffee it foamed up in yellowish suds. Leona had inland water.

One late afternoon two men came out of the Paradise Store, one of them carrying a grocery bag, their feet kicking up puffs of dust from the road. Leona called to them. "Obie. Will. Evenin'."

"Evenin', Leona."

"Come over here and meet my churren." I loved the way she said "churren"; it sounded like what a mother bird would say at bedtime in the nest.

She laid her hands on our shoulders and gave us a gentle shove forward. "These are my white churren. Barbara and Nick, shake hands now."

Nick scowled horribly and pushed back to hide behind Leona, but I held out my hand and the man called Obie took it in his long cool fingers, and the one called Will said, "Pleased to meet you, Barbara."

I felt we had been let in, like joining a secret club. Now I could come back to Colored Town whenever I wanted, an honorary member, because Leona was a person who mattered here and her children were under special protection.

Mother told me it was the nasty law here that nobody from Colored Town could leave and go east of the railroad tracks after dark without a signed and dated reason from a white landowner. I nodded sycophantically and agreed that this was mean. Privately, though, I didn't see why anyone in Colored Town would want to leave it, ever.

Early one morning Nick and I got bored waiting for breakfast so we went down to the beach, along the wobbly, bleached boards through the sawgrass. Sometimes interesting things had washed up in the night. I found one of the shiny brown pods we called sea-beans; I'd told myself they were good luck, like a rabbit's foot but not so gruesome, and if you kept one in your pocket and fondled it, it developed a fine brown sheen, signifying luck.

The waves hissed quietly and receded. And then we saw it, a lifeboat, a big, serious lifeboat with room for maybe ten people, run aground in the sand.

It was on our beach. It was our lifeboat. At first I hoped it was left by an enemy landing party that might be lurking nearby, but when we got to it and climbed in, the words were in English. The name of its ship was on everything, the life preservers, the neatly stowed lockers of food and provisions. Joyfully we set about looting it, and opening the boxes and rummaging among the gear.

The Coast Guard Jeep roared up and plowed across the beach and two officers jumped out. I suppose their early plane must have spotted it before we did. They shooed us out and quickly, efficiently, stripped it of everything that came loose, every identifying mark, and stowed it all in the Jeep. Then they stood us up together and looked at us hard.

"You can read, can't you?" asked one.

"Of course," I said, stung.

"Did you read the name of the ship? On the life preservers and all?"

"Of course."

"No, you didn't." He fixed me with a serious military stare. "You didn't see the name. You don't remember it, do you understand? You won't ever remember it. Either of you. Will you?"

I felt so important I almost fell down. "No," I whispered.

"No what?"

"I won't remember."

A minute later, I didn't. I still don't. Nick doesn't either.

I thought afterwards maybe it was the name of a state, but Mother said probably not, since that would mean a battleship and surely we'd have known if something so important had gone down. We wouldn't have, though. In the war, we weren't allowed to know anything, which meant we got to invent it all. Everyone invented it all, and posters appeared warning fiercely against spreading rumors—LOOSE LIPS SINK SHIPS, THE WALLS HAVE EARS—but we couldn't help it.

The lifeboat itself was too big for the Coast Guard or the tides to take away, so it stayed, and worked its way deeply into the sand, and shipped water full of small skittering sea-life for Nick to chase. At high tide, you could dive off its stern. We were inordinately proud of it.

And then we piled into the Plymouth and went home, and I turned back into my previous self. As I struggled my arms into my outgrown coat to trudge to school, I was sure that the other me was still barefoot up in the Australian pine tree, rocking in the salty wind, watching for ships and tunelessly shouting songs of her own devising. She seemed several sizes larger than the northern me.

*   *   *

Briefly, that school year, my teacher was a man, a riveting novelty. Mr. Weis was forbidden by law to lay violent hands on bad boys, but nobody'd said he couldn't throw chalk at them, and he threw with amazing speed and accuracy. It stung, and the boys yelped. Alternatively, he crept up behind them and whacked their desks with the wooden yardstick provided for drawing lines on the blackboard. The crack was satisfying and everyone jumped. Often the yardstick broke. I don't know what the supplies office thought of the way he went through yardsticks.

School was punctuated by air-raid drills, an improvement over the fire drills of yore for which we had to stand in long shivering lines on the playground while our teachers counted us, and then wait until, presumably, the flames died down and we could go back inside. For air-raid drills, we trooped instead down to the basement cafeteria, where I'd never been before, smelling of cement and steamed broccoli, and sit against the walls with our knees over our ears. It was warmer than fire drills.

One day somebody got the signals crossed and announced a genuine air raid headed our way. We were to go home in an orderly fashion, not to dawdle nor to panic and rush out into traffic, and head straight for our basements and sit with our knees over our ears as previously instructed. (Why we were sent to the cafeteria for a pretend air raid but sent home for a real one is another mystery.)

Mr. Weis did not turn us immediately loose. He unfurled a map of the world and showed us how far away Germany was, and how the danger of its bombers was probably exaggerated. He made us sit at our desks while he laid out a few facts about the war itself, and how the Treaty of Versailles had given

Germany the rack-and-thumbscrews and made this war, and Hitler, inevitable.

We were aghast. Nobody had ever told us anything so subversive before. Hitler and his countrymen were mad dogs, ravening fiends from hell for whom no excuse could be made nor reason found. A week or so later Mr. Weis vanished between Tuesday and Wednesday without saying goodbye and was never heard from again. Maybe his opinions reached the authorities and got him fired, or maybe he just found a job more suitable for a grown man.

I went home in an orderly fashion and found Mother reading on the couch. "The Germans are coming," I told her. "We have to go down to the basement. It's an air raid, a real one."

She looked up and struggled to focus on me. "Oh, I don't think so," she said.

"But it's true! They closed the school and sent us home!"

"I expect it's a mistake," she said.

I stood there awkwardly in the middle of the room, the bearer of momentous news like a torch that had sputtered out in my hand. I could hear Viola singing to herself and the thump of her iron, and smell the steaming shirts. Mother turned a page. All was peace and order. Germany was clear across the ocean, and even the ocean now was far away.

I went out to play.

Mother went out to work.

IN WHICH MOTHER CONTRIBUTES TO THE WAR EFFORT

With all those men away at war, the Government viewed the work force with alarm. Who would make the guns and tanks to keep the war in business? For that matter, who would hold the fabric of civilian life together, drive the buses and taxis and ring up the groceries? With an audible wrenching shudder, the Government told women to go to work. For the war effort, women, even married women, even Mothers, should tear themselves away from their beloved kitchens and go out in public to work at actual jobs. Their husbands would understand. Patriotism called.

It was easy, when all the world was young, to hold two or more conflicting visions at once. On the one hand, all proper women stayed home, either demurely waiting for a husband or, after they'd got one, fussing with dishes and laundry. On the other hand, all proper schoolteachers, nurses, waitresses, file clerks, telephone operators, and secretaries were women. It could be argued that these were either women still trolling for husbands or women of a lower caste who simply didn't count; this wasn't true, but it was convenient to think so. Still, unmarried women could quite correctly go out and do jobs that no sane man would dream of doing, like typing letters and answering phones. The great taboo, then as later, was to take a job that a man might want, because a woman only worked for money to buy frivolous hats and jewelry, while a man used money to support his family. There was even a strong current of resentment that women were paid at all for their two top jobs, nursing the sick and teaching children, because these were women's natural roles in life and should be, like childbearing, gladly performed for free.

In some circles, well into the 1960s, the only proper paying job for a married woman was giving piano lessons to the neighborhood children, because she could do it at home. If she emerged from under her roof to go to work, the neighbors might see her and assume that her husband was a financial failure, shamed in the world's eye. To this end many little girls spent reluctant sunny afternoons practicing their scales, as insurance against marrying a failure.

No nice woman would take a job of any importance, even if one were offered, because what man would marry such a woman or, if she already had a husband, what husband would put up with such a wife? Our sweet pediatrician, Dr. Deyrube, was a woman, but she was a foreigner, Austrian I think, with a lovely lilting accent, and there's no accounting for foreigners.

Long later, well into the feminist seventies, there was a sort of riddle people asked each other. I forget the framework, but the point was that the surgeon was operating on this kid, and the kid was the surgeon's son, but the surgeon was not the kid's father. How could this be? What was the answer? I didn't get it. Nobody got it. People came up with tortured genetic scenarios to explain it, but nobody I talked to ever got it right.

Once in a great while an important woman would surface, by heredity or marriage, like European queens and Eleanor Roosevelt, but personally earned importance was freakish. Carl worked for a woman, Roosevelt's Secretary of Labor Frances Perkins, first woman in a cabinet post, and it was clear from the dinner talk that he considered her a freak, a joke, and something of a personal insult.

According to the posters, such now was the national emergency that women were supposed to roll up their sleeves and work on assembly lines, welding and riveting in munitions factories, building tanks and ships. Mother went to work as a display artist in a department store. She would have made a splendid welder, fast and efficient—I can see her in the face-shield and spark suit—but this was Washington and factories were scarce, and besides, display artist was the only job on her resumé.

After my parents had left college and walked into the waiting jaws of the Depression, they went, for reasons unexplained, to Pittsburgh, where Mother worked in Hess's display department and my father was a floorwalker, prowling the aisles in search of shoplifters. Every few weeks they cut Mother's pay again, and when she was down to six dollars a week, she quit. They both quit. Willingly or not, she was pregnant with me, and they went back to Washington and moved in with her parents. Parents, in those years, saw a lot of their grown children, who often came home accompanied by deserving friends, and couches were crowded.

Mother didn't work again until the war came and gave her permission. As for Carl's permission, I don't know. I was a diligent eavesdropper and as good as a cat at slinking around in the shadow, but I never overheard a word of private talk between them. I don't suppose there was an argument; Mother never argued except about abstract matters like my taste in poetry.

I think she always had more leverage with Carl than she

thought of using. Socially, he had married up, from immigrant Irish shopkeepers into a family that came here so long ago they were called settlers rather than immigrants and even the women went to college. This gave him a sneaking admiration for her ways, even while he needed to stamp them out and impose his own. She was gentry, though her Socialist mother would have been outraged at the thought. He wanted to be gentry too.

With streaming head colds, he refused to touch common Kleenex and used only mountains of monogrammed linen handkerchiefs that had to be scoured free of mucus and washed and ironed by hand. And in the evenings after dinner, in pleasant weather, when he and Mother took a sedate walk around the block he always carried one of his collection of well-polished walking-sticks, flicking it insouciantly at bushes and hedges, a boulevardier, a flaneur. I expect his parents at the general store in Woodville would have laughed.

Anyway, however the matter was settled between them, one Monday morning Mother went downtown to work.

No great upheaval followed. Outdoors we continued to prepare for the German invasion; indoors Viola, calm and competent, continued to sit at the kitchen table and adjudicate our lives. Nowadays the problems would have been staggering, with cars and drivers needed for soccer practice, swim meets, music lessons, ballet lessons, tennis lessons, Scouts, hockey, basketball clinics, play dates, track, and karate, but in that long-ago suburb we simply walked to school and walked home again.

In the big mulberry tree by the back porch I found a suitable crotch and built a crooked platform of scraps of wood and some hundreds of nails that always bent because Mother's advice—

"Hold the hammer by the *end* of the handle, down here, so you can put some swing in it"—was wasted on me. I rigged clothesline to an abandoned Easter basket and hauled up books and graham crackers and spent long afternoons in my uncomfortable perch, crooked nails denting the backs of my legs. In its season the mulberry tree produced millions of inedible fruits that rained down on me and speckled my already dingy clothes with purple stains.

I read. The eye doctor threatened blindness before I was thirty, but I couldn't stop. I read my way through the children's department at the library and into the eclectic family bookshelves. I read much that was unsuitable and much that was simply bewildering; I found Maxim Gorky's *My Childhood*, which sounded as if it might be fun, but it wasn't, and I can still see the corpse glimpsed through cracks in the shed's wall, and the woman shrieking in the agony of childbirth with her relatives running in circles wringing their hands.

I read poetry, miles of poetry, often just for the luxury of crying. Like Pavlov's salivating dogs, I can still bring forth tears at the very thought of some of my favorites, like "The Forsaken Merman" ("Come, dear children, let us away; / Down and away below") and Hodgson's

> 'Twould ring the bells of Heaven
> The wildest peal for years,
> If Parson lost his senses
> And people came to theirs,
> And he and they together
> Knelt down with angry prayers
> For tamed and shabby tigers

121

And dancing dogs and bears,
And wretched, blind pit ponies
And little hunted hares.

Almost anything in Kipling's Jungle Books was good for a cry, and of course Ernest Thompson Seton and that infamous dead fox with her starving kits trying to nurse, anything at all sad about animals. I couldn't stay away from them. I must have loved to cry, and perhaps it was good for me, since tears about one's own lot were the ultimate sin in our household, as in all proper middle-class homes. I lavished them on *Black Beauty* and *The Yearling* instead, but at least they didn't go unshed.

At school, goldfish had given way to Early Man. We were told about cavemen, Cro-Magnon Man, Neanderthal Man. He painted on the walls of his cave; he speared woolly mammoths; he discovered the uses of fire. Once in a while Early Woman appeared in an illustration, huddled in a corner with Early Baby, but she was never mentioned in the text and can't have been numerous. (Her scarcity was confirmed just a couple of years ago when *National Geographic* announced that the Americas were explored, settled, and populated by bands of restless, adventurous young men, a genetic feat deserving further study.) In our later lessons we learned that the Egyptians, Greeks, and Romans were also all men except for Nefertiti, and even she was nothing but a head and neck.

I was part of a tiny minority, then, a scant handful sprinkled over the world, inaudible, all but invisible. It was a heady thought. Minorities had it easy. We could say what we pleased because no one would hear us; our legislation would never pass so we weren't held responsible for its consequences. Women had no consequences. We few, we happy few, were exempt from history; neither were we obliged to spear mammoths and build pyramids. I would be light and fleet of foot and zip around the world like Puck, eavesdropping and playing tricks, glimpsed only rarely by a lucky few and then vanishing again. I didn't bother to consider the Mother factor or attach this light-footed vision to the stationary women I knew.

My own mother, in the meantime, flourished. Fathers, by tradition, came home from the day's work exhausted and surly. Mother came home sparkling all over as if from a light fall of snow. She got prettier. She laughed. She never went so far as to sing in the house, but on Saturdays, setting out on errands or to take me to Grandmother's, she started singing when she turned the key in the ignition, all the nonsense songs from her college world. She sang

> The Sultan's wives
> Have got the hives
> From eating anchovies and chives.
> There will be trouble.
> There will be hell.
> When the old man
> From the war
> Gets home.
> The Sultan's sons
> Those sons of guns
> Have stolen the Sultan's favorite ones.
> There will be trouble . . .

Then, one day, Mother and Nick and I were in the car and setting out for errands. Mother pulled away from the curb and began to sing.

> O I went to a house
> For to get me some bread,
> But the lady said Bum, Bum,
> The baker is dead.

Nick moaned and doubled over and pressed his hands to his ears. "What's the matter?" she asked.

"Don't sing. Please don't sing. It sounds awful."

I was stunned. I suppose Mother was even more stunned. We had thought Nick was one of us, and suddenly he was one of them, one of those who, like my kindergarten teacher, knew what singing was and silenced those who didn't.

Forever after Mother never sang again, never once, even when it was just the two of us, and car trips never felt quite the same. I forgave Nick, but grudgingly, and a rift opened between us. It healed, but I didn't forget it. Long later, when he was at Stanford, he mentioned buying season tickets to the orchestra, and Mother said she thought nobody paid to listen to symphonic music except from motives of outrageous snobbery, but that was the only hint she ever gave that she'd been hurt, or that she missed singing "Casey Jones" in the car.

Viola fed us children at six, and then Mother and Carl came home, and Mother lit candles on their dinner table. From the living room we heard her talk about work, and strange names were mentioned—Al Dorfman, Gene Florimbio, Hal Melnikov. It seemed to me slightly shocking that she knew people, men even, that Carl had never met, and spoke freely about them and their doings in this other life of hers. It may have shocked Carl too.

With her own money and her employee's discount she sometimes, when she thought of it, brought us clothes, socks, underwear. She'd always had to ask Carl for money for children's clothes, spring and fall, and she must have been wary about asking for money for mine, so she bought me everything two sizes too large, hoping they'd last longer, but somehow I grew out of them without ever growing into them, and they shrank up my arms and legs and popped their buttons and their hems pulled out and hung down. In Mother's book, thinking about clothes at all was vulgar, so I never did, but considering our respectable demographics, I must have been an odd, even threatening, sight among my peers. The Hecht Company, with its generous sales, helped.

When there was no school, I was allowed to visit her new world. I'd never been to the Hecht Company. Back then, stores had individual characters, and this wasn't one we shopped at—Grandmother went to respectable old Woodward & Lothrop and Mother, when she was forced to shop at all, went to pragmatic Sears. Pretty Aunt Peggy went to luxurious Garfinckel's. Hecht's was slightly raffish, promotional, Jewish, bustling, energetic, and its display department was flavored with a merry cynicism and elaborate practical jokes. Everyone called Mother "Mother"; apparently her maternal condition and her working there among them with hammers and saws was a good-natured joke in itself.

In those days, retail displays were built from scratch on the premises. It was all in one enormous noisy room, and everyone was glad to see me and everyone seemed to love Mother, and they strolled around carrying stepladders, chatting, borrowing each other's rubber cement. As I sorted it out, they were roughly divided into artist types, often female, and carpenter types, male, and only Mother was both. She had a big hungry-looking table saw for rough work and an agile little hand-held electric job called a Cut-All for carving pictures out of plywood; she had colored chalks and powdered temperas, great rolls of colored paper and a glue pot and a staple gun. Tools.

I sat on a stool and watched while she sawed out the life-sized outline of a little girl. With big shears in her small hands she cut out paper clothes, a white blouse with puffed sleeves and a blue jumper, and pleated and bent them and stapled them to the outline so they stood forth in three dimensions; a paper sculpture. In the same jeans and sweatshirt she always wore, she leaned over her table and worked fast and confidently, with no waste motion. The distraught Mother unstrung by her quarreling children, the helplessly clumsy Mother in the kitchen, disappeared into a woman who moved like a ballet dancer and smiled to herself while she worked. It occurred to me how sad it was that women always had to live like women, even if they weren't any good at it.

According to the general wisdom, it was Mothers who were happy all day, running the vacuum cleaner and tending babies, while the Fathers toiled grimly toward exhaustion, but the thought peered over the edge of my mind that it might be more fun to go forth and work among merry companions who didn't need their diapers changed, doing work that wouldn't need to be done all over again tomorrow, than to be a Mother alone with her house.

With the blade of the shears she curled wisps of yellow paper into hair and glued them on. A pinkish wash covered the face and then she painted in the features, crooked smile with a missing tooth and cocky eyebrows. She cut scraps of ribbon to tie in the hair, and then stood the girl beside the table, next to a spotted dog and a running boy in overalls who looked like Nick. They were part of a frieze, she said, that she would nail up around the whole children's department for Back to School, chalking the school buildings and yellow buses, lawns and trees directly onto the walls, easily rubbed out to make way for Halloween and Christmas.

At lunch time the whole display department downed tools and headed together for the employees' cafeteria, where they had a permanent table staked out. Here they absentmindedly ate lunch while fiercely playing rummy. The rummy game had been going on forever, for longer than anyone remembered, and it was played with intense concentration for a quarter of a cent a point that nobody ever collected and nobody ever paid. Mother, at this point, was several hundred points ahead of her closest rival, her boss Mel, and they played as if the family farm rode on the outcome. She won again.

After lunch she took me out on the street to show me her window. Windows were usually a group effort, so she was flattered that Mel had given her this one with no strings attached, only its frightful designated merchandise. The Pictures-and-Mirrors buyer had gone overboard and acquired a boxcar or two full of framed pictures so awful that not even those who buy art in department stores could be persuaded to bite. They'd been marked down, and still they lingered, and they had to go.

Instead of trying to make the best of them, Mother had simply heaped them in the window, layered them on its walls, dangled them from its ceiling, piled them on the floor in an epic jumble of landscapes, seascapes, flowers, bug-eyed children, covered bridges, puppy dogs with bones, kittens in baskets, barefoot black boys with fishing poles, red barns, and lone pines. With white paint directly on the window glass she drew a larger-than-lifesize Peter Arno–style matron in a floppy hat facing the *New Yorker*'s Eustace Tilley, with lorgnette, who was saying, "Egad, Drusilla! Veritable masterpieces for only 99 cents!"

Whether any pictures were sold, I know not, but she must have entertained the passersby on busy F Street. Certainly she'd entertained herself.

Mother was having fun. Surrounded by people who loved and admired her, working at something she did well, laughing and chatting and climbing on stepladders with paint can and brush, she was having a wonderful war.

Subversively, she had shown me a crack in the wall, a crack in between the lipstick of entrapment and the floor wax of motherhood. The Hecht Company gleamed through it and, if a department store can be said to smile, it smiled at me. Someday, I thought, I can go there and surely, even though I can neither draw nor saw, such nice people will find some use for me, and I too will be happy there. And, when I needed my first permanent job, I did, and they did, and I was.

In the middle of the war, neighbors persuaded Mother and Carl to walk up the street for dinner and I was left in charge of Nick and Judith in the early winter dark. Someone knocked on the door and I opened it to a young Japanese man who said his name was Jack Hirose and he had come. He carried a small satchel, and smiled.

Mannerly, I invited him in. On the East Coast we were at war with Germany; if he had said, *"Achtung! Ich bin Fritz,"* I would have patriotically killed him, but since Japan was a mostly legendary enemy to us I offered him Carl's chair, the Father's chair, and he sat down. He looked tired. Nobody had mentioned him; nobody told me he was coming, but of course journeys were a grab bag then, trains canceled or shunted onto sidings for troop movements, and who knew how many days or weeks it would take for a young man, even carrying nothing but a clean shirt and his precious camelhair brushes, to trek from the internment camp in Colorado to a doorstep in a dark suburb in northwest Washington? How did he even find the house?

Stared at by three unknown children, he took a harmonica from his satchel and played, and Nick and Judith and I danced for him in the living room. "Turkey in the Straw," I think it was. Jack remembers the scene more clearly than I do. Mother called from the neighbors' house up the street to ask if I'd put Judith to bed, and I said, "Jack is here." I think she was flustered and said she and Carl would come right home, and I said, "No, you don't have to come home. We are all dancing."

Carl, I found out later, had been handed the thankless job of winkling out some of the Japanese-American internees in the camps, driven from their homes by panicked Californians, and bringing them to jobs and sanctuary in the East. Jack was a graphic artist, and I suppose Mother had promised him work in display art. He moved into the attic and, with the Oriental delicacy in close quarters, slipped quietly into the family.

Others came. Kosumai, pretty Kosumai, showed up and

immediately came down with mumps. She lay in state in my bedroom, I was smuggled out to Grandmother's, and everyone else was quarantined. Kinu came, Jack's fiancée. (" 'Fiancée' is Japanese for 'girlfriend,' " I explained to Margie.) Eventually Jack's tiny Issei mother showed up too, but only bowed and smiled.

In time Jack prospered and opened his own display-art company and grew rich, and when he turned up at our weddings and funerals he always saw me and came over at once to touch me and smile. Looking back, it's nice to think I was a happy occasion. The roundups, the confiscations, the internment camp. The waiting. The chance. The long discontinuous journey toward strangers on a series of trains, jostled in the dark by tired soldiers and their duffel bags, the waits. The strange station, strange city. Taxis? Were there taxis? And somehow finally the suburban house and a ten-year-old girl in pigtails opened the door, and showed him to the Father's chair and danced for him.

No child would recognize or even imagine being the bright ending to a grownup's tunnel, and I never thought about it before, but no wonder Jack always looks for me at funerals and comes over to touch my arm.

For Christmas Mother made me a dollhouse, on company time I presume, with leftover company materials. It was an imposing structure, two stories high with a staircase, and shutters on the windows that opened and closed, and painted braided rugs on the floors. On the dining room wall were three round portraits no bigger than my thumbnail of me and Nick and Judith. It was a work of art. But what was I supposed to do with it? Rehearse my future as a housewife? But its floors and dishes never got dirty. Make up stories about the inhabitants? But the boy and girl, Father and Mother, in some unforgiving bendable substance, resisted invention, and the black-haired Father looked menacing. Perhaps I was too old for dollhouses. Perhaps Mother hadn't expected me to play with it; perhaps she made it just to be making it, not for me but for fun.

Just last year I heard from Cynthia, she whose mother gave me the Bible, remembering a birthday party of mine, the most memorable party of all. Mother had drawn full-length paper doll portraits of all the little girl guests, cut them out of construction paper, and dressed them in copies of the party dresses they were wearing. Cynthia treasured hers for decades and grieved when it disappeared. I don't remember, not that party or any other party for me, and certainly not a paper-doll of myself. It seems ungrateful of memory to have lost it, but again, perhaps she was doing it for herself, because she liked drawing little girls, and not for me.

For Christmas, Valentine's Day, Easter, Summer, Back to School, Halloween, Mother splashed the walls and windows of the Hecht Company with splendor. At home, nothing changed. Home stayed so always the same it stopped being a comfort and became an irritant, especially the walls. I don't know why our pictures were so boring. Mother was the one with the artist's eye, but it was her sister Lois who hung the explosive close-ups of fruit and sinister flowers and Georgia O'Keefe, and her sister Peggy who hung Navajo rugs and sinuous, rhythmic moderns that made her rooms dance. Things to look at, not just to endure. We had Renoir's *Girl with a Watering Can*.

She hung in the dining room, in the same place, year after

year after year, and I loathed the little red-faced twit. When you stepped in through the front door, you faced Van Gogh's vegetable garden with its immovable blue wheelbarrow, and to your right, by the stairs, a group of dark-blue card players by Cézanne that I hated most of all, hated them for their mulish concentration, their absolute refusal to look up and acknowledge me. For them, I was invisible, I was nobody, because they were men and had important things to deal with, cards to inspect. I slammed my schoolbooks onto the dresser and tried not to look. In the living room, over the couch, a brown racetrack scene by Degas. In the upstairs hall, a framed letter of thanks to Carl from President Roosevelt and several Winslow Homer boats. In Nick's room, its walls and furniture aged and bruised by tantrums, over his bed, a Raphael Madonna tentatively holding a naked, pale, and hideously deformed child as if she didn't much like to touch him, and small wonder.

Generic pictures such as might hang in a sample apartment. They stayed in their ordained places for so long that they burned themselves into the walls, the way your snapshots burn their way onto the plastic sleeves of your wallet. Even if, in an unthinkable rage, I had pulled them all down, they would still have been there, the skittish brown horses, the blue card players. The house has been sold and new people remodeled and painted and moved in, but even they must sometimes look up suddenly and see the shadow of the girl with the watering can blistered onto the dining room wall, under the fresh paint. When they get up late at night to go to the bathroom, a Winslow Homer boat probably gleams in the faint shine from the streetlight outside. After so long, no mere human could expunge those artworks.

Nothing else changed either. No furniture was moved or replaced until it decayed into uselessness. Mother lived in her house like an overnight customer in a motel. After her first mad flurry of painting and building, she simply abandoned it. Once I complained to her about a friend of mine who had bought a derelict shell of a brownstone and spent four years restoring it, haunting demolition sites for molding and mantelpieces, camping out in the kitchen while he finished it room by room, even finding an art deco piano for the fourth-floor ballroom and somehow getting it up there. Then, when it was finished, he suddenly sold it to a rich lawyer and moved to an apartment. How could he leave it, after years of work?

"I understand perfectly," said Mother. "Once you've finished it, you aren't its creator any more. You're just its janitor."

Janitors never hang different pictures or have the couch recovered. I suppose the pictures were an act of defiance. She would live here and behave herself, but she would not take part in the place. She was always good at holding back.

It was decided that I was old enough to take Nick downtown on the bus, weekends and holidays, to the Mall, the world's largest toy. The journey was fraught with perils, since car sickness could strike and we'd have to grab a transfer from the driver and hurry off to throw up; the intersection of Connecticut and Van Ness was best, with a friendly sheltering woods.

At the Mall, the great marble museums of what Nick called the Mifsonian were free. Any child could walk penniless through their doors and wander all day at liberty through halls of gems

133

and crystals, the brutal weapons of primitive surgery, the bones of the extinct, the working models of coal mines and steam engines. Nick, who couldn't say "Smithsonian," had no trouble with "diplodocus" and "trilobite." He was laying down strata of his scientific education; I of the scattershot mind didn't discriminate, just piled it uncataloged into my head's jumble, where saber-toothed tigers bedded down with Old Ironsides, early printing presses, and the Sioux.

It was ours, all ours. We set our sneakered feet down firmly on the marble floors, landlords of infinite resources. Elsewhere, in later life, people charged me money to look at things in their museums and art galleries, and it never felt the same; plainly the contents were theirs, not mine, and my feelings were hurt by the admission charge. Only the Smithsonian's treasures were ours by right.

And only unsupervised children could have had such fun, since any school or parental trip would have involved long pauses and explanations at boring exhibits, but we passed them by, found our own things, and I read the labels and messages to Nick, and we marveled and moved on. Mother gave me money to buy hot dogs from the carts outside, and we covered ourselves with mustard and struck out across the grass, detouring to chase pigeons, toward Arts and Industry, with the sun-blinded Capitol on our left.

Many years later, we ran into each other there. This doesn't seem peculiar, except that Nick was living in southern California at the time and I was living in Philadelphia and neither of us knew the other was in Washington. I was prowling a visiting exhibit at the National Gallery of Art when he came up behind me and said in my ear, "His palette gets a tad self-indulgent, don't you think?" I was surprised, of course, but not greatly astonished: where else should we meet, who if not us should converge here, in our childhood playground?

Sometimes I was deputized to take him down to Chevy Chase Circle, a longish walk, for a haircut. The barber shop was on the same street as the library, a proper, men-only barber shop, and I waited embarrassed and dwarfed in one of the huge black leather chairs, Fathers' chairs. It was unseemly for a woman of any age to sit on leather, and almost indecent for a girl. Nobody there ever smiled, least of all Nick, who perched on a board laid across the arms of the barber chair, engulfed in a black cape, while Andrew J. Bible, a very solemn man, solemnly cut his hair, and ran the clippers up the back of his head and around his ears, and anointed him with manly and powerful perfumes.

All little boys and many big ones wore Army-style crew-cuts, and a fresh one prickled deliciously under the hand like a baby hedgehog. When we got home, Nick went ritually around the family presenting his head to be touched and smelled. Men and boys got haircuts; Mother cut the female hair, including her own. She liked cutting hair, and long after we were grown she stalked us, clicking the scissors, anxious to take off just a little, just to get it out of our faces.

She took us to the zoo. We did the zoo slowly, carefully, attentively, visiting personal friends. An enormous brown bear did tricks for a man who showed up regularly with a bag of bread. He said, "How do you feel about the Democrats?" and it reared heavily up on its hind legs, slowly, high in the air, and batted its enormous paws together, and the man threw it a piece of bread. Who was he, and why had he invested so much time,

135

maybe all his time, in teaching a grizzly to applaud the Democrats? Nobody asked.

A formal wooden sign on a grassy knoll said:

LOST CHILDREN WILL BE TAKEN TO THE LION HOUSE
THE LIONS ARE FED AT 3 P.M.

The war trundled on and on, and as I got older it was less of a lark. At school, the gung-ho fight songs of the early war had darkened and taken on an elegiac note ("On the island of New Georgia in the Solomons / Stands a simple wooden cross alone to tell . . ."). I stopped digging booby traps in the garden for the Wehrmacht and took to sneaking the evening news. The news came on the radio at eleven, brought to you by Mobil Gas, at the sign of the flying red horse, and Mother and Carl always stayed up for it. So, privately, lying awake in the dark, did I, and then crept barefoot across the upstairs hall and down the closed staircase—the second step from the top still creaked—to where a heavy curtain covered the opening to the downstairs hall, lest precious warmth escape up to the bedrooms. I crouched invisibly listening.

The news was the radio's only purpose besides baseball. Mother and Carl, especially Mother, were passionate baseball fans, and Mother in youth would ditch her afternoon classes at Central High School and slip over to Griffith Stadium to catch a game; she had watched the great Walter Johnson pitch. The Senators gave their followers many stressful seasons and were rarely out of the basement, but Mother always said, "Any fool can be a Yankees fan. It takes talent to be a Senators fan."

Riding my bike around the neighborhood I could hear,

through all the open windows, the same words coming from all the different radios: "There's the pitch . . . and it's low and outside. *Ball two.*" The sound of summer, the radio's sunny side. The news was its dark side.

Radio was our ear on the world. The newspaper explained things that had happened, but the radio told us what was happening. Not just in movies but in real life too people actually said, "What was that? Did you hear that? Something's happened! Quick, turn on the radio!" and it was Pearl Harbor, or a fire, or a storm: the radio knew. Brown, and shaped like a shoebox, it was warm to the touch while it was talking, and glass tubes inside it glowed in the dark like the magical eyes of a little pet dog that could see the whole world. I liked just walking past it in the living room knowing it would talk to me if I turned the knob. It inspired trust, unlike the television anchor with his blow-dried hair, because it was a disembodied voice, as the Lord spake from on high. "It's true, I heard it on the radio" carried weight. Who has such faith in television?

Every night at eleven it told us what was happening. Europe had slipped out of focus, Eisenhower displaced by MacArthur, and now we fought our way island by island across the Pacific, losing and winning and losing, coral atolls and kamikaze pilots and names like Okinawa, Corregidor, and Mindanao that tasted so warm and soft it was hard to connect them with killing. How could blood be shed in a place called Mindanao, a song of an island, surely, a golden circlet in the blue water, probably with mermaids untangling their long wet hair? "Mindanao," I whispered in the dark staircase.

Geography exploded and whirled in my head, and then

scattered like sparks. The war had swollen past thinking about. Probably it would simply go on forever, with nobody winning or losing, until the surface of the earth was all ragged and frayed and the animals hid in holes in the ground.

When the final galloping Mobil Gas music came on, I slipped back up the cold stairs to my room, my head a sleepless rubble of Marines and blue water and flaming planes.

THE MOUNTAIN: A PASTORAL DIGRESSION

Summers, I was sent up to the mountain, to be out of Carl's way and to keep Alfred company in that lonely place. I don't know for how many summers, or for how long I stayed, because on the mountain there wasn't any time: if the ironweed is blooming, it must be August. Searching the cabin in memory, I don't see any clocks or even a free calendar from the hardware store tacked on the kitchen wall. There was no radio and no newspaper, so the war didn't so much recede as freeze, with a flaming fighter plane suspended halfway down the sky. There was no telephone, no running water, and no electricity. A trip to the nearest town for groceries was a solemn event.

Hardy souls sometimes pack up a sleeping bag and stomp off into the wilderness to live this way on purpose, at least for a few days, but this wasn't a camping trip, and lacked glamour. The cabin, built before the Civil War, down in a fold of the northern Blue Ridge, was originally a single square room with a sleeping loft overhead and a woodshed attached. At some later date, a kitchen was added, with sloping rough-hewn rafters and a door of its own to the outside, and a kerosene stove and a plank shelf for the washpans and buckets.

The place was primitive even by primitive standards, and it occurs to me only now to wonder why nobody ever dug a well and installed a pump, a pump with a curved wooden handle such as one sees in farm museums. Pumped water would have been easier, and probably innocent of tadpoles and mud; the water Alfred and I hauled so far from the spring had to be left to

141

settle for an hour, so the undesirable ingredients could sink to the bottom of the bucket or swim to the top and get skimmed off.

We brushed our teeth standing outside the kitchen door and spat into the bushes. At night we went together to what was delicately called Down the Hill, or sometimes the Little House, with the flashlight skittering along the path in front of us, and sat together, for company, in the spidery dark, playing the light around the walls, with their cobwebs and flaking whitewash, and into the mouse nests in the corners, fluffy with shredded toilet paper, where the beady eyes of the frightened babies stared back.

Sometimes I asked myself, Why am I doing this, why am I here? But I never asked anyone else. It would have been rude.

I was there because long ago in Central High School Mother took up with a girl named Adelaide, whose family for generations had been medical missionaries in northern China. Her two sisters had stayed there, but for reasons of domestic amity she had been sent to America to live with an aunt and go to school here. I suppose she wasn't happy. She wasn't happy in the years I knew her either; but somehow she and Mother stayed friends. She was Mother's only friend, only private, personal, long-term friend, though I never understood quite why.

Adelaide married her cousin Horace, and they had a son, and divorced. I'd heard that it wasn't a good idea to marry cousins, and I could see why: the names got confusing. Adelaide called her former father-in-law "Uncle Julius" and Alfred called him "Grandpa Julius."

This Julius had a farm of sorts, on a mountain west by northwest of Washington, but you could hardly call him a farmer. He was an eccentric, like his son, Alfred's father, and

142

like many of Carl's relatives. Eccentricity was a calling then, as maybe it still is in England, and entitled its male practitioners to collar, bore, and frighten all comers, while the females, like Carl's sister, expressed themselves by showing up at the bank wearing a hat, pearls, white gloves, and nothing else.

What happened to eccentrics? I suppose for a while we locked up the impecunious ones, and then we just medicated them all, and after that it was no fun anymore and they faded away.

I think Mother told me that Uncle Julius had been Bob La Follette's campaign manager in his 1924 run for president on the Progressive ticket. It seems like a good match. Julius was always full of theories. He had theories about sheep, agriculture, housekeeping, nutrition, politics, and rabbits and, aside from the usual cows and chickens, he harbored a constantly shifting population of enthusiasms that were going to revolutionize the world but frequently perished of neglect as he moved on to fresh theories. The farm had once raised apples, and even now the occasional renegade apple tree, grown monstrous tall, blooms in the spring, but it's hard to work up a rousing theory about apples.

As part of the divorce settlement, Adelaide was given the little cabin and a few acres, half a mile or so away down the wagon track, and Uncle Julius guarded the only way out to the road, like a Wagnerian dragon. Two farm gates had to be opened, sagging on their hinges and urged on by shoulders, and then closed again, and Uncle Julius could hear us coming. At the second gate, he put his foot on the running board and his head in through the window and explained his theories.

Washington was a good place to get out of in the summers, and to the cabin Adelaide repaired after school was over, and took her son Alfred, who hated the place, and thither I was sent, throwing up every couple of miles, as company for him.

Alfred and I never liked each other much, or had anything at all in common, but we served our families' purposes. At any rate we never quarreled, having no mutual battleground on which to spar.

We slept in Mole End, on iron cots, wondering about the rustlings outside which could very well have been bears but more likely raccoons and possums. Mole End had been a chicken house in fairly tumbled condition, but Mother came up one weekend and nailed it more firmly together and painted it barn red and wrote over the doorway MOLE END in elegant Gothic letters as it says in the book. Up in the cabin, *The Wind in the Willows* was our evening reading, supplemented later by T. H. White's *The Sword in the Stone*, as we sat in the foul-smelling light of the kerosene lamps, at the round table covered with blue and white oilcloth.

Alfred complained and fidgeted. He despised all fictions equally because they were simply *not true* and left to his own devices read nothing but *Popular Mechanics*, of which he kept a large stack by his cot. A peculiar offspring for poor Adelaide, Central High's star English teacher, who was always given the plummy advanced Shakespeare class and the supervision of the annual Shakespeare production. He regarded her with contempt; she regarded him with bewildered consternation.

In the mornings we went for water. Two buckets apiece. Across the shaggy grass and down the twisty path in the woods, across rocks, snagged by brambles, stamping our feet and shouting to alert the snakes; the mountain had a flourishing population of copperheads, and in a dry season they came to

Indians. Over the dresser hung a framed enlargement of an ancient photograph, Indians, a campfire, and Aunt Cornelia as a little girl. Her father had been an Indian administrator. Sometimes we just sat, Alfred and I, and she lay peacefully in her bed, and the afternoon rolled past the house.

The behavior of grownups was always a mystery not to be questioned, and I didn't ask if perhaps Uncle Julius had simply sent her up to her room, as Nick was sent to his, with instructions to stay there forever. Mrs. Reid took up her food.

Mrs. Reid was a short square Finnish woman with a heavy accent who had somehow, on an unlucky day, married a local man. Mr. Reid spent his days in their cabin, Cripplegate, down below the pasture, doing nothing. Mrs. Reid took care of Skyfields, tended the chickens and the vegetable garden, cleaned the house after a fashion, and cooked. She milked the cows, squatting on a stool in a circle of barn cats, doling out their allotted squirts of milk in rotation, into their waiting mouths. She was busy, but I have no reason to suppose she ever forgot to feed Aunt Cornelia.

There was no heat in the bedroom. Uncle Julius had a theory about that, often explained: the windows faced south and east, and in order to trap the maximum warmth from the sun he had had the walls painted yellow. Sunshine on yellow walls would keep the room cozy all winter. No need to waste money on radiators. Even at the time, I wondered, and now after a dozen winters on the mountain, I think of whining winds, thin walls, the thermometer below zero, and the long weeks with no sun at all, or only a glimpse of it, low on the horizon and far away.

At some point, between one summer and the next, Aunt Cornelia disappeared and became a non-subject. Nobody said

147

she'd died, but she wasn't there anymore. I try not to think she froze to death, upstairs in the yellow room, waiting for the sun to shine.

Over time the rabbits, too, disappeared.

Chores aside, we ran loose on the mountain. A fragment floats up from memory: we had our bare ankles dusted with a yellow powder to discourage chiggers, and the name "Flowers of Sulphur" seems to come with it. Could that have been its name, and if so, why have I held onto it all these decades, since it never reappeared in my life and didn't work very well even at the time? Was it really spelled "sulphur"? Did it really come in an oval tin box with a tight-fitting tin lid, like a box for lozenges, or have I just made that up?

A memory is so gelatinous, waffling into this shape and that, until you say it out loud or write it down and it turns to stone, right or wrong, a fact. Places slither around too. Early memories seem to take place in dozens of different houses and gardens, but when you nail them down, they were the same house and the same garden seen from dozens of different perspectives that never quite mesh.

What does remembrance look like? I'm told it's all, all those years, crammed into the left frontal lobe, in a cerebral groove called the fold of Broca. Will they ever discover a way to unwrap it—painlessly, of course—and let us look down into its contents in all their rich, untidy, embarrassing, roiling stew; perhaps poke a long-handled spoon in and stir and watch the stuff churn up and sink again, old phone numbers, a pool table in somebody's basement, a page in a geometry textbook, faces without names, names without faces, a row of rickety houses seen from a train window, *Clair de Lune* picked out on a piano, and the smells of pine trees, low tide, shaving lotion? The name of a town we drove through twenty years ago? Flowers of Sulphur?

Alfred's father had given him a BB gun, perhaps to annoy Adelaide, and we went looking for things to shoot, crows mostly, though we did manage to score several large frogs around the spring. I had heard that the French ate frogs' legs, and somehow we prevailed on Adelaide to cook them up for us. They were all right but unexciting; the French version owes much to garlic, unknown in those days to white-bread Americans. Then there was something about moles, or possibly mice, that memory has mercifully smudged. This was my project, and I was going to make something, a little purse for coins, with satiny soft furs sewn together. Did I trap and kill moles? Or use mice from the kitchen mousetraps? I must have skinned them myself, and then tried to cure the skins, and I suppose they stank and I was persuaded to bury them. Forgotten, and just as well.

One year we collected the roots of young sassafras trees and talked Adelaide into making root beer. It smelled lovely, and was put up in mason jars on a shelf in the kitchen, and exploded. The jars blew up one by one at long intervals, usually in the quiet of the evening when we sat at the table reading, and we all jumped, and Adelaide would go for the mop. One year we concentrated on archery, with bows and arrows we whittled by hand, and practiced. We stood sideways to the target and squinted our eyes like professionals, and even I got fairly good, considering how crooked our arrows were.

One year we had butterfly nets and jars of formaldehyde that nearly knocked us out as cold as our unfortunate prey. Sometimes we found Indian arrowheads. Sometimes we poked around the abandoned cabins on the mountainside, with little left of them but a tumble of stones, a stone fireplace, a cellar hole fringed with wild daylilies down which we never quite fell and broke our legs, and the remains of a trash heap, blue glass medicine bottles and the lids from mason jars. Sometimes we hitchhiked down to the river.

I was there, it was me, but even so it's hard to believe. Adelaide was certainly not an irresponsible guardian, and yet there we go in memory, two children eight, nine, ten years old, trudging across the pasture and down the long steep mountain road, unpaved then, that gilded the trees with dust in August. At the east-west highway we stood by the roadside holding up our thumbs. Presently somebody pulled over and shoved open the passenger door and gave us a ride, down the curves and dips of the long long mountain to the Shenandoah.

No driver seemed surprised to see us; none molested or kidnapped us. During the war when gas was in short supply, it was patriotic to offer wayfarers a lift, and later, in the sixties, a whole generation thumbed its way around the country and met only occasional trouble. College students regularly thumbed their way back to school, holding up signs with their destinations, Oberlin, Cornell, Penn State. Hitchhiking was a mode of transport. Offering a lift was a mitzvah. Sometimes you met interesting people. Something fundamental seems to have changed, though I'm not sure quite what. Maybe it's just prosperity: who would offer a ride to a stranger so low, so outcast, so peculiar and possibly deranged as not to be driving a car of his own? Or maybe it's part of the paranoia of privacy, like never sitting on our front porches anymore.

We hitchhiked to the river and plunged in, wearing our cotton shorts and shirts that, like our flesh, hadn't seen a washing since

June. Again, nobody expected us to drown, any more than they expected us to cut off our fingers with our pocket knives or shoot out our eyes with the BB gun. Somehow the safety of children, a subject of obsessive, passionate national concern today, simply didn't bother anyone I knew. Maybe this was good for us. Maybe it made us brave and carefree. Or maybe reckless and foolhardy. Or all of the above. At any rate, like most children we survived unscathed except for poison ivy and occasional bee stings when the wild grape was in bloom.

By the time we were bored with the river we were shriveled like peach pits and our teeth chattered. Somewhat cleaner than before, we hitchhiked back up to the Gap, then walked the steep mile up Bear's Den Hill, and on across the pasture's dusty cart track, arriving sweaty and dirty again in time to go for the evening's water.

One afternoon I went up to the breathlessly hot, fly-buzzing attic, where army cots lay waiting for extra visitors, in search of something new to read. Exiled up here on rickety shelves and in orange crates was a stash of books from the world of Adelaide's missionary family, probably from earlier generations. My shirt sticking to my back, I opened a volume of improving moral tales for children.

The first tale told of a little girl who was given a kitten and was so entranced that she spent her days playing with it, ignoring her former companions. One night a couple of boys took the kitten and strangled it by a cord around its neck and hung the body from a branch outside the girl's window, where it was the first thing she saw in the morning.

I turned the page to see what righteous punishment befell the little monsters, but no. I'd missed the point. The boys were right. They had done the right thing, done it, all selflessly, to teach the girl a valuable lesson, that it was wicked to lavish attention on a brute beast and abandon her human companions, who were made in God's image with Christian souls.

What world was this? I tried the next story. Somewhere in the northern plains lived a family in an isolated cabin, and one evening the parents had to take the horse and buggy to town and leave the children alone. The father told them that they were not, under any circumstances, to open the door to anyone, for any reason, and off they went. So a great blizzard blew up and the snow drifted deep against the house, and somebody pounded on the door. The oldest girl called out that they weren't allowed to open it. A man cried piteously that he and his wife and tiny baby were lost in the storm, but the girl stood firm. The man said that his wife was trying to keep the baby warm under her cloak, but they'd been wandering for hours and were all in danger of freezing to death, right there on the doorstep. The baby was blue with cold. After some more back-and-forth the oldest girl couldn't bear it any longer and opened the door.

Well, of course it wasn't a lost family at all but a traveling murderer who chopped up all the little children with an ax, and served them right too. The author didn't quite say they all went straight to hell, but we could assume it: disobeying a Father was the worst sin a child could possibly commit, the equivalent of cocking a snook at the Lord Himself, and anyone who even thought of it deserved to get chopped up with an ax.

Soured by my wanderings in the Old Testament, I was sure the murderer was a plant. What sensible, actual murderer would be out wallowing through drifts in a blizzard, dragging an ax, in the lone hope of finding some children to chop? No, he'd be holed up in the hotel in town, waiting for better weather. That murderer had been conjured up and sent by God Himself, as a test of the children's obedience, and instructed to slaughter them if they disappointed Him. The gulf between me and Christianity gaped even wider and I put the book back in its orange crate and went outside to look for snakeskins.

Why are all my sharpest memories to do with books?

When the flesh-and-blood missionary world came to the mountain, it wore a rather merrier face.

On the other side of the earth, the Japanese invaded China and the Japanese army marched up to the door of the little hospital founded by Adelaide's father and now managed by her two sisters and widowed mother. The young lieutenant in charge came to the door. Adelaide's mother, Mrs. Hemingway, opened it. She was a tiny little woman in white sneakers, with white hair wrapped in braids around her head, and since this was early days in the war, the well-brought-up officer bowed in respect for her venerable age. He spoke perfect English, having been educated at Columbia. "Oh, please sit down," said Mrs. Hemingway, "and tell me about your years in America. Do you ever miss it?"

The officer had been sent to strip the hospital of its equipment and medical supplies, but it would have been rude to brush her aside. He sat down. He said what he missed most about America was apple pie. "You sit right there," cried Mrs. Hemingway, "while I bake you an apple pie!" And she bustled off to the kitchen.

Now, in all the years I knew her I never saw Mrs. Hemingway

make anything more challenging than a cup of tea, but I suppose there were servants in the hospital kitchen who hadn't fled at first sight of the troops. Anyway, according to the story, the lieutenant waited respectfully while the pie baked, and cooled, and then he ate it and paid his compliments, bowed again, and ordered his troops to come in and sack the place.

There was nothing left. While the pie baked and Mrs. Hemingway chatted him up, Adelaide's sisters, Izzy and Winnie, had supervised the emptying out of every last syringe and bandage and aspirin tablet, out the back way and up to be hidden in the hills. I suppose in the more desperate stages of the war they might all have been raped and skewered on bayonets, but they weren't, and somehow Izzy and Mrs. Hemingway got to the coast and sailed on the *Gripsholm*. Of neutral Swedish registry, this virtuous ship prowled slowly over the world's waters, flying the Red Cross flag, picking its way through mined harbors and collecting and redistributing prisoners of war, nurses, doctors, missionaries, and other marooned expats. Months passed. The passengers learned, and taught each other, dozens and dozens of different ways to play solitaire.

Winnie, the youngest, stole a mule and started off overland. It was a strange journey: every village and town she came to was empty, deserted, fires still smoking but no one to ask for food or water or directions. Finally she met an old man, crippled, unable to leave, and asked him where everyone was. "They were afraid," he said. "They ran away."

"Afraid? Of me?" She explained who she was, and the old man laughed until the tears ran down his wrinkles. The villagers knew that the Japanese army was coming, but they'd never seen a Japanese army, or even a picture of one. Neither had they ever seen a blond, blue-eyed American woman riding bareback astride a mule, so it seemed reasonable that she must be it, and they fled.

Winnie laughed too, and went on her way chuckling, over the high mountain passes, meeting many kind and interesting people along the way, and down through India, and so to the coast, where she too found a ship and went home. Only of course it wasn't home at all, for any of them; north China was home and always had been, but it was not in their nature to repine. All of them wound up on the mountain, where they were very merry.

I have these stories, I think, at second hand, by way of Mother. I hope they're true.

I fell in love with the wayfaring women. As different as possible from the anxious, diffident Adelaide, sent to America to lead a normal life, they were happy and brave. They'd had brave adventures. I'd been brought up to believe courage was a strictly masculine attribute; women were allowed only fortitude, or endurance. Courage implied action and a certain grimness: brave men never had fun. Winnie and Izzy, though, sang at their various jobs all day.

They whipped us into shape. They had no patience with Alfred's whining or his threatened asthma attacks in the face of chores; they marched us off on expeditions. We went to pick blueberries at Raven Rock, on the other side of the Gap, striding along in line, Winnie ahead with her staff leading us in song, belting out

> O the night was thick and hazy
> When the "Piccadilly Daisy"
> Carried down her crew and captain in the sea-ea-ea!

Raven Rock was as somber as it sounds, a scattering of boulders with a dizzying view to the west, infested with copperheads sunning themselves. We picked our buckets full of blueberries and then marched back home singing.

We made butter. It was Winnie's and Izzy's idea. Butter was severely rationed or perhaps just not to be had, and the patriotic were told of the joys of margarine instead. The butter people wouldn't let the margarine people sell it colored yellow, so it came white, with a capsule of coloring included, and it was some child's duty to mash the stuff long and hard with a wooden spoon to spread the coloring through it. This never worked. It was always streaky, and never tasted like butter anyway, or felt like it in the mouth. Judith once found and ate a quarter-pound stick of real butter, probably the entire family's ration for a week. She wasn't scolded because, Mother said, she couldn't have known it was precious, but it seemed to me that nobody who didn't know it was valuable would bother to chew down a whole stick of butter like a banana.

Over at the farm, Mrs. Reid milked the two cows night and morning, producing far more milk than anyone needed. It was kept in mason jars in the springhouse, a stout little stone structure with a heavy wooden door and a trough of spring water running through it. I suppose most of it soured.

Alfred and I carried many jars of milk back to the cabin, and they were left to sit while the cream rose yellowish to the top. This was poured off into another mason jar, and we shook it, there being no butter churn in even the dimmest recesses of the barn. We stood in a circle around the table and shook the jar savagely until our arms gave out, then passed it to the next person, while Winnie sang something with a good beat to it, like

"Onward, Christian Soldiers." After a long time the cream began to solidify. It was scooped out into a bowl and pressed until a thin pale liquid oozed out and was poured off, and what was left, with a sprinkle of salt, was butter, real butter, fit for a pre-war king. Proudly we stored it in the slimy box by the spring.

At the spring, Alfred and I surprised a thirsty copperhead and dropped our water buckets with a great clatter and ran for the house. Winnie picked up a garden spade and strode down the path and chopped it in half. She flipped the pieces, still twitching, into the woods and whistled us an all-clear; she had a one-note whistle fit to wake the dead and no one disobeyed it.

When they had grownup matters to discuss, they spoke Chinese, and they called each other by their Chinese names, meaning Oldest Sister, Middle Sister, Youngest Sister. They organized grand picnics high up in the pasture. Alfred and I gathered mountains of firewood and helped carry the food and dishes from the cabin. A fire was built on the short, sheep-clipped grass (sheep were Uncle Julius's current theory) between two boulders, food was cooked over it and eaten, and we threw our chicken bones into the flames.

The rest of the wood was thrown on to make a towering pillar of fire, visible far across the valley, and the aunts sang hymns. Even I could tell that Winnie in particular had a wonderful clear, carrying soprano that rang out over the dairy farms below in "Swing Low" and "Old-Time Religion" and "Jacob's Ladder" and, as the flames died down, "Abide with Me." Then we gathered up our dirty dishes and marched, singing, back to the cabin in the velvet night. There were more stars in those days and we could see the Milky Way flung out in reckless extra-vagance across the sky.

In the evenings, *The Sword in the Stone* had been retired and Mrs. Hemingway told stories. Alfred hated them. They were even more untrue than our books, and he complained and fidgeted but he hadn't much choice; it was either sit and listen in the circle of lamplight around the oilcloth or retreat to his dark cot in Mole End. Without electricity, domestic life was a communal affair.

Mrs. Hemingway's voice, like Winnie's and Izzy's, rose and fell in musical variations from a lifetime of speaking Chinese and flowed around the room like silk. Her stories were too long and subtle to be considered folk tales, but neither did they seem to have roots in our Western fairy stories, and certainly none in Christianity or even basic morality. I grieve that I didn't write them down before it was too late.

Of "Raven Uncle," the longest, I remember only the title and a couplet, "Silver bullet, bright and pliant, / Save us from the frightful giant." In "Pearlino," a beautiful princess is dissatisfied by all her many suitors and resolves to make herself a perfect husband. Her recipe called for a hundred yards of the finest white silk, a hundred pounds of the finest white sugar, and other delicate ingredients, including the pearls for which she named him. He was very beautiful but, not surprisingly, dumb as a box of rocks and so gullible he kept getting led into bizarre scrapes from which she had to rescue him, and I forget how it ends. Nobody had heard of tape recorders.

Mother did catch and write out the shortest, simplest one, "The Filial Tiger," and had it published in a children's magazine:

It seems there was an old woman, and she a widow, who had an only son, and the son took care of her and fetched the wood and water. One day a tiger sprang out of the forest and killed and ate him, and the old woman was very angry. "Who will take care of me now, and fetch the wood and water?" she demanded. She took the tiger and marched him off, three days' walk to the nearest town that had a magistrate, and told the magistrate her story, and the magistrate was very angry. He said to the tiger, "You have killed and eaten this old woman's only son, and she a widow, and now she has no one to fetch the wood and water. From now on you must be this old woman's son, and take care of her as a son should do." So they went back the three days' walk to their village, and from then on the tiger lived with the old woman as her son, and fetched the wood and water and brewed the tea. After many years the old woman died, and the tiger buried her with all the proper ceremonies, and lay howling and mourning on her grave for seven days and seven nights. Then he went off into the forest and nobody ever saw him again.

And then we went to bed, following our flashlight's dancing spot, and lay on our cots listening to the owls converse across half a mile of dark.

THE LONG DARK NIGHT
OF JUNIOR HIGH SCHOOL

Without ceremony, I arrived at the end of the elementary school across the circle and was remanded to Leland Junior High School, far away in alien territory.

Junior high schools have been renamed "middle schools" because the word junior was an affront to self-esteem, but the idea remains the same. Mother, who went through school under the old eight-and-four structure, thought it was a terrible idea, segregating children during their three most disastrous years so they could exercise the worst possible influence on each other.

Apparently other parents agreed with her and took action. Nobody walked with me to Leland. My whole neighborhood went off to private schools instead. Margie and her sister and brother went to Whitehall, in the company of exiled princesses. Tracy and her brother went to Sidwell Friends, stronghold of respectability. Lucille went to Holton Arms, where the children of senators went. Mother said there was nothing wrong with Leland except the age of its inmates and those families were simply showing off. (Does it mean something that "showing off" is no longer bad but a talent in its own right, leading to headline celebrity and television talk shows? Perhaps this is just as well; all that modesty must have been oppressive.)

Not that Mother knew much about Leland. On parents' night at the beginning of the year, my English teacher, who was young and flustered, surveyed the room-full and began, "Quite frankly, just between you and I . . ." Mother made a sound somewhere between a gasp and a hiccup and never willingly went near the place again.

Nobody writes about these years. Psychologists descend on the elementary schools and analyze growth and learning; everyone has a theory on high schools, test-makers and politicians obsess on them, and their graduates write novels about them. The three years between are the missing tooth, the blank. Everyone's trying to forget.

In this holding pen or isolation ward, the inhabitants are a motley lot. The boys who have started to grow are gangly and hairy, the ones who haven't are round and pink-cheeked. Some of the girls have breasts and wear lipstick and some, like me, are still in pigtails and baffled. It's an age of cliques. Friends and who they are and how many of them are the great obsession, and the more peers you can call friends, the more popular you are, and popularity means you will find a safe place in the world. You're going to be all right.

I wasn't. At home, friends had simply appeared through the hedges. At school, I didn't know how to go about getting them. My classmates, all older and more sophisticated, seemed potentially more like enemies, and I kept my distance. Sometimes, just the same, they attacked. In one class, for alphabetical reasons, I sat in front of a girl named Kitty who was the most popular as well as the noisiest girl in seventh grade and moved through the halls in a chattering cloud of admirers. She tapped me on the shoulder and said, "Let me borrow your pen for a sec."

How does one learn to say no? I handed it over to her. She smiled and uncapped it and smashed its nose into the wooden desk top, crumpling it over double. Then she handed it back. Strange how people know things: how did she know how I felt about that fountain pen? I had bought it—it was out of reach behind the counter and couldn't be stolen—with baby-sitting money, and I loathed baby-sitting, sole source of income for girls between eleven and fourteen. The pen was an Esterbrook with a wide nib and its powerful track across the page, like the slash of a miniature sword, made me feel invincible. It lived on manly black ink, never girlish blue, and it was the only possession I'd ever taken care of.

I took its wreckage back from her and dropped it on the floor without a word, and went up to the teacher to borrow a pencil and got scolded for coming to class unprepared. I didn't say anything. I was learning. And I didn't cry, or even glance at Kitty. I think I owed much to Winnie and Izzy on the mountain—certainly I've been fortunate altogether in my women-folk—or perhaps it was simply the work of time, but I was less abject. Sometimes I even threw a snappy comeback to my tormentors. Inside I was growing, if not an actual spine, at least some gristle; my head was still bloody but less bowed.

Leland was a wasteland of compulsory boredom. There was more time than curriculum to fill it; apparently nobody had decided what, if anything, to try to teach us in these hiatus years. In the last year, ninth grade, I would be allowed to start Latin, but in the meantime we marched in place. This at least has changed now, and I understand the middle-school years are packed to the bursting with math and technology, but luckily for me, those barely cast a shadow over the days back then. What math there was, I was always on the edge of failing.

The wicked, as the wicked will, found alternate employment to fill the long hours. I was in the wickedest section of them all, 7-A, and we were notorious. Handsomely paid war work had sapped the staff and our teachers weren't of the sharpest, and tended to take long sick leaves, perhaps looking for better jobs; almost any jobs would have been better. Substitutes came and left again, sometimes in the middle of a class or even the middle of a sentence. Our reputation had spread among the substitute pool and even the most financially desperate of them were reluctant to come. Sometimes the principal had to take the class.

Our home-room teacher, official overseer responsible for our days, was a Miss Steis, who told us in the beginning, freely and frankly, that she had been in a mental institution and then released on compassionate grounds as the sole support of her brother, who was apparently in worse shape than she was; it was whispered among us that he had two heads and lived in a bottle. When the bad boys acted up, she cried. Sometimes the principal came in and lectured us on our lack of compassion. Never, never ask the seventh grade for compassion.

She had only one teacherly dress, a shapeless black wool that had never been off her back for long enough to visit a dry-cleaner, and as the fall progressed she smelled worse and worse. Bad boys made a great fuss of fanning their faces and opening the windows on even the coldest days, and at Christmas they took up a collection and bought her a present, and wrapped it and set it on her desk. She wept again with sentimental gratitude and said we did, after all, have good hearts. And opened it. It was a bottle of Air Wick, an evil-looking green preparation with a thick spongy wick that, when released, was supposed to absorb bad smells. She cried so hard she had to leave the room, after which the bad boys organized a fist-fight and a desk got broken.

We took a year-long course called Health, involving a movie

projector and screen and many animated films produced by the government. One explained, as had Miss Dobbins in fourth grade, the unwisdom of digging your well downhill from your outhouse, and showed animated sewage seeping into our water and what happened to us when we drank our own shit. Outside, the green trees shaded the green lawns of suburbia, while inside we watched another film assuming that most of our relatives had tuberculosis. We were shown what happened if we slept in the same bed with fathers or uncles who were coughing and spitting blood, and the bacilli were seen charging through our blood-stream and into our lungs, which they ate.

The boys were luckier than the girls and took Shop, in which they learned how to build birdhouses and the shoeshine kits they'd need if the Great Depression came back, with compartments for polish and rags and brushes. The girls took Home Economics, which somehow swelled and burgeoned and seemed to swallow entire days. We made peanut butter cookies, over and over, apparently a basic life skill, and the cooking room was in the basement next to the cafeteria so the smell of scorched peanut butter drifted out and mingled with the smell of yesterday's designated lunch, called the hot-plate, closing the back of the throat with loathing and nausea.

We sewed. Claire Benson's mother, long before, had told me most graphically of the time when she ran a sewing-machine needle clear through her thumb and out through its nail, and I was sure that no matter how careful I was, I too would end up skewered. My thread was always tangled and always broke, and I wrestled over and over with bobbins and dropped them and chased them under chairs. We were supposed to complete the course by making a blouse, but mine wasn't even recognizable as a garment and, in my struggles, grew revoltingly grimy.

More restful was the section on Flower Arranging, another basic life skill. The teacher obviously knew nothing and cared less about it, but she passed around lavish books with pictures showing a single flower and some stones, and read to us about the Japanese philosophy of the art and the spiritual significance of its essential balance of yin and yang, the helpless passive feminine beside the vigorous manly yang.

The longest Home Economics section was called Grooming. We learned that brunettes should wear red, blondes blue, and redheads green. Never should any shades of blue and green be seen on the same body or even in the same room, because they clashed. Clashing was bad. Horizontal stripes made you look fat, vertical stripes made you look thin. The perfect face was oval in shape, but if we were born with defects—a brow like Rita Hayworth's, apparently, or a jaw like Ingrid Bergman's—we could disguise the problem by the way we wore our hair, or by shading our pancake makeup around the trouble spots from light to medium to dark, to make them seem larger or smaller. Diagrams were provided in the textbook.

There was nothing frivolous about this; it was in truth our core curriculum, the arsenal of essential skills needed for our designated career, but I rejected it furiously. Boredom possessed me like a rage. The world out there was bursting with things to be learned and books to be read, and the hours of school were deliberately, purposefully, spitefully keeping me from learning anything at all.

In English class, the year was devoted to outlines. The teacher explained that nothing, not even a letter, could be written without first composing an outline, and we trudged through pages of topic sentences arranged in descending order from Roman numerals to capital letters to Arabic numerals to lower case letters. I couldn't imagine how, after all that, and knowing how you were going to finish the thing, you'd have the interest or energy left to go back to Roman numeral one and start the actual writing. Besides, suppose, after you'd written the beginning, you realized it was going to carry you off in a different direction from the one you'd outlined? It often did, and got you a failing mark on the paper.

The first bright spot on the gray horizon was the school song. We had none. The principal announced in an assembly that we needed one, to unite us in school spirit, so there was to be a competition to write one and anyone, even lowly seventh-graders, could enter. Finally, something interesting to do. I went home and started work.

It went to the tune of the "Battle Hymn of the Republic," or in my lexicon, "Solidarity Forever." There were four or five verses, of which I can remember only one:

> O there may be cafeterias where they like the hot-plate more,
> And there may be cafeterias where they keep a cleaner floor,
> But no other cafeteria has the rattle and the roar
> Of Leland Junior High!
> 'Ray for Leland Junior High School!
> 'Ray for your school and for my school! etc.

I was very pleased with it. Rousing, it was, and easily memorized, and I looked forward to a modest immortality as I turned it in. When I was summoned to the principal's office, I went with happy step.

He closed the door behind us. He was, he said, saddened as well as angry. Saddened that anyone so young should be so rotten with cynicism, but angry that I had given vent to my hostility in such a mean-spirited way, with such selfish disregard for the feelings of others. How did I suppose the cafeteria ladies would feel if they saw what I'd written about it? Hatred, he said, always does more harm to the person who hates than to the object of that hate, so I was really to be pitied, and he did pity me, but it was his job to protect the school from people like me, and of course I was to show no one these nasty verses, and he would make sure they went no further than his office. Ostentatiously he tore up my neatly typed pages, across and then across again, and dropped them in his wastebasket.

"And now," he said, "I think you owe me an apology."

I apologized, I suppose; how not? but I can't have looked very repentant, merely stunned. I'd even shown the song to Mother, and she'd laughed out loud, which was praise from Caesar.

"I'll be keeping my eye on you," said the principal as he ushered me out.

I don't remember anything about the winning song in the competition, except that the tune was rather limp and the theme was pledging lifelong loyalty to the walls and halls of Leland unto death. To the best of my knowledge it was never performed in public, and probably never in private either.

Once again I had badly misunderstood the world and wound up the villain instead of the hero. It was my first and last foray into school spirit.

We took a course called Library Science, which consisted

entirely of memorizing the Dewey Decimal System and being tested on it over and over. All I remember is "000 to 099: Religion and Philosophy," and even that may be wrong. We never went near the school library and, in retrospect, it seems most of my visits there were illicit. Nice Mrs. Bender, the librarian, never asked where I was supposed to be instead. Gym class, probably.

The new twist to gym was uniforms. We were required to undress, in the middle of the school day, in the dank basement locker room, and replace our loafers with sneakers and our clothes with a navy blue, one-piece suitlet with elastic-bottom bloomers. After gym, we were supposed to take this thing off again, and our underwear, and join our classmates naked in a group shower.

This innovation was bluntly explained to us in Health class: when we were younger, we were odorless, like Adam and Eve before the Fall, but with our ripening years we developed a pungent sweat after exercising, and no teacher should have to teach a classroom packed with foul-smelling post-gym students. In theory, we were to take the suit and sneakers home regularly to be washed but somehow I never got around to it. Not that I worked up much sweat at actual sports, but I made do with the shameful sweat of anxiety and my locker stank like a swamp. I never showered either, and shuddered at the Hieronymus Bosch spectacle of my naked peers jostling their baby-fat together under the taps.

Sometimes we played kickball; I was no good at it but at least I understood the principle involved. Mostly we played basketball, which was terrifying and incomprehensible, though everyone else seemed to understand, and screamed at me when I accidentally came into possession of the ball and quickly passed it off on the nearest person who seemed to want it, who was on the other team but how was I to know? they all wore the same suits. With the glad connivance of my teammates, I practiced oozing backward off the basketball court toward the stairs, waiting till an exciting scrimmage distracted the gym teacher and her whistle sliced through the din, then slipping down to safety in the locker room.

On school mornings, I tried almost daily to convince Mother I was sick. I learned that if she leaves you alone in the room with a thermometer under your tongue, you can whip it out and shake it upside down to produce a fever—not too hard, as anything over a hundred and one would rouse suspicion. Presently, hating contention as always, she simply gave up and let me stay home.

I was very happy. Being theoretically sick, I wasn't allowed to leave the house, so I prowled the bookshelves. Mother had lined the whole back wall of the living room with shelves, and it occurred to me that the books on the top shelf might be up there for a reason, so I stood on the back of the couch to check, and they were.

Lady Chatterley was heavy going. Lots of stuff about how the Industrial Revolution had despoiled the English landscape, and my usual confusion with the English caste system: the problem seemed to be that the gamekeeper was hired help. I knew from English children's books that being kind to the servants showed a noble character in the young hero or heroine, but getting personally friendly with them or their children was somehow sinister, wrong, dangerous, or at least odd. The lady and the gamekeeper got personally friendly, but just what they were doing to each other was murky and philosophical and didn't sound like fun. Probably if she'd been doing it to the lord next door, it wouldn't have been worth writing about. I never did go back and reread the thing in later years.

I settled down with Mother's typewriter and began writing a novel of my own. This blissful situation went on for a long time, weeks I think, until finally Mother sent me back to school. "I was thinking you'd get bored, hanging around the house," she said, "and *want* to go back." My brilliant mother's flashes of stupidity always astonished me: how could anyone be bored while being let alone? Boredom was a punishment inflicted by other people on their captives. And how could she imagine that anyone would go to school who wasn't forced to?

I survived the first year, in spite of dangerously bad report cards—"Does not participate in class," "Does not take part in class discussions," "Fails to grasp basic mathematical principles," "Failed to complete sewing assignment"—summered gaily, and then hauled myself into eighth grade as if into Charon's rowboat.

The school's compulsory lunch always smelled awful, perhaps because the basement cafeteria wasn't ventilated and smells accumulated and layered in the air as the days and lunches went by, and wartime food shortages didn't help the menu. Mostly we ate what the Army calls shit-on-a-shingle, a soupy bun-topping of unknown ingredients that actually, with its carrot flecks, looked more like vomit than shit.

I found myself in line next to a girl named Amanda that I knew slightly; she lived on the margin of my neighborhood. "You know," she said cheerfully, "there's someone in my class who's just as weird as you are. You ought to know each other. There she is over there. Come on."

Still unable to say no, I followed, tray in hand. "This is Gloria," said Amanda. "This is Barbara. You'll like her, she's weird too."

Gloria, sitting alone, looked up like a startled deer. I can't remember what she said, except that it was the kind of defensive, in-your-face crack, probably literary, that I'd used myself to fend off tormentors, and I replied in kind. Maybe it was a quote and I capped it. I wish I could remember, because it was a landmark. In the flick of a moment I was saved.

FROM WHICH I AM RESCUED
IN THE NICK OF TIME

I could have blended invisibly in with my classmates, all of us with our standard European genes, but I tried not to blend. The hair du jour was called a page-boy, shoulder length and curved inward at the ends, with bangs. Those whose hair curled too vigorously for this wore it short, and this was called a poodle cut. In defiance, I'd kept mine in pigtails, known as braids now that I was older, and wrapped them around my head and anchored them with hairpins, like a Scandinavian immigrant girl. I don't think it was very flattering, but it was definitely unique. I'd given up trying to assimilate.

Gloria came from a different mold. There's a painting by Goya of a Señora Sabasa Garcia that has something of her air of delicate hauteur, but mostly she resembled the ladies of the court of Versailles, and Mother said it was a shame she couldn't wear the eighteenth-century gowns and elaborate wigs that would show off her long neck, sloping shoulders, and high waist. Blue jeans were unkind to her rounded hips. In her gym suit, with her freakishly long legs, like a stork in bloomers, she dodged away from the basketball with her who-are-these-*people*? look that called for a feather fan. She had grass-green eyes in a pointed face and an aristocratically arched nose that, in future times, on anyone else, would have cried out for cosmetic surgery.

I looked at my hands and at hers. Mine were small and square and I'd bitten my nails to the quick since kindergarten, so that now their remains were splayed and edged with blood; I gnawed my knuckles too, and one of them still carries a lump that marks the time I was working on actual bone. Gloria's hands and fingers were long and white and looked boneless, like the hands of ladies in Flemish paintings, and her nails were long arched ovals.

I was a poet; she was a painter. Her drawings and pastels were stunningly good, even by Mother's standards, and gave off a muscular self-assurance quite alarming in a girl of twelve. Looking back, I can see something of Degas in them, and something of Daumier. I rummaged in her trash and smoothed out the discards and saved them. A young girl drying her hair on a balcony, with a French door open behind her. A ballerina looking upward and her upraised arm, hair caught back with a ribbon. A fat lady, seen from behind, walking down a street with a shopping bag. I wish I still had them.

She could write, too, which seemed unfair; if I couldn't draw, how come she could write?

We lived, for three years, a kind of joint life, though our circumstances were different. Gloria was the only child of a rather ordinary couple whose sole point and purpose in life she was and who seemed awed by her—Mother said something mean about a pair of ducks who'd hatched a swan. Gloria was always nice to them, though, and perfectly obedient, without a trace of condescension. They lived in a bungalow on the far side of the high school, and after supper Gloria washed the dishes without complaint as a daughter should.

We were of one mind. Trapped in school, we strained every muscle toward freedom like racehorses locked in the starting gate, desperate to plunge into our futures. We were wolfishly hungry to learn and know and swallow and digest the whole world. By then, geography was no longer taught in the schools,

178

and still isn't, so that an American can grow up and get elected president without being able to locate Europe on a map; the educational authorities seem to feel it disloyal even to think about countries other than our own. Gloria and I dove into foreign lands as if they were forbidden arcana, more exotic and various than sex.

We wanted it all. We read "Mother India" and Marco Polo and Pearl Buck's Chinese novels; we read "Heart of Darkness" and Somerset Maugham and Isak Dinesen and the adventures of Richard Halliburton and Sir Richard Burton; we even tried to read Doughty's *Travels in Arabia Deserta*. Everywhere: we were going to go there. It was waiting out there. No hasty tourists we, though; we would spend a year in each place, watching and listening, eating and drinking, sketching and writing, until we'd taken possession and absorbed it into our flesh, and then move on. Nepal was calling, and Portugal and Spain, Brazil, and Brittany, and Morocco.

What would we do for money? It didn't matter. We would travel on foot and by local bus, or hitchhike, or stow away on ships, and Gloria would sell sketches of passersby in the market squares. We would sing for our suppers and someone would feed us, or if not, we would forage or steal and sleep in a culvert and go on our way rejoicing.

Some of our favorite places disappeared. Constantinople, Rhodesia, Persia, Siam, Ceylon, Zanzibar detached themselves from geography and drifted away like Atlantis but kept up a disembodied life, still smelling of nutmeg or tigers, their ghost populations still busy in their bazaars or coffee plantations.

Gloria's father belonged to the National Geographic Society and we were allowed to go downtown alone at night to its

179

programs in Constitution Hall, and reel out afterward giddy with the news of camel caravan, Mayan temple, Siberian lake, medieval fortress, African veldt. We never tried to make a list or plan of our destinations, because one place would naturally lead to another until the whole world was ours. We wouldn't hurry.

Surely no two children our age today could possibly be so naïve. Still, our rainbow wings were a great solace at the time, and if Alfred's aunts could hitchhike through India and ride a bus across Turkey, why shouldn't we? Sometimes even now, just before waking in the morning, I think it all happened, and we went. I can see us in the sun-blasted square, Gloria with her sketch pad on her lap drawing a little boy's profile, me scribbling at a rickety table on the cobbles, drinking brandy like Somerset Maugham.

Marriage being out of the question, we would have affairs, passionate but brief, perhaps one in each country. Our work would be brilliant. We didn't consider the rewards of fame and success—we rather scorned them, and expected to go unrecognized until long after our deaths: dying undiscovered and penniless in a Tunisian desert or Tibetan monastery was far more romantic than money and fame. The brilliance of our work was the only point, and we would struggle always for excellence. A touch of madness would be a good idea too, for inspiration, and we toyed with inducing it. Not totally round the bend, like Van Gogh, but maybe halfway round, like William Blake, with a taste for absinthe thrown in.

Meanwhile we were students, bad students, at Leland Junior High School. Except for the waste of time, I no longer minded much. I had an ally, and an ally makes all the difference. Two freaks are better than one. A lone freak is a rabbit fleeing the hounds with its ears nailed back. Two can cast withering glances over their shoulders at the tormentors who follow calling out, "Hey, say some long words for us!" Gloria was wonderful at making faces, another art I never mastered; all I could do was stick my tongue out, which was childish, but she could cross her eyes and screw up her features into a whole castle's worth of gargoyles until our tormentors were quite unnerved and fell silent, wondering if we might just possibly be dangerous after all.

Reinforced, we became insufferable. We must have made it clear that we were at school under duress and expected nothing of any use from our classes. We marched through the halls chanting poetry. From time to time we were called to the principal's office for our attitude. I was never as good as Gloria at the attitude thing—it was her face, her contessa look, the hint of a lip delicately curled in disdain, without actually curling the lip, which would have been insubordinate; the faint surprise at finding herself in such unworthy company; the gently courteous replies.

Heavens, what a pain we must have been. Except for occasionally skipping classes or slithering out of gym, we never did anything severely punishable, and this must have made us more enraging than the real miscreants, the petty thieves and locker-smashers. The authorities could find no cure for us in their instruction books. We had suffered much, and we extracted payment in full.

I suppose today we'd be forced into counseling, with a kindly licensed psychologist to probe for our problems. I'm afraid we would have found it hilarious.

We were so entwined that we could never remember, the next day, whose idea it had been and which of us had said or done it. We talked. When we got home from school, we called each other and talked on the phone until Carl put his foot down: no call to last more than three minutes, with an egg-timer standing sentinel by the phone. After that we wrote to each other, long letters in the evening to be exchanged at school in the morning. We talked at lunch. We went places and talked walking.

Everyone walked back then. Not Mothers, because whenever they went out they came home with groceries and needed a car, but Fathers walked home from the bus stop or the train station, and the young walked everywhere. Walking was transportation, not exercise. (The word "exercise" was rarely used except ironically, as in "Good exercise" after moving the couch or push-starting a stalled car.)

Gas rationing must have helped reinforce the rule: except to buy sneakers at Sears, nobody drove children around. If you couldn't get there yourself, you didn't go. Bikes were important for long hauls, but their tires were often flat and at the destination they had to be parked and padlocked, while feet you had always with you. Winter and summer, we walked automatically, almost catatonically. Half an hour to the ten-cent store, half an hour in the other direction to the library, forty minutes to Gloria's house, twenty minutes to Leland. If alone, we meditated in long slow waves; if companioned, we talked. There was a special quality to ambulant conversation. Walking stimulated the vocal juices, but also pardoned pauses, and sometimes offered sidebars, as of a barking dog or a baby crying on a porch, before swerving back to the main theme. Someone might walk a friend home six or eight blocks and then, since they were still talking, the friend would turn around and walk the other back to the starting point. If parents were snooping or siblings squabbling, friends walked to nowhere just for the sidewalk's privacy.

Gloria and I went downtown whenever we could, walking to and from the bus stops. (If you don't waste your lunch money on lunch, it can serve as bus fare instead.) Washington in the 1940s wasn't exactly Samarkand, but it was a lot more interesting than Bethesda. We went to the Mall, in those days clotted with a jumble of temporary shelters for war work, and skipped Nick's dinosaurs and commandeered the National Gallery of Art; we strode through it handing out approval and rejection left and right. No to Monet, Renoir, David, Cézanne, anything pretty, most of Picasso, most portraits of the holy family, and most landscapes either American-rugged or English-sweet. Yes to Brueghel, Manet, Gauguin, Da Vinci, Vermeer, Sisley, Courbet, Goya, Matisse. The decision of the judges, as they say, was final: we told ourselves we were simply right, and tramped smugly over miles of marble to visit our anointed.

It might be argued—I'm sure our teachers would have argued—that we needed a good, old-fashioned thrashing to wipe that smirk off our faces and teach us respect, but oh dear, it did feel good. Sometimes we said to each other, intoning solemnly, "We know everything there is to know about everything there is to know about," and then burst out laughing at the pure pleasure of being us. Shriveled by years of ridicule, our egos rose up and stretched and bloomed in each other's light. Bloomed grotesquely, the principal would have said.

I followed Gloria easily into the world of the eye, but the ear was harder. She played me her records, Stravinsky, the Brandenburg Concertos, Chopin nocturnes, Vivaldi, and I listened till my ears ached, but I had to hear the same piece over and over before it carved out a groove in my mind. I was slow of hearing. All my life I've been making resolutions to work harder at it, but I'm still slow.

In return, I had poetry for Gloria. I'd discovered Browning, and made her listen . . .

I stop and stare at what I've just written. *Am I making this up?* How old are we by this time, thirteen? How many ordinary suburban thirteen-year-olds do I know who read each other Browning, listen to the Brandenburg Concertos, know where Medina is, and prefer Manet to Monet, all on their own, for the fun of it? Browning? How did I even *find* Browning?

I rummage in the fold of Broca where memory lives and come up with a favorite book, Kipling's *Stalky & Co.*, written in 1899 about three bad boys in an English boarding school. They're joyously, creatively insubordinate and well worth imitating. One of the roommates reads Ruskin for fun. I looked into Ruskin in the library and put him right back on the shelf. Another reads Browning and quotes some lines I liked, so I went and got Browning. That's all.

Like the countries we planned to visit, one thing led to another. Laurence Olivier's *Henry V* came out, and we hiked over to the Hiser Theater and saw it, and I got silly-drunk on Shakespeare and went straight home and memorized the speech before Agincourt and "a little touch of Harry in the night," which always made me cry. Still does. For good measure I learned the sonnet "Not marble nor the gilded monuments" and recited it to myself, with gestures, walking to school. It was good to memorize stuff, so you didn't have to carry the books around.

Nobody guided us, except that Mother said *Wuthering Heights* was trash, overwrought and self-indulgent, like so much of the nineteenth century, compared to the cooler heads of the eighteenth. She suggested I read Pope and Dryden, Sterne and

Smollett, so I didn't. Nobody encouraged us and if they had, we might have taken up something else instead, like housebreaking, but nobody noticed. Perhaps we were unusual—I suppose we were—but most children were unusual then. Different, one from the other. Various in flavor. It was before the invention of teenagers.

In fifty years we've grown used to the concept, but if you go back only as far as fiction and memoirs around World War II, there are no teenagers, only boys and girls evolving into adults at various speeds and along various paths. When Gloria and I were there, teenagers were barely visible on the horizon. I think it started with Frank Sinatra's early fame as a crooner and the hysterical young fans who mobbed him, when some journalist coined the term "bobby-soxers." Bobby socks were our standard floppy white ankle socks, and I promptly took mine off, to distance myself from the mob. I walked miles in all weathers with my feet bare in my loafers, raising blister upon blister until my heels were leprously misshapen.

A new comic strip appeared in the papers. Formerly the funnies had featured adults, animals, and sometimes small children—or possibly dwarfs—like *Nancy* and *Orphan Annie*, but this one showed an entirely new creature. I think her name, and the strip's, was *Penny*. She seemed to be about fourteen, and divided her time between drinking Coke with friends in a drugstore and prattling with friends on the phone, sprawled backwards in a chair with her legs flung over its back, bobby socks aloft. She was a "teenager," and she was nothing else: her character consisted entirely of her age. The *Archie* comics joined her and offered fare for the slightly older, with romantic predicaments in a self-contained world of the sub-adult.

The nation's marketers sprang to attention with whoops of joy. With the right propaganda, a vast population, crossing the whole socioeconomic spectrum, could be isolated from the older and the younger and assigned its own clothes, food, music, and rituals. Once they'd been corralled, it would be easy to sell them the movies and sodas and records they'd need as its citizens.

The teenagers loved having a name, and a uniform, and attention. They'd never been a group before, only under-age and in need of teaching. Now they were a powerful union, courted and studied, and they turned their backs on their kinship clans and cleaved them only unto each other. On their private island they had their own songs and dances, their own heroes, their own language, and only minimal, compulsory contact with the outside world.

Television moved in and reinforced the vision, with sponsors to sell them their own special needs. Money was made by the sack-full. A whole new literary classification, called Young Adult and peopled only by teenagers, rolled off the presses and commandeered sections in the libraries. Later the Internet, chat rooms, and instant messaging reinforced their bonds. Teenagers were forged into an indigestible lump in society, as separate as Amazonian Indians but more numerous.

I can think of no neurological reason why a person between twelve and eighteen couldn't read Browning and listen to Bach, but the social reasons got pretty overwhelming: step out of line and you get your passport confiscated.

Rejected by our peers from the start, Gloria and I went on our merry way.

MOTHER RETURNS TO DUTY, PLUS CONSIDERATIONS OF SEX & BABIES

Mother quit her job and came home and had another baby. Years later I asked her why she'd quit, when she was having so much fun. She said she realized she'd been kidding herself and her job didn't contribute one iota to the war effort and was simply a cop-out, when her proper work was at home. That is, she quit *because* she was having so much fun, a concept not as bizarre at the time as it seems now. Duty cocked an eyebrow at her. Whatever your duty might be, fun was a fairly clear sign that you weren't doing it.

I'm not sure of the chronology; did she quit after she got pregnant? Why did she get pregnant? It could have been an accident, I suppose; the females in my family are grossly fertile and defy contraception. Grandmother once warned me that, with us, if a man gives his trousers a good shake in the house next door, you're pregnant. Or maybe Mother quit and then, having taken the measure of the children she already had, got bored and decided to have another one, just to see who it would turn out to be. She hadn't a motherly cell in her body but she did quite enjoy children, especially girls between five and eleven and boys under twelve; she disapproved of puberty.

Roosevelt died. Young Edward up the street, good Republican son, came and banged on the back door to tell me, sticking his tongue out and thumbing his ears in the classic *nyanh-nyanh* gesture, and I snatched up the cat dish and threw it at him. He danced a clumsy little jig and went on to bang on the next door while I called "Liar, liar!" after him. I went to Mother for reassurance. She turned on the radio and lo, it was true.

There was consternation all around, especially among the young, who thought "President" was Roosevelt's first name and couldn't imagine what we'd call this next man. Washington was a small town then, and a company town, and Roosevelt had been mayor and CEO. Wheelchair or no wheelchair, after three terms most locals had caught a glimpse of him. I had. I suppose it was his second inaugural parade, so I was almost four, and some grownup took me down to Pennsylvania Avenue. Whoever it was—could it have been my father?—slung me up on his shoulders for a view across the crowded sidewalk. The presidential car rolled by, and Roosevelt saw me on my perch and smiled directly at me and tipped his hat. He looked nice.

One day a torrential rain roared down our block and flooded the basement, and all hands were pressed into service, including my friend Margie from next door. We all waded in the dirty water, mopping and bucketing and fending off the flood, until her sister Mary came for her. "Come on, you've got to get cleaned up, we're going to the White House for dinner."

"Do I have to?" asked Margie, soaked and filthy.

"Don't you want to?"

"I'd rather stay here and help. This is more fun."

She was persuaded that breaking a White House date needed a stronger excuse, if not an actual note from the doctor, and left reluctantly. Carl, for once, looked amused, that Margie would rather bail out the neighbors' basement than dine with the Roosevelts. Probably he told it around the Labor Department. Or maybe not: he wasn't much of a one for sharing amusement.

I suppose Franklin or Eleanor had said, "Why don't you come

on over for dinner Tuesday? Bring the kids." It was like that. After he died, the town drifted catatonically for weeks, as if a primal Father had vacated the primal Father's chair.

Then the war in Europe was over. The concentration camps were liberated and the newspaper ran photographs of skeletal survivors and ghastly stories. I wrestled with them, trying to believe and not believe in the same breath, wanting not to know that people, not mere maniacs like Hitler but plain people, had done such things to other people deliberately, slowly, over a long time, in cold blood, and having nothing to do with fighting a war.

It was an unsafe feeling. Just possibly, after all, if Gloria and I roamed the world together, people wouldn't offer us a ride and a place to sleep. Maybe people weren't to be trusted. Weren't even very nice.

Then we dropped the bomb. The mushroom cloud covered the newspaper pages, shaped like a bad dream oozing out from under the bed. Grandmother said, "When the crossbow replaced the longbow, everyone thought it meant the end of the world then, too." This wasn't completely soothing, since surely the crossbow could kill only one or two people at a time and didn't poison the air and water. I brooded. The whole world brooded. Then the war was over, and Becky was born.

With this, we outnumbered the bedrooms and I was moved to the attic. I preferred to think of it as a garret. Sara Crewe in *A Little Princess* was banished to the garret after her rich father died; poets in Paris lived in garrets. Insane relatives were discovered hidden in garrets. I was still in the house but not of the house, removed but not totally removed, like a cousin, and watching from above the fray.

It was cold up there. There was no heat and nothing was caulked or particularly insulated, and the wind came through. Mother got me a small electric radiator that I pushed up against the bed; curled over it I stayed warm enough to read. Summers were bad, though.

From 1801, when John and Abigail moved into the half-finished White House in its sea of mud, until the mid-1950s, when air-conditioners started spreading from the movie theaters into the bedrooms, summer in Washington was infamous. People died. It put the British in mind of Calcutta and their diplomats drew hardship pay. The government fled into long recess, leaving parking places on the downtown streets and a population reduced to a straggle of somnambulant tourists. The president and his friends went to the Catoctin Mountains in Maryland, to the place Roosevelt called Shangri-La, after a mythical monastery in the rather dizzy novel *Lost Horizon*, and Eisenhower, not a reading man, renamed after his grandson David. In the Catoctins it wasn't all that much cooler but the air weighed less by the cubic inch.

For the native born, like my mother and her children, summer was a fact of life. Not much got accomplished, nobody slept well. In elementary school, on particularly stupefying days in June and September, a kindly teacher would lead her class out to the hall to line up at the drinking fountain, and each child in turn was allowed to run water over the insides of the wrists. This, the teacher said, was where the blood ran close to the surface, and the cold water would cool our blood, and therefore us, from inside. It sounded plausible, but we got only a few seconds apiece and I'm not sure it made much difference.

In offices and shops, heavy black table fans roared all day, the more sophisticated of them turning with gracious dignity from side to side, like Queen Elizabeth II waving to the populace, to blow papers off alternate desks. Children shrank from them, having been impressed with the vision of their severed fingers spiraling across the room spraying blood.

Downtown, then as now, fire hydrants were opened to flood the gutters and the marble fountains filled up with the squealing children of the poor, while the policemen, sweating through their uniforms, turned away and let them be. In the suburbs the Good Humor truck came jingling by, and if money could be coaxed from Mother, we bought Good Humor bars, vanilla ice cream on a stick, enclosed in a thin, brittle chocolate coat. Nobody had figured out how to stabilize chocolate, so it flaked off as we ate and dotted our clothes and our bare feet, and then let go completely and slid down over our hands. Popsicles were easier to deal with and could be sucked down to an interesting sharp point, but they were basically nothing but ice.

Suburban children ran in the hose. That's what it was called, running in the hose. Every lawn had its sprinkler. Some sprinklers had a twin-armed jet that either jerked back and forth or swirled around and around; others had a single bar with many small jets and moved slowly back and forth like a big silver comb, pleasant to watch but less satisfactory for standing in. The smallest children wore only their white cotton underpants, while older girls wore bathing suits. It was bad for the lawn. As the children scampered and pushed each other, the grass collapsed into muddy squish and the smallest ones fell down in the mud and sat there wailing, tears and water running down their faces, until a sibling yanked them out of the way and wiped them down roughly with her hand.

193

No matter how cool you got, even blue and shivering, night clamped its hand down. People rustled around in the darkness. No house was ever quite still, ever quite asleep. A shower might run, or just water in a basin, to splash over the face. In the kitchen the refrigerator door opened with a wheeze of gaskets. Every refrigerator held a bottle of cold water, properly in an empty green prune-juice jar, courtesy of Sunsweet, flat-sided for tucking up against the side wall out of the way. Nice people poured it into a glass; others, standing half naked in the cool light from the open door, drank from the bottle. Topped it off from the faucet before putting it back. Sleeping babies whimpered with a rash called prickly heat. Sheets thrashed.

Waves of polio alarms closed down the neighborhood swimming pools, and conscientious mothers wouldn't let their young go even to the movies, oases of air-conditioning, because polio worked crowds, or so some believed. Nobody really knew. Polio was the faceless stalker. The hooded Horseman. It slunk around in silence, it crept up on small children, leaving them twisted; it had found the very President himself. Every school had at least one crooked, half-paralyzed child in a wheelchair or on crutches. Nobody knew what polio looked like or where it lived, in the air or the water or the food, on your own unwashed hands or your neighbor's breath. Nobody ever did find out. The vaccine finally slew it, but it died still faceless.

Mother, true to form, paid no attention. Still, our local swimming pool remained closed.

In my attic, there were no screens in the windows at either end of the long room and bats flew in and panicked. I like bats, I like to watch them darting overhead in the dusk, I like to see a pair of them tucked in for the day on a window screen, asleep with their wings folded like wonderfully complicated little leather umbrellas. Trapped in the attic, though, they barged hysterically into the sloping sides of the ceiling and scrabbled and squeaked, and I felt my way down the splintery staircase and opened the door into the real house and woke Nick up. He came, all sleepy, and coped with the bats, urging them back out the windows. Once he got badly bitten and bled all over my bed. They have teeth like needles.

Mother had a theory about an attic fan. She felt that, with a sufficiently powerful exhaust fan installed in the window by my bed, if all the windows in the house were closed except for one over the laundry tubs in the basement far below, then the fan would suck concrete-cooled air up through the various stairways and cool the whole house. It didn't. It was stifling in the attic and the fan's roar was ear-damaging, like the engine room of an ocean liner and probably the same temperature. The bed shuddered. Sometimes, late at night, I defied orders and opened the other, opposite window; bats were better than suffocating.

The new baby, Becky, was a hit. Judith had a look in her eye that meant she'd like to get some of her own back, pass along the tortures she'd suffered from me and Nick, but we circled the wagons around the feisty new one. Not that she needed much protection; right from the start, she seemed quite ready to tackle Judith, or anyone else who kindled her easy wrath.

I lugged her around with me like a favorite kitten, and sometimes neighbors phoned Mother in horror when they saw me swooping through the streets with Becky stuffed into my bike basket. When she learned to talk, she spoke mostly to invisible people and her collection of familiar spirits; I remember one group was called the Streamliner's Babies and lived in bureau drawers, emerging at night to commit outrages.

Having a swarm of children was no cause for comment at the time: having children was what Mothers did. Stopping at one was selfish, because an only child was lonely and spoiled and neurotic and came to a bad end, never having learned to share his toys. Condoms were fragile, diaphragms a nuisance, and vast numbers of children were accidents, usually greeted with resignation, abortions being hard to arrange and sometimes fatal. Once they'd arrived, the accidental turned out to be just as nice and funny as the deliberate, but they did strain the budget and bulge the bedrooms.

If stopping at one was selfish, choosing to have none was unthinkable. Who would be so shiftless and irresponsible? Children were what you did when you grew up: you registered to vote, married, had children, and thus became a fully vested adult, certified grown. The childless were the subject of public pity. Women praised the nobility of a husband who stayed married to a barren wife and they grieved aloud over her affliction, but secretly they wondered. Of course there must be a medical reason, some internal ailment it would be indelicate to discuss, but hadn't Freud told us how medical matters were swayed by the secret heart? A woman without children must have made her womb an unwelcoming place, slammed its door against the unborn, and very likely she was a chilly fish who lay reluctantly in her husband's arms, or turned him away altogether.

It was pretty late in the world's day for a fertility cult, but there it was. As a woman's everyday virtue was her clean house, so her permanent value was fertility, the quantity and quality of her output. At forty, her work was done. A man at forty had a quarter century of usefulness ahead of him, but a woman heard her fortieth birthday approaching like the footsteps of death; she was still raising the children she'd had, but there would be no more. There were many sad, bitter jokes about turning forty, after which a woman was extra baggage and a bit contemptible, hanging around like that after she'd finished her work. Rather a nuisance, too, as she was expected to degenerate into a scold or a whiner, at least until the grandchildren came along. Only after the grandchildren grew up and the husband died was she free to become what was called, affectionately, a crazy old bat.

Later, with the baby boom in full roar, good folk sometimes worried about overpopulation using too many resources and crowding out the natural world and urged us to draw the line at two. For a while the population bomb was a popular cause, but then we realized that the more people we had, the more gross national product we could produce and consume, so the problem retreated to the lunatic fringe. Then the contraceptive pill came in, making babies more optional and opening alternate careers, at least for the middle class. By that time Mother had five.

What did Becky look like? She has no baby pictures. During the war and its aftermath of mercantile confusion, there was no film for civilians. It's a curious legacy of global war, these vacant spots in all the world's photograph albums. What did Nick look like at six, what did I look like at ten? Here I am on a beach, holding a shell, a skinny seven-year-old with a bathing-suit strap hanging down one arm, and on the next page, here I am with breasts.

I wish I could see us all in those years. We were there, I know

197

we were there, but I can't prove it. Probably there are people who don't need photographs, who can carry around in their heads clear snapshots of their relatives, year by year, mentally labeled and dated, but I can't. I can feel us, I can hear us, but I can't see us, as if we'd gone up in smoke and drifted around bodiless until film returned to the drugstores.

In the centuries before the Brownie box camera, itinerant portrait-painters traveled the roads, capturing the precious flesh just as it was that day. Snatching the momentary look before it got elbowed aside by the next look. The little boy in the velvet suit and neck ruff, staring stiffly ahead and holding the string of a pull-toy, will stand like that always, and the bride in her white dress will still be a bride long after the flesh has withered: the time moved on, out of sight around the corner, but the footprint stayed.

The infant Becky passed through without leaving a print. I remember only that she had a fearsome scowl and narrow green eyes, but that's no great feat; she still has.

Babies came of what happened in the dark between husbands and wives, called sex. There was a subtext to sex, though, that had nothing to do with babies. Nice people call it fondling, angry people call it molesting, and the girls call it nothing at all because they don't want to think about it. Later, much later, it turned out boys sometimes had the same troubles, with camp counselors or parish priests, but that was an even darker secret at the time, and the boys didn't talk either. When the scandals finally broke, those involving boys were considered immeasurably worse than those with girls, being doubly unnatural.

Speaking only as a girl, though, it was always beastly, frightening, sickening, and best forgotten, and I suppose it happened, one way or another, to every girl in the world, as an inescapable part of being young and female, like menstruation. As long as nobody found out and made a hideous fuss, no counselor urged us to talk and talk about it, most of us recovered.

According to the few known facts, it's usually an older man, an uncle, a neighbor, a teacher, a friend of the family, known and trusted. It happens without warning. Maybe he starts with an impulsive kiss on the cheek, perfectly friendly, and then grabs you. He puts his hand up your skirt or down your pants, he holds on tight, breathing harshly, clutches your bottom and backs you up against something. (Remember?) Because of who he is, a grown man, a neighbor, all you can do is keep whimpering "Please, please!" You can't even say "Please don't," because you can't say "don't" to a man. Besides, he seems to be pretending he isn't really doing what he's doing, so it would be rude for you to notice. It would make him angry. Struggling would make him angry. You want to join him in pretending it isn't happening, because you're so hideously embarrassed that it is.

The memories surface briefly, like a mullet breaking water, and slip back down again. Once it was the kindest man I knew, the only grown man I trusted, and when he grabbed me I burst into spontaneous tears of such sorrow and loss that he let me go and backed away and left.

The loss hung on, though. It meant he'd never really liked me, was never being kind, he just wanted to put his hands all over me, for urgent, manly reasons that had nothing to do with me. After that, I tried to avoid him, but I couldn't. I don't know which of us was the more embarrassed. Me, probably.

MOTHER FINDS A WAY OUT & GRANDMOTHER REBUFFS SENATOR McCARTHY

Against all odds, Mother found something to do. There was a splendid children's magazine in those years, called *Story Parade*, and its editor, Hazel Wilson, author of the "Herbert" books, lived near by. She may have sniffed Mother out somehow and prodded her, or maybe Mother went to her first, maybe with Mrs. Hemingway's "Filial Tiger" story. However it happened, Mother started up a monthly comic strip for it called *The Merry Mice*.

My own first work was "The Happy Mouse Family." What is it with mice? Some shy self-effacement of starting out small? Or is it a good thing to be a mouse, quick and agile and opportunistic, darting under the line of vision to seize the crumb? Mother's mouse family was more conventional than mine and lived in a human household, secretly, like the Borrowers, with their small adventures recounted in rhymed couplets.

A less ambitious woman would have started a novel. Once, poking around in the boxes in the sultry family attic among the wasps, I found the first twenty pages of a novel, a murder mystery I think, that began with a man looking at himself in the mirror while shaving. She hadn't thrown them in the trash, but she hadn't gone on either. She—and her father—had expected the world of herself. Suppose she wrote a novel and it wasn't great? Suppose she stretched her wings and fell down, with everyone watching?

So she drew pictures of mice.

Inking and lettering on bristol board, she worked all morning in her bathrobe at the dinner table, the pot-bellied jar of India ink standing open at her elbow, and as deadline approached she would say very little except "Don't jiggle the table." (The table, all its long life, had crooked legs and jiggled if you looked at it. It was also too tall for its chairs, so the whole family formed the habit of reading the newspaper standing up in order to focus, and we still do, leaning over bracing our hands on its pages, on all the tables of our various lives.) The best light in the dining room was at the head of the table, the Father's chair, the captain's chair, the one with arms, but she never worked there. She worked in her own chair at the foot of the table, far from the window.

Even such a small self-imposed assignment must have been a joy after the floppy shapelessness of home life—that it had to be done by deadline, and her name was on it, and when it was finished it was finished, unlike babies, and she took it to the editor. She and Hazel Wilson got to be friends. Someone else, later, told me of coming to the offices when Mother was there and hearing the shrieks of laughter from far down the hall. Mother had found people to talk to, and talking, talking and laughing with like-minded people who, as she put it, "spoke the language," was the only form of entertainment she understood. Being entertained by professionals, as with radio, movies, television, while she had to sit silently until it was time to applaud, struck her as a kind of violation. An invasion of the self. An insult, really.

Her conscience was clear because she worked at home where duty lay, but sun flickered in through the cracks in the walls. She graduated from mice to illustrated stories. They centered on an ordinary suburban neighborhood like ours, a boy named Billy and his friend Fats and the various trouble they got into. The occasional girl in the stories was always a bossy little snitch. Having grown up with two sisters, perhaps Mother's vision was skewed, and besides, it was no fun to write about girls. They never had adventures, or got into interesting trouble. Later, when Becky grew older and took up horses, Mother wrote about girls with horses, but her heart wasn't in it.

We all posed for the illustrations, so Mother could get the arms and legs right. Marshall Gibson, up the street, was quite honored to pose for Fats. Nick was Billy. Becky was any baby sister. I had to be the odd grownup, holding still even when my nose itched, in bone-aching positions such as leaning out of a window or sprawled on a sidewalk where I'd fallen with a bag of groceries.

Her old Royal portable chattered and muttered late in the night, its bell dinging at the margins, and more India ink flecked the dinner table. Some secret tension in the house, as of a wire hidden in the walls that was stretched too tightly and vibrated, relaxed and stopped thrumming. Mother worked, but in her bathrobe, at home like a lady.

Knopf collected and published the first batch of stories in a book called *Billy Had a System*. The second collection was called *Billy's Clubhouse*. They were nicely received. Mother, longtime author of illustrated verses for people's birthdays, became an official author, an official illustrator, and since the world of children's books is a tight one, more friends appeared. She met writers we already admired, like Hilda van Stockum and the d'Aulaires, and artists like Wesley Dennis and Dagmar Wilson, and they autographed books for us and drew little sketches on the flyleaves.

Wriggling through suburbia's fingers like a greased mouse, she joined the Authors' Guild and found a New York literary agent who was a kindred spirit, and some merry editors, and took the train to New York from time to time to lunch and talk and laugh. Publishers sent her corporate Christmas presents.

More books followed, proper chapter books instead of collected stories. Most of them are long forgotten, being about middle-class white children with such middle-class problems as wanting a dog or dropping a library book in the bathtub, but at the time they did well. Presently she developed a sideline and was sought after in the Washington area to visit schools and give chalk talks, lugging a big flip-pad of newsprint to draw on. For these occasions she bought herself, every three or four years, another navy-blue suit at Sears, and checked the skirt in the mirror to make sure it would be decent, on stage, to the eye of the audience. Artist, writer, and actress, together at last. (The scholarly legal historian had been left behind, probably in some delivery room or other.)

And she had some money. She didn't have to ask Carl. It makes a difference, having money, even modest amounts. Then Random House invited her to write and illustrate one of a group of books they were planning for the very earliest readers. Beginner Books, they would be called, written to a strict vocabulary list. By this time I had left the house and Andrew had come along to fill the vacant room; he posed for the pictures. *A Big Ball of String* came out in company with, among others, the instantly famous *Cat in the Hat*, and sales were sumptuous. Suddenly she had more than a modest amount of money. She had more money than could be swallowed up by summer day camps and autumn school shoes.

She bought a piece of land on the mountain, up the hill from Adelaide's cabin, and built a little summer house. A house of her own, more than an hour's drive from her family. Below her, the view spread out over dairy farms, and late at night, if she got up for a drink of water, she could see the lights already on in the milking barns. Carl rarely went there. He'd grown up in the country and hated it. She was alone for the first time in her life.

She scrounged around rummage sales and secondhand shops for odd bits of furniture and mismatched china. After a lifetime of scorn for owning things, she took an interest in old patchwork quilts and early American pewter. She dragged in cartons of used paperback murder mysteries and built more bookcases. In a rebuff to the *Girl with a Watering Can*, she matted and framed engravings of wildflowers and hung them on the walls. When she died she left the house to me, along with her collection of murder mysteries, blue sweatshirts, ankle socks, straw hats, flannel nightgowns. I live there now. Her ashes are scattered under the biggest oak tree, the one where the driveway turns. Four good carpenter's saws still hang on the wall of the tool room downstairs, rusting.

There is only one bedroom. She didn't plan to invite her family. Even getting from the steep dirt lane to the steeper dirt driveway involves an unwelcoming two- or even three-point turn, cursed by FedEx trucks. We came anyway, of course, and brought our own children, and built dangerous great fires in the stone fireplace in March and lolled on the deck in August, but if she knew we were coming, she stayed in town. If we came while she was there, she left.

All this over decades, of course. In the meantime the rest of us grew older. Memories slide back and forth across each other like colored gels, changing the mood, and nothing files itself by date. Gloria and I got caught shoplifting at a drugstore down on Pennsylvania Avenue.

Having an allowance, she wasn't the experienced thief that I was, but the most generous allowance would be strained by the sudden proliferation of paperback books flaunting themselves on racks in every drugstore. Who could resist? It amounted to entrapment. I wish I could say I was caught heisting Kierkegaard or Tolstoy, but I clearly remember it was *Lost Horizon*, the Shangri-La novel. I knew it was about Tibet, and since Gloria and I would be going there, I needed to read it.

We were escorted to the manager's office, which was much like a principal's office. He sat behind a large desk. We stood in front of it. He didn't lecture. He must have been a smart man as well as a kind man, and he said he wasn't going to call the police, but he was going to call our parents. He asked for their phone numbers.

We froze. I would far rather have taken my chances with the police. I could imagine Carl's rage; it would be epic, and very likely this time he really would throw me out of the house, as a criminal element and undesirable influence on his own children. He had the bourgeois horror of getting what he called *involved*: "I don't want to get involved," he would say, meaning anything public or civic, anything with his name on it. This was involvement of the first degree. And his reverence for the law, any law, was religious. From time to time he did pro bono work as a public defender, but it was clear from his stories that he didn't consider the defendants even marginally human: they came from the class of people that broke laws.

We must have made a pathetic sight, still clutching our ill-gotten loot, stricken with horror. Very well, he said. He wouldn't. This time. Put the books back where you found them and give me your solemn word that you won't do this again, anywhere, ever. Gasping like fish with relief, we gave our word. It was hard to keep, very hard, with new titles constantly blooming on the racks, books that weren't in our staid library, Wodehouse and Benchley and Dorothy Parker, but the terror of that moment and the humiliation that washed over us afterward kept me lawful.

One day a week, Gloria went downtown to the Corcoran Gallery for drawing lessons, and another day she had ballet lessons in a second-floor studio near the movie theater, across the street from Mother's old elementary school; family history used to stick to you more than it does now, leaving visible landmarks. Sometimes I walked down there with her and waited for her in the library. She wasn't planning on dancing seriously but she liked the idea of ballet, the discipline, the movements, and besides, it was a good place to take a sketch pad. She studied the rituals of Asian dance too, and she could ripple her arms and hands in the gestures as if they were made of a single stream of water, her neck moving above them as supple as a snake.

Once I asked Mother if I too could take ballet lessons, and to her credit she didn't laugh, just gazed at me in astonishment. I wasn't visibly clumsy, but neither was I on friendly terms with my personal flesh. There was nothing much wrong with the flesh, as flesh; I had nice legs and a narrow waist and wide shoulders, all quite de rigueur, and presently developed acceptable breasts. I just didn't have much contact with it. The inner and the outer Gloria were on comfortable terms. She inhabited her flesh, while I sort of drove mine around, manipulating it from a command post behind the eyebrows. I could make it walk and run and ride a bike, but I would never be able to make it dance, or even play basketball. It wasn't really mine. We had nothing to say to each other. Later in life it discovered sex, when it would snatch the reins and gallop away with me, but afterward it stepped aside again.

I suppose I haven't taken very good care of it. It has to eat whatever's handy, spend long dull hours at a desk, and rarely gets taken out for a run. If my flesh were an employee, it would quit.

Gloria and I finally arrived at the ninth grade and were allowed to start Latin, the first solid tuft of land in the great squashy bog of Social Studies and peanut-butter cookies. The first dignified use of our time in a landfill of ruined hours. *Marcus puer est. Flavia puella est.*

It's fallen into disuse now, and students no longer wear long-sleeved shirts on test days to hide the verb endings inked inside their wrists, but at the time it was still the ancient dividing line between the aspiring intellectuals and the future lowbrows. I expected it to be the scalpel in my hand for dissecting English, and besides, Mother said that with a couple of years of Latin under the belt, anyone with an ear could pick up Italian or Spanish almost automatically. Gloria and I planned to spend a lot of time in Italy and Spain.

We weren't very good at Latin—it was anti-romantic, mechanical, like an Erector set, a boy's game—but we persevered, for the first time in our school careers. We would rendezvous before school and drill each other, cracking open the grammar piece by piece like walnuts. Somewhere I stumbled over the phrase "*Lente, lente currite, noctis equi,*" and understood it. It unwrapped itself in my head, all shiny with translation, and spread its wings like a butterfly hatching, or like strands of colored silk teased through a blank square of canvas.

The second year, alas, brought us Caesar's Gallic Wars. It had always been thus in the second year, because the educational authorities adapt slowly and for centuries only boys studied Latin, and dispatches from the battlefield would keep their ears pricked. Gloria and I slogged through tactical maneuvers and crossed and recrossed the flumen like conscripts, grumbling. A few pastoral odes might have kept us going, but they weren't on the menu. I remember very little except the ongoing fuss about *impedimenta*, translated as "baggage" but, from the way Caesar complained about it, maybe included a straggle of army-issue prostitutes dillydallying along the via, giggling and picking Gallic flowers.

I dropped Latin after that. Nick, later, stuck it out through Virgil and lorded it over me chanting passages from the *Aeneid*. (For a biologist, he did turn out reasonably literate, thanks no doubt to the endless hours I spent, when he had measles, reading him the Arthur Ransome books, which are all right in their way but a drudge to read aloud.)

The war had been almost immediately replaced, in Washington, by Senator Joseph McCarthy and the House Un-American Activities Committee. My leftish family and their lefty friends searched nervously through their pasts and found unacceptable friendships, meetings, donations, magazine subscriptions, and radical girlfriends therein. They weren't the only ones searching.

Suddenly almost everyone needed a security clearance and almost everyone was under scrutiny, their records combed and sifted far back into their wild youths. Washington cowered under the great witch-hunt. My sociable aunt Lois stopped giving parties, because you never knew. Make a joke about HUAC to the wrong person, and in the morning you have no job and a black mark against your name, your wife has been thrown off the charity committee and your kid thrown out of Little League.

One of Carl's colleagues, a nice man who'd been over for dinner, jumped from a hotel window rather than face the Committee. Doubtless he had reasons.

Communism, the new enemy, was more dangerous than Hitler because it was invisible, and everywhere, like polio. Your next-door neighbor might be pretending to be an ordinary person, with kids and a lawn-mower, when he was really a Communist in disguise, and simply living next door to him might infect you, invisibly. The most innocuous book or movie or even comic strip might be sheltering invisible messages that would creep into your brain and infect you all unbeknownst.

McCarthy is our national junior high school, the embarrassing years we all want to forget, and mostly do. Anyone who does remember remembers it as a Hollywood thing, with blacklists and rat-finks, because Hollywood is more interesting than Washington and actors, or even screenwriters, are more interesting than bureaucrats. But Washington too was a strange place in those years, uneasy and stinking of cowardice. The people who should have spoken out thunderously were afraid to thunder and the people who should have split their sides laughing were afraid even to smile. Only the cartoonists took up their pens, and those who were there remember their McCarthy, the paranoid little fat man with the darkly unshaven jaws by Herblock or Walt Kelly. But cartoonists, alone behind their drawing boards, live relatively protected lives. They went down on the lists as com-symps and fellow travelers, of course, and many newspapers expunged them, but they went right on drawing rude pictures, as cartoonists always have.

One of McCarthy's most fervent crusades was purging the Federal government of homosexuals, down unto the lowliest mail clerk. The FBI's J. Edgar Hoover ferreted through the trash of possible queers, looking for letters in an effeminate hand addressed to someone named Alexei. It wasn't that homosexuality predisposed you to Communism, exactly, but it did make you an easy mark. Any Commie agent could come up to any homosexual and say, "Be a Communist or else I'll tell everyone you're queer," and so, being sissies, they would cave at once and start handing over government secrets. Happened all the time. Unacceptable risk. Men's toilets were bugged all over Washington and some had peepholes, the better to track down sissies and root them out.

This is how it was explained to me, and I marveled, balanced halfway between believing that the grownups must surely know what they were doing and finding the whole thing alarmingly silly. I had been, in McCarthy's word, brainwashed, and early. Grandmother had explained governments to me long ago, and Socialism sounded like a lovely system, sweet and gentle, a motherly government that let no one go hungry or untreated by doctors, and the rich couldn't bully people and even the children of the poor went to college. Suddenly it was the ultimate evil and worst imaginable fate. Bumper stickers bloomed—it was expedient to display them—saying BETTER DEAD THAN RED, and I was miffed. I, personally, expected a long future and I'd *much* rather be Red, or green or blue, than dead, but as the Cold War heated up, it began to seem that I wouldn't have much choice in the matter.

Grandmother was of an age to retire from teaching, but her principal tried to talk her out of it, his best-beloved history and civics teacher. She wavered. She really loved teaching; it was the natural expression of her life. First, though, he said, if you stay, you do have to sign this, and he handed her a loyalty oath.

I suppose it was a simple thing, swearing only not to be a Communist, nor to urge her students to overthrow the government by force and violence.

Grandmother read it and laughed. "Mercy," she said, "I couldn't sign *that*," and handed it back and went to clean out her desk.

For years after she retired, cards and letters kept coming from her former students, thanking her for pointing out the road to Socialism. I'm sorry McCarthy and J. Edgar never actually found her out and hauled her before the Committee. She would have thoroughly enjoyed herself—"Now you listen to me, young man"—and it would have been great fun to watch.

AN EMBARRASSING EPISODE
IN WHICH GLORIA & I SET FORTH
ON OUR TRAVELS & COME BACK AGAIN

On a warm day in early spring, the wide world called to us and Gloria and I set out for the Chesapeake Bay.

I don't remember why. The Chesapeake is nice but it's hardly Nepal. A modest destination indeed, where people speak English. Did we plan on a quick swim, and then to come home? Was it a practice run for our global wanderings? Or did we expect to find a ship bound for the Orient and stow ourselves aboard?

I remember packing supplies, a paper bag containing a handful of dried apricots and some cold biscuits from the night before, but why we went at all I don't remember. Memory has saved the cold biscuits and discarded the larger picture. If indeed there was a larger picture. We were in some ways very young for our years. Maybe we were just traveling to be traveling, in a restless time of year.

This was before Washington was belted and rayed with roaring highways, and its modest streets made foot travel feel like a reasonable option for seasoned walkers like us. The north-south roads were Wisconsin and Connecticut Avenues and Sixteenth Street, with Massachusetts Avenue slicing slantwise across them. The Chesapeake lies due east of Washington, as we must have known, after tracing all those Maryland maps in grade school, but we headed south, down Connecticut to Military Road, where we cut across to Rock Creek Park and walked down it. I like to think we were planning to follow the Potomac south to where it joins the bay, but on the other hand we may simply have placed our faith in destiny: if we were in motion, destiny would take charge.

We walked all day. We ate the apricots and biscuits. Our feet began to bleed. Penny loafers, especially without socks, were never designed for serious hiking, but they were the only shoes we had and our faith held strong. We were always going to go traveling, and now we had stepped forward to accept our journey. Limping, we went on our way, down through Georgetown, and across a bridge into Virginia. I don't remember which bridge. Night fell.

We were somewhere in the Virginia suburbs and by this time we must have been heading west, away from the bay. Were we in Rosslyn? Arlington? Alexandria? We'd lost anything like a main road, and strayed aimlessly in small dark streets. A quick cold shower of rain fell and soaked us to the skin and the wet leather of our loafers gnawed pitilessly into our heels. Shivering, we took shelter on someone's porch.

It was late and the house was dark. We sat on the porch floor hugging our knees, teeth chattering, and for almost the first time since we'd met, a silence fell between us. Then one of us sneezed, hard. A light in the house went on, and then the porch light, and a man opened the door and stuck his head out. "What's that?" he said. "Is somebody out here?"

We scurried away into the night. If we'd presented ourselves, and explained, then surely the man would have arranged for the police or our parents to come and escort us home, but faith had deserted us. Without a word between us we set about trying to find our way home.

It was the end of childhood, long delayed. Whenever I think of the loss of foolish innocence, I see that dark porch somewhere in

218

Virginia, and the light going on, and two girls running away in the dark. Perhaps we were the last romantics, or anyway the last of the romantic children. Tatters of Rimbaud and Gauguin fell away as we limped off into the night hoping to find the way we'd come.

Tolerant fate must have forgiven us, because somehow, after hours of wrong turns, we found a bridge back across the river into Washington. The one clear vision I still have is the lovely sight of an empty, lighted, clanging streetcar; we must have found Wisconsin Avenue, and we must have had the ten or twelve cents for fare, because the streetcar took us as far as Friendship Heights. From there we walked through dark Bethesda and over to dark Chevy Chase to my house, which was closer than Gloria's.

Amazingly, the lights were on, the only lighted house on the block. People were still awake. Mystified, we blinked like moles in the lighted front hall. It was four o'clock in the morning.

Mother called Gloria's parents. Carl was furious, of course, but apparently not at me. He was angry, terribly angry, at Gloria's father, who had insisted on calling the police although it was quite unnecessary to get the police involved. Gloria's parents came and took her home.

Nobody scolded us. I was confused by not being punished, and kept waiting, but it never happened. Were they relieved? Had they thought we'd been kidnapped?

Here memory boggles. What was the matter with us, that we thought we could just walk off on our travels and no one would notice? I may have had some excuse for feeling I wouldn't be missed, but what of Gloria, her parents' adored one-and-only, always so dutiful? We were far too old to be so thoughtless.

Decades later I read *Stuart Little* to my sons, Matt and Ben, and when Stuart sets off to search for Margalo, Matt burst into a storm of tears. "He didn't tell his parents," he wept. "He never told his mother and father he was going, and they must have been so worried." Matt was five.

People grow up, if they grow up at all, at different speeds.

Gloria and I set the whole episode aside and never spoke of it again. Instead, Gloria began to talk of going, not to Lhasa, but to New York to the Art Students' League, and she set about polishing and culling her portfolio. There were no schools for writers, so I shouldered the weight of my own education. I stopped reading about Bedouins and took up the books I thought had to be read.

I'd never heard the word or the concept of a "canon," but it was easy enough to identify the essentials: they were mentioned in other books and referred to with reverence, and they were still in print after maybe hundreds of years. They sat massively on the shelves at the library or in the living room.

I don't remember any new books coming into our house, no book still in its dust jacket, no popular novel. There were the books that had always been there, and then Mother and Carl went out in the evenings, their only outings, two or three times a year, to Lowdermilk's, a great warren of a used-book store downtown. They brought back cartons of bargains, like the complete Dickens and complete Kipling missing only the most popular volumes; *Dombey and Son* but no *Oliver Twist*, *The Light That Failed* but no *Jungle Books*. Whatever else I needed, the library had.

I read the books that I understood had to be read. The experience was, as the critics say, uneven.

I read all of Shakespeare's tragedies and most of the comedies and histories. I loved Boswell's *Life of Johnson*, *La Morte d'Arthur*, and Burton's *Anatomy of Melancholy*. Nobody could see if my light was on in the attic without opening the door in the hall and peering up the stairs, which nobody did. I could read all night. The complete Poe was spotty. Dante's *Inferno* had riveting Dore illustrations but the repetition of agonies passed from horrifying through interesting to monotonous, and I didn't understand the gradations of theological sinners, schismatics and such.

Down to the south of me a generation of future writers was learning its craft in afternoon kitchens and evening porches, where the soft voices of neighbors and relatives told stories, stories about real people, townsfolk, ancestors, ghosts, crimes. Nobody in my family told stories about people. Nobody gossiped. So I huddled in bed in the middle of the night with Ibsen, Shaw, Strindberg: strict education required reading the long-winded philosophical prefaces too. Only a habitual insomniac like me could have persevered.

Rabelais was disgusting, but Cervantes was swell, and *Canterbury Tales* was great, well worth the extra trouble of a glossary; imagine writing such wonderful stuff so long ago, under the handicap of such knotty language. *The Education of Henry Adams* was a challenge. I kept counting the pages left to go and congratulating myself on those already traversed. I did finish it, but I was none the wiser.

Milton stopped me cold. I tried, I tried hard, I tried several times, but each time I stuck fast and had to back out. Finally I slunk away defeated, convinced that forever after people would keep asking me what I thought of *Paradise Lost*, and I would have to confess and be scorned.

So far so good, but I keep my fingers crossed.

BEING A TREATISE ON
THE ORIGINS & USES OF AUNTS

To digress. My aunts had dressing tables. Do aunts still have dressing tables, dressing tables with skirts, their mirrored tops sprinkled with face powder; silver-backed hairbrushes and cut-glass scent bottles with frosted-glass stoppers?

Mother had a lipstick. She kept it in the medicine cabinet next to the Band-Aids, in the hall bathroom we all used except Carl, who had his own, and I think it must have been a free sample, an inch or so long. Pinkish, in a gold-colored tube. She used it for state occasions like dinner parties, and it lasted her all through my childhood, even though I sneaked an occasional smear of it.

Looking back, I think Mother's lack of vanity was an extreme form of vanity in itself. She'd always been pretty, maybe the prettiest of all, but she scorned it. She was her inimitable proud secret self, and artificial devices like nice clothes or face powder would have meant an appeal, on false and frivolous grounds, for the world's admiration. Only her own and her father's approval mattered. Her self was like an agate she'd found out walking alone and always kept in her pocket; you wouldn't put powder and lipstick on it. Respectably, she washed her face and combed her hair. She made her children wash their faces and comb their hair. Any lengthier consideration of the mirror would have been frivolous.

The aunts had dressing tables.

When I was a scruffy, scabby-kneed child standing around, my aunt Peggy would tip up a tiny bottle and then touch its stopper once behind each of my ears, and I walked away with scent swarming around me like a cloud of bees, my head balanced carefully so as not to disperse it.

For that matter, do people still have aunts? Available aunts, that is, not just Christmas aunts? Once, whole families stayed in the same area for generations, which seems peculiar now, and boring; now an uncle will find a better job in Seattle or a brother's company move him to Newark, and children scatter like sparks; my own nieces and nephews wouldn't recognize me on the street.

Grandmother and her three daughters, with their husbands and children, all lived within a ten-minute drive of each other. Peggy and Bob lived just down the hill from her, their kitchen doors scarcely sixty feet apart, on the two deep wooded lots they'd bought before my grandfather died. Every evening at bedtime Bob would take the dogs out for a run and stop in to say hello. He liked Grandmother. They sat at the table and argued politics and world affairs, and I was impressed: it was an uncommon compliment for a man to argue with a woman. Then he whistled for the dogs and went back down the hill. I don't remember Peggy stopping in.

Something was amiss in Mother's birth family. I could smell it even when I was quite small. Mother drove me over to Grandmother's on Fridays for my weekend stay and stopped in the driveway, engine running, while I got out with my paper bag of clean clothes. Then she drove away. I remember once, for some forgotten reason, she came into the house and sat down with her raincoat still belted, perched on the edge of the couch like a social worker, and she and Grandmother discussed whatever it was. Mother was using her formal voice, the guarded one she used on bus drivers and automobile mechanics. She didn't eat or drink anything and nothing was offered, and when the issue was resolved she left. I pondered. This *was* her mother, wasn't it? Who talks like that to their mother, as if they'd never met before?

Grandmother came to our house for dinner only rarely, maybe once a year, but that I could understand: she tried to argue with Carl, who took argument as a personal insult; I could have told her that, but I don't expect she would have stopped. We never went to her house *en famille*, but then Carl rarely went anywhere.

One year Peggy did invite us all to dinner. The whole family for dinner, I think she said. I'm sure she said. The next day I was in my aunt Lois's little bookstore and lending-library in Bethesda, and I said I'd see her at Peggy's. "I'm afraid not," she said coldly. "We weren't invited. This is the first I've heard of it."

Horrified and contrite, I went to Peggy and confessed. Peggy sighed. "I'll just have to invite them, then," she said. I don't know how she explained the tardiness of the invitation, but they came. This made us too many for the dinner table, so the Ping-Pong table was hauled out of the basement and set up on the deck. Luckily it didn't rain, but I was faced all through the meal with the awful evidence of what I'd done. But she *had* said the whole family. Lois was her sister.

It came to me only slowly, and much later: all four of these women had been in love with the same man, which in close quarters breeds evil feeling. If he'd lived a little longer, I'm sure I would have joined them. Grandfather was tall and kind and distinguished-looking and smoked a pipe. His was the only lap I ever sat in, and ever after I fell easy prey to pipe smoke.

When she was in her sixties and he was long dead, Grandmother told me at breakfast, embarrassed, that she'd had a most unladylike dream about him.

Even the boyfriends his daughters brought home adored him and remembered him always. More than one man, I heard, fell in love with all three sisters, one after the other, perhaps hoping only to marry into the magic spell. He entertained dinner guests with tales of his work. A parasitologist with the Department of Agriculture and a pioneer in the fields of hookworm and heart-worm, he had memorably disgusting case histories to tell, chuckling, while he carved the chicken.

Grandmother, who had lived all her adult life in northwest Washington and its suburbs and taught for decades at the same high school, had made no close friends and scarcely any acquaintances. I suppose her husband was enough.

Were Mother's jeans and carpentry the remnants of an eldest daughter appointed as an honorary son? Probably they were. He wrote verse. He wrote and had printed a slim volume of mediocre verses that I seem to have lost, and Mother, aged twelve or thirteen, was chosen to illustrate it.

If you have three daughters, you can't choose all of them all of the time, for all purposes, but the others are always watching.

He died unexpectedly, in his fifties, of a botched operation for gastric ulcer while Mother was in the hospital having Nick. Nobody dared to tell her. Nobody realized she would simply ask the nurse for the morning paper, and there he was, with a picture and a feature story on his work. This accounted finally, years later when I found out, for the darkness and sorrow that swallowed the house when Nick came. I'd thought his arrival was the occasion of grief; I was sure he'd be sent back, or thrown out, with me, into the street. Nobody told me Grandfather had died and snuffed out the light in Mother's life.

Lois was the luckless middle daughter. She had her little bookstore and it made her feel important, but she didn't seem to enjoy it much and her manager, Louise, was the beloved of the customers, just as Lois's housekeeper was the beloved of Lois's children.

I paid duty calls on her for decades, and she always cross-examined me sharply about my siblings, hoping to hear that they were far gone in drink or living in a box under a bridge. When I'd finished glossing over their troubles, she told me again about her own children, and all their advanced degrees and important careers. More advanced, more important, than those of her sisters' children.

It was from Lois that I learned, here and there, the few facts I ever did learn about my father and Mother's marriage to him. Since the marriage had failed, she was happy to tell, though never more than a sentence or two at a time, with a sniff. Their life had been rackety, I gathered, with hungover guests found sleeping on the couch in the morning, though this seemed a thin reason to take up with Carl. Why Carl? They had friends, my parents, some of them merry, some of them later successful. She could have chosen among them, surely. Maybe she was rebelling against her life and Carl was of all of them the least likely to be found on a couch in the morning?

When Lois was ninety and beginning to slip, she asked her husband, over and over, "Is it true my sisters are dead? Both of them? They're really dead?" Her husband assured her they were, and she said, "What a shame," and smiled. Once she turned to me and explained, "I had two sisters, and one of them was very bright and one was very pretty, so naturally they had an extremely high opinion of themselves." Poor woman. Envy is the only one of the seven deadly sins that's never any fun at all, even briefly, and she spent ninety years with it, waiting for her tall blond father to choose her first.

As for Peggy, the petted youngest, lighthearted Peggy, nobody would want to be Peggy's sister. Half Washington was in love with her and her parties were the most fun to be had for a hundred miles around. Half a century ago, before the word was bludgeoned out of all its juices, what she had was called style. This meant that everything she did, or wore, or bought, or cooked, or grew in her garden was something you'd never thought of before but as soon as she did it, you realized it was the only right and perfect thing.

During the war, silk was made into parachutes and silk stockings were not to be had for love or barter, so party-going women tried to dye their legs tan. The dye was meant to look like stockings, and sometimes a black stocking-seam was traced up the back with eyebrow pencil, but the effects were only so-so. Like the dye in margarine, the dye on legs came out streaky. In the summer it rubbed off on the furniture and in the winter you froze, barelegged. Peggy rebelled.

I was hanging around her house when she came up from the bedroom, ready for a downtown party in a merrily flounced black cocktail dress and bright red knee socks. She looked wonderful, but then, she always looked wonderful; if she balanced a magazine on her head, it looked like the priciest hat in town. Within weeks, fashionable Washington was wearing red knee socks instead of leg dye, but somehow they never looked quite the same on anyone else.

It was Peggy's pleasure that infected her world. She enjoyed herself. Even when she was washing dishes, enjoyment hung around her like a golden haze. This was utterly foreign in my. life, and I lusted after it. Once I went down to her house at midday and she was eating lunch, alone, in the chair at the head of the table that should have been sacred to Bob. She was eating a cold red soup streaked with white that she told me was borscht, borscht she'd made herself, of course, since nobody sold it, with sour cream.

I'd never heard of borscht; I'd never even heard of cold soup except as a liability; I'd heard of sour milk but never sour cream. Even her solitary Saturday lunch had style. Mother at that moment would be eating a peanut butter sandwich while finishing the morning paper. Mother felt that caring about food beyond the subsistence level was just as decadent as caring about clothes beyond the warmth-and-decency level.

At the other end of Peggy's table the mockingbirds' raisins lay in a pretty glass dish. She'd started feeding them outside in the usual way, but presently for convenience she opened the top half of the window for them and served their lunch on the table. The dining room thrashed with wings. Mockingbirds are big. Sometimes she'd hold a raisin between her lips and a mocker would tread air in front of her face to pluck it.

She sometimes made cutting, astringent remarks that hurt your feelings, but you could count on Peggy to do the right thing. When I was maybe seven, I was playing in Grandmother's long front yard on a chilly fall weekend and, having nothing better to do, smashing acorns with a stone on a flat rock. If you have a nose attuned to acorns, smashed acorns smell like food, and a baby squirrel came to inspect them. He was tiny, an infant, and hungry, but so young he couldn't cope with even smashed acorns, and he was cold. He climbed onto my bare legs, and then inside my dress, his baby claws like spiders, and up my front, where he poked his head out of the neckline and rested, warming himself on my skin.

Holding him gently in place, I crossed the driveway and went to find Peggy. I didn't need to say anything, just lifted my chin and showed her the small gray face under it. Without a word she found a shoebox and lined it with soft things, and got an eyedropper, and punched open a can of Carnation milk to warm in a pan on the stove. I went back up to Grandmother's knowing the orphan would be all right.

Curly was better than all right. He grew up to be a major pain in the neck and a Washington legend. There was the night, for instance, that a guest in his cups lingered long after the party was over and it was time for Curly's evening romp. As was his custom, he frolicked wildly over the back of the couch and pranced on the mantelpiece.

"Jesus Christ," said the guest. "Look at that. I don't believe it. It's a squirrel."

All unrehearsed, Peggy and Bob looked at each other, and looked at their guest, and said, "What squirrel? I don't see any squirrel."

The guest left. It was said he never drank again.

Peggy had had her radiators recessed into the walls and covered, with a shelf over them, and in the warmth and darkness under them Curly built nests. When Bob's paychecks stopped coming, he raised hell with his employers and much strife ensued, before the cleaning woman rooted around under a radiator and found the shredded remains of assorted mail, including a small fortune in paychecks and many an unpaid bill.

After a long and happy time, Curly bowed to natural forces and went out and found a wife, but he came home often to visit. His wife stayed back at the edge of the woods, lashing her tail and calling him forty kinds of a fool.

Peggy's rooms were all lightness and air. She took up with the Indians of the Southwest long before fashion discovered them—I believe she wrote some indignant papers on their behalf and made herself a nuisance at the Bureau of Indian Affairs—and from her prowlings through the desert she brought back woolen rugs made with the old vegetable dyes, and baskets and pottery and copper jewelry that look familiar to eastern eyes now but seemed miraculous at the time.

She went to galleries in New York and brought back elegant witty drawings for the walls. Her living room admitted nothing as bulky and pompous as a Father's chair, but Bob was so amiable a man that he just sat wherever was handy. The house was made for parties, and there were always parties.

Carl's associates were labor lawyers and arbitrators and judges who spoke of serious matters, drank sparingly, and liked to get to bed early; Bob's were from the news world, journalists and radio and television people, and Peggy hung on the fringes of theater and art and brought home people she found there. Nobody went to bed early.

In June, they gave the wild-strawberry party. Across the road lay a broad patch of abandoned fields, earmarked to disappear soon under a wave of executive homes, but in the meantime blanketed with tiny, startlingly sweet wild strawberries. When they were ripe, the party assembled. One friend was the harpist with the National Symphony Orchestra and she brought her harp, and the men carried it across the road and set it up in the heart of the strawberries, and she played while everyone else got a container and fanned out to pick.

Picking was undignified work; you had to crouch or stoop and grope through the underbrush, turning up the green leaves to find the red berries. (The under secretary of interior got excused because he couldn't find a single one, and realized for the first time that he was red-green colorblind.) When the buckets were full, they trooped back to the house to drink gin-and-tonic while Peggy made shortcake and Bob whipped mountains of cream. Everyone gorged, but so lavish and so generous were the wild strawberries that everyone got some to take home. With whatever was left, Peggy made heavenly jam for Christmas presents.

Even during the war, nobody ever ate anything boring there. Bob made frequent forays down to the waterfront for dripping burlap sacks of oysters and crates of scuffling blue crabs. Peggy found spices nobody else had ever heard of. Decades ahead of everyone else, she found bean coffee and a coffee grinder; she found peppercorns and a pepper grinder. She and Bob found strange-smelling ethnic markets in areas of the city where nobody else had ever been. Everything in their world, even breakfast, was an adventure.

At Christmas, presents from Peggy were pure joy. Mother wrapped everything in the cheapest printed roll-paper from the ten-cent store, but Peggy made the same creation of a package that Mother made of her tree, and there were paper cut-outs on them, and foil stars, and flurries of ribbon. While all the children were little, she found perfect things to give, not just what you'd always wanted but something you hadn't known enough to want. When I was six or seven she gave me a clock, an ordinary bedside clock. I didn't know a clock was something a child was allowed to have. Grownups had clocks, as they had money and car keys, because they were in charge, and the children were told when to get up and when to go to bed.

I remember taking it out of the box, and staring and staring at it, and giving its key a couple of experimental turns. It ticked. The minute-hand jerked. It was real, not a toy. It was for me. I felt powerful.

Not that Peggy's talents were all domestic. She was a crack shot with a rifle, and when she and Bob went to county fairs, she figured out the crooked sights on the shooting gallery's guns in the first round, then adjusted her aim accordingly, fired again, and always won the top prizes. They staggered home laden with giant plush pandas and frightful plaster birdhouses. When Grandmother looked up and saw a large menacing snake draped over a branch high above her vegetable garden, she called Peggy, who brought her rifle and broke its back with a single shot. It dropped in wavering loops down from the tree and fell dead among the cabbages. Peggy shouldered her gun and went back to her house.

Was this Grandfather's ghost again? Did he admire her marksmanship? Teach her to shoot? Was it something she could do that her sisters couldn't, or didn't try? All three women seemed to carry the print of a father's hand. I can't see Grandmother's mark on any of her grown daughters, only his, and that might have been sad for her, except of course she was in love with him too.

When one person in a family is so ardently loved by all, it

upsets the balance and blights their feelings for one another. Love can undermine the whole structure far more effectively than hate. My grandfather was the story of their lives, of all their lives, and I blundered into the rubble after it was over.

What sort of a mother had Grandmother been? I can't bring up the picture. Practical, of course. Strict. Sensible. Enemas, cod-liver oil, galoshes, homework. No cuddling, of course; people like us didn't cuddle or gush. But perhaps our current emotional reading of motherhood is something new, and back then, being a mother *was* galoshes and enemas. Responsibility. Common sense.

Peggy and Bob had two daughters, Judith's and Becky's ages, and I envied them their lives, but somehow they didn't make much of a dent on the household. It wasn't a children's world. Perhaps Peggy wasn't, at heart, a mother; perhaps all three sisters were trapped by their first love and, like a Hans Christian Andersen story, stayed frozen forever as daughters.

I remember the great swing, surely one of the world's highest. With her gun, Peggy had shot a string up over a tree branch, then attached the string to a heavy rope and pulled it up and secured it. The seat was a round board with the rope knotted through a hole, and the arc you could make on this was nothing short of majestic. At its height you looked down on the roof, down the chimney. But in memory that isn't a child on the swing, it's a pretty woman, and she's kicked off her shoes and her skirts are flying up over her face and she's shrieking, holding the rope with one hand and a drink in the other. There are no children in sight except me, somewhere on the sidelines watching.

Peggy and Bob went to New York for theater, and came back

and bought the record albums. They'd been to marvelous parties with Noël Coward; they played all his records, some of them privately cut, and his rhymes made me curl my toes with a pure and ancient joy, now mysteriously lost to the world; when Stephen Sondheim goes, the last rhymes will go with him. I sat on their floor hugging my knees while Coward and "Where's Charley" and "Finian's Rainbow" and "Kiss Me, Kate" and "Annie, Get Your Gun" poured into my head and the lyrics layered up over Horatius at the Bridge and The Ballad of East and West.

Nothing in our house was strange and wondrous; everything in theirs was. A colleague on assignment to the North had sent Bob the long, strong bone from a walrus penis, with a note saying "If you don't think a walrus has a bone in it, you try it in water at thirty below zero."

When I got my hands on some nickels, I played their slot machine. It was a splendid machine, huge, massive, gaudily embossed and embellished all over in brass. Back when he was a cub reporter on the night police beat, Bob had been rather a pet with the cops and they let him come along on a gambling-house raid. The raid was successful and yielded plenty of loot, and the police kindly gave the boy from the *Daily News* a nickel slot to take home. They must have helped him carry it; it weighed a ton. I was warned over and over of the futility of gambling, and how my hard-earned nickel would simply disappear into its maw with nothing to show for it but the sight of revolving cherries and lemons, but in truth I made out pretty well. It was adjustable, and Bob had adjusted it for the most generous payoff so as not to fleece his guests. At the end of a month of parties its house box, Peggy said, usually held just enough to pay the paper-boy.

237

On the radio Bob's pleasantly granular, whiskey-and-cigarettes voice could be heard reporting on the wide world. Once I heard him broadcasting from a plane over a South Pacific battle; through the static and gunfire he sounded as if he was having a wonderful time. After he graduated to television's evening news, though, I lost him. We didn't have a television at home, and wouldn't until after I was long out in the world and Mother and Carl had to give in, for the baseball. (We were none of us early adapters. In 1963 I listened to Kennedy's assassination and funeral on my little brown radio.)

Peggy and Bob didn't have a television either. When Bob's superiors at NBC found out, they brought one over to the house and forcibly installed it. Peggy said it was hideous and had a pretty little cupboard built into a bookcase and hid it in there, opening the doors only for Sid Caesar's *Show of Shows*.

Much as I loved and envied their world, I always knew it wasn't mine. I was the awkward child lurking on the fringe of the party, eavesdropping on the laughter, sneaking into the kitchen to stick my finger in the strange food and taste it. I could never go prancing through life like that. It wasn't in me.

Once, after I had started high school, I was at Grandmother's for the weekend and got caught in a sudden rainstorm and soaked, with nothing to change into, and Peggy lent me a dress. I remember it vividly. Soft wool, in an odd black-and-green plaid, with a crisscross bodice. It fitted me exactly and was possibly the first garment I'd ever worn that fit; certainly it's the first garment I remember at all, which is probably just as well.

I looked at myself in Peggy's mirror, another luxury. At home there were no full-length mirrors. There was a mirror over the mantelpiece in which you could see the top of your head and another on the bathroom medicine cabinet in which you could see if your face was clean, but nowhere to see yourself whole. I looked pretty good. I looked grown, in Peggy's dress.

For the flicker of a moment I imagined the joy of actually becoming Peggy, followed at once by reality. Peggy was Peggy so effortlessly, and for me to try to be her would be work, exhausting, full-time work, and doomed to failure. Growing up is the process of learning how many things you can't do and how many people you can't be. When you've winnowed them out, what's left is you.

I was always grateful to her, though, for showing me all those toys. How else would I ever have heard of Noël Coward, or chutney? Her world has always been a happy lightness in my life, like a bunch of flowers or a new song.

Peggy, the youngest, was the first to die, of various lung complaints, or perhaps she didn't want to get any older; some of my relatives seem to have a knack for pulling their own plugs, from inside.

Years later, I was in Washington for some family occasion and had brought along my twins, Matt and Ben, who were maybe seven or eight, and the three of us were sent to stay with Bob. I bedded the boys, and Bob and I stayed up to see the cereus bloom. Peggy had brought it back from the southwest and it lived in a pot, a scruffy, unprepossessing cactus-type bush. Once a year, on a midsummer night, it blooms with a single amazing flower, or so I was told, divinely beautiful and scenting the air for acres around. At sunrise it closes down for another year.

We sat on the patio beside it, staring at its swollen bud and chatting of this and that. At midnight we decided this wasn't the night. Perhaps the next night, but I'd be gone by then. We went to bed.

In the morning Ben stomped grumpily up from the bedroom. "I couldn't sleep with you all talking all night," he groused. "Yammer yammer yammer. Especially that lady."

"What lady?"

"The lady who kept talking and laughing all night."

"There was nobody here but me and Bob."

"Yes, there was. There was a lady. Not you, the other lady. I heard her. I couldn't tell what she was saying but she kept on talking." He was quite firm about it, and cross and sleepy.

I suppose there was another lady. Of course there was. Of course Peggy would come back to see if her cereus bloomed, and stay up late talking and laughing. I was sorry I'd missed her.

CONTINUING EDUCATION

Gloria and I moved on, several blocks to the north, to Bethesda–Chevy Chase High School, which, Mother assured me, was highly thought of on the national ranking of public high schools. I'm sure it was. Certainly it was full of school spirit.

We were told in assemblies that school spirit was far more important than academic studies, since school spirit built character as no mere learning could. Nobody explained how, exactly; it was supposed to be self-evident. School spirit was tightly wound around and inextricable from sports. It meant loving not just the red-brick building itself but all its sports teams, with a deep personal love, and defending its honor on the playing fields or in the bleachers, especially against the forces of our satanic rival, Montgomery Blair.

At the high-school level all the educational authorities were men. It never entered their minds that some students, perhaps perfectly decent in other respects, might not care much whether or not we beat Blair. Beating the Nazis had made sense; beating Blair, whose students, like us, were compelled to attend and indistinguishable from ourselves except for living in a different suburb, did not.

There weren't any female players outside of gym class, of course, only female cheerleaders, but girls were required to care equally. It was wrong, bad, cynical, and even punishable not to care. Not caring, like Communism, might prove contagious and infect our fellows.

Gloria and I had been caught slithering out of compulsory pep

243

rallies and escorted back to them. At pep rallies, our assistant principal led us in prayer, asking divine intercession in the big game on Saturday. God, Who by rights should be paying attention to the looming possibility of nuclear war with Russia, was implored to look with favor on a few touchdowns for our side, while at that very moment, over in Silver Spring, Blair was pleading for the same blessing. God was to drop everything, weigh the respective prayers of two suburban high schools, and decide on Saturday's winner. Nobody else seemed amused by this, or if they were, at least they had sense enough to shout "amen" instead of choking into their fists.

Saturday's game wasn't compulsory and nobody took attendance, but the authorities knew perfectly well who wasn't there. Us. Sometimes, just on general principles, we were called to the office for what British schoolboys call a jawing.

We were taking all the same courses but the only class we had together was Latin, since there was only one second-year class. Because we weren't half as cynical as they thought we were, it never occurred to us that word had come over from Leland and efforts were made to break up our unholy alliance.

The busywork of junior high receded and we were offered, besides the pep rallies, real stuff to learn. As previously mentioned, we slogged through the Gallic Wars, and we started French. French was definitely an improvement, romance-wise, and we spoke Franglais to each other, and I settled in with a dictionary to make my own translation of Baudelaire's *Fleurs du mal*.

In Biology, with Mr. Zimmerman, we learned about the division of cells. Mr. Zimmerman showed slides. Fiddling to adjust one, his fat hand appeared enormously on the bright screen as he said, "Now this is an example of mitosis." I couldn't stop myself. I think I'd thought the whole class would join me in a chorus, but only I spoke out to say, "Those aren't your tosis, those are your fingerses." Nobody laughed and Mr. Zimmerman gave me an F for the day. Other than that, I remember the loathsome life cycle of the bott fly, the flagella of the paramecium, something about the circulatory system of trees, but not much else.

In Algebra, I actually understood the principle, I just couldn't work the problems, and spent a lot of time mooning over them, making up stories about these two pigheaded people rowing in opposite directions in boats that leaked, though not equally. I knew something about boats from Florida days; how often, since the protagonists were presumably alone, did they have to stop rowing and bail with a rusty coffee can? And surely the one headed upstream would be swept backward during this hiatus while the downstream one drifted forward, and why wasn't this factored in? In my heart I faded out of algebra class and into a rowboat with Nick, my feet in the warm bilgewater beside a couple of dead fish, blisters on my palms . . .

Early in the year, in warm September, the girls of my gym class marched out to play softball. Those waiting for their turn at bat lounged on a grassy slope behind the catcher. I lounged there for three full innings, unmourned in either the batting lineup or the outfield, until the teacher marched up. Mrs. Quayle was her name, and she was short and square and furious, with the most ripplingly muscled calves I have ever seen on man or woman.

"What's your name?"

I told her. She wrote it down on a clipboard. "I've been watching you," she said. "I saw what you were up to. And I'm telling you right now, I am giving you a failing grade for *the whole year*."

If she'd given me Paris, I couldn't have been happier. "Since you're failing me anyway, I guess it doesn't make much sense to show up for class then, does it?"

She glared and marched away swinging her clipboard like a mace. Maybe she hadn't quite planned for that, or she'd been hoping I'd wail and promise to reform so she could relent. Or maybe she was glad to be rid of me. Nobody told me there'd be a stiff price to pay for the carefree gym hours I spent in the library, and my school days cheered up immeasurably, brightened by Mrs. Casey.

Mrs. Casey, may the angels sing her praises, taught English. In the first weeks of school, to take our measure, she assigned an informal essay on a subject of our own choosing. Fully half the class elected to write a description of their bedrooms at home; I chose a picture in the French textbook that baffled me. A black-and-white photograph showed a stiff, solemn man in a suit standing beside a perfectly enormous and equally solemn pig, and the caption read simply "Truffle-Hunting Pig in France." There was no explanation in the text and I'd never heard of truffles, so I forged ahead with an account of the truffle hunt, and the pigs, specially bred for their speed and spirit, galloping over the fields and leaping the fences in pursuit of the fleet-footed truffle which, when caught, would be stuffed and mounted and hung on the wall.

When Mrs. Casey returned our papers, she'd written in her neat teacherly hand in my margin, "It's never too soon to think of publishing, you know."

Going to school got less painful.

Teachers, in theory, are supposed to teach, to pour information into the empty vessel. Sometimes, though, a teacher appearing at the right time in one's life can do miracles with only a nod of recognition. Mrs. Casey never praised me either in class or in private, except to treat me as an equal. After listening to half a dozen silly answers, she would sigh and call on me, and I would give my opinion, and she would say "thank you" and move on.

In the same school five years later Nick too got lucky. Nick had never had any doubt since he was four years old that he was a scientist, any more than I had doubted my own calling, but his grades in science classes were even worse than his other grades. He pursued his studies privately. In school, he failed to complete the assigned projects because, as he explained to his teachers, they were stupid projects. He refused to press autumn leaves between two sheets of waxed paper, and label them, and call it science.

Scowling and intractable, he slouched into high school, trailed by Judith's blazing comet of straight As and honor rolls just behind him. A science teacher recognized him on sight. The gods will remember his name, but I've forgotten. Smith, we'll say. He took Nick under his wing, or, rather, picked him up by the scruff of his neck and set him on his path.

Nick, said Mr. Smith, must first have a solid liberal arts grounding, for which he would go to undergraduate school at Carleton College; Mr. Smith would see that he got in. After that, he would take his master's and doctorate at Stanford, with its excellent marine biology department, and spend summers making himself useful at the research facility at Woods Hole. Oh, and he must also learn Russian, because so little Russian research had been translated. Not to worry about the money, the

National Academy of Sciences would pick up the tab. Doctorate in hand, he would seek out the right mix of teaching and research.

It all came to pass as Mr. Smith decreed. For a general science teacher at a suburban public high school, he must have had unusual clout. He took Nick in hand personally too. On the day the yearbook pictures were to be taken, Nick showed up at school in his usual sagging T-shirt, and Mr. Smith popped him in his car and drove him home to change. I wasn't there, but I like to think of Mr. Smith rummaging brisky through Carl's closet and bureau drawers looking for a suitable shirt and tie.

Gloria didn't need a teacher. In art class she took advantage of the supplies to pursue her own projects, politely ignoring little Mrs. Clapp, who fizzled with rage but had to subside, sulking, in the face of what Gloria could do. Mrs. Clapp was always grieved by the occasional unclothed body in her art history books and turned the page quickly, before we could focus, saying, "We don't want to be that way, do we, class?" At an easel Gloria calmly went on with a watercolor of a bare-breasted brown woman leaning from a window, framed in pale curtains. Mrs. Clapp turned her back and lectured the class furiously on the importance of keeping a clean mind, but nothing could be done about Gloria and how good she was.

As teacher's pet in English class, I might have been shunned, but somehow I wasn't. Most of my classmates knew me from Leland: I was a freak, and freaks were expected to be expert at something useless. Teacher's pet in English wasn't a coveted position anyway, and besides, I came in handy.

Mrs. Casey assigned the class a sonnet to write. It needn't be glorious poetry but it had to be technically correct, in either the *abab* or *abba* rhyme scheme. (Nobody pretended this kind of folderol would get us better jobs or defend the country against Communism. It was just the old way, up until Russia launched *Sputnik* in 1957 and America raced to catch up, the old way of handing down gobbets of pure useless civilization from one generation to the next.) By the end of the school day I had nine supplicants. From Friday afternoon until late Sunday night, I wrote classical sonnets of steadily declining merit and in the morning before class I handed them out, reserving the best for myself.

The sentiments were hogwash but the rhymes were dead on and my iambic pentameter flowed like tap water. They all got the highest marks. Mrs. Casey made no comment. She asked no questions. But as we were leaving the room after class she brushed by me and murmured, dryly but not unsympathetically, "You must be exhausted."

Sometimes one is enough.

And then I lost Gloria, lost her as suddenly as I'd found her.

EVERYONE LEAVES, EVERYTHING CHANGES

She came in very late for Latin class, looking dazed and strangely wispy, and collected some assignments from the teacher, stared around the room as if searching for my face, and then left, never to come back.

She had rheumatic fever. Like polio, this scourge has been lifted from us, but at the time it followed upon a strep infection untreated by the antibiotics not yet invented. Apparently nothing could be done for it but rest. Years of rest. Gloria called it "romantic fever" and wrote me professing to be pleased with the vision of herself wasting away on a couch like Elizabeth Barrett Browning, but she was ever a proud noncomplainer.

Weeks later, I was allowed to come visit her, and I sat on her bedroom floor all afternoon and we talked and talked, as always. She was still looking forward to New York and the Art Students' League; her parents had promised she could drop out of school at sixteen, as soon as it was legal, and take up her real education. I suppose at that point her parents would have promised her anything.

That evening she took a turn for the worse and the doctor came. My visit had been too exciting. I was not to come back. Her only visitor would be Marianna, a placid neighborhood friend from childhood who went to Catholic school and never excited anyone. We weren't to talk on the phone, either.

I never saw her again. We wrote. Constantly at first, then less often. For three years we had lived as one person with scarcely a separate thought, and then she was gone, like a moth flittering out of my hand.

At about the same time my family moved to Florida.

Memory here smudges over and breaks apart into fragments. Years of connective tissue have rotted and dropped out of the fold of Broca and my self flickers here and there like a lightning bug trapped in a dark room, or like a family's abused scrapbook, with the baby pictures still intact but the later pages ravaged or ripped out and only those little black stick-on triangles left where the pictures had been, and maybe a shred of newsprint left from the corner of an article.

Carl's eccentric aunt Mary died. (The last words in her diary were "Carl was here with those horrible brats of his.") As her only relative, he inherited a modest three-story apartment building in Fort Lauderdale, on the bank of the New River. At some point he'd sold the happy cottage out on the beach; the Lauderdale Arms apartments, in the sun-struck town a long bus ride from the ocean, was less lovable. It was also in a state of disrepair and infested by aging long-term residents with grudges.

I don't remember family discussions or decisions, or being told anything at all, but perhaps I wasn't paying attention. They found tenants for the house in Chevy Chase and went south to supervise the Arms. Carl taught economics at Coral Gables; Mother repainted all the pastel apartments in funky dark greens and blues. I went to live with Grandmother.

In the next scene, I'm at Grandmother's, and riding the little puddle-jumper bus that plied the far-out suburbs in those days, carrying commuters and schoolchildren in one direction and cleaning women and yard men in the other. On school mornings, if I was late, the driver stopped at the foot of the driveway and blew his horn.

Somewhere in there I must have boxed up my books and clothes and said goodbye to my attic, my mother, my brother and sisters, family cat, neighborhood friends. Viola, I learned later, went to work for a rabbi, a widower with a well-behaved little girl. I never saw her again. I remember nothing. How and when does memory decide what to save, and how does it decide without consulting us? Whose life is it, anyway? When our lives break apart like that, do weeks and months dribble out of the torn edges, never to come back? Was I stupefied by what's now called depression, or simply by adolescence?

The end of the school year delivered a nasty shock: the year's blank in gym class would have to be made up by double gym classes the next year. If you failed Algebra you would have to repeat it, but only for five hours a week; the penalty for failing gym was ten hours a week, ten hours of throwing balls under the vengeful eye of Mrs. Quayle. In Maryland, as in many states, sport was the single most important element of education and no one could graduate from high school without paying it full tribute in years. I announced that I simply wouldn't go back. I would rather go to prison. I would run away to sea and be a sailor.

Grandmother pulled some strings. She got me across the District line into Washington, her old stomping grounds, and registered in Woodrow Wilson High School, where nobody cared about Maryland's gym classes. But first I was sent to spend the summer in Florida.

It was hot. I staggered around in a daze of heat. Sometimes Nick and I would rent a little boat and go out to catch killer sunburns and scrappy, nameless little fish that the cook refused to fry up for us on the grounds that only colored people ate that kind of fish. (She took them home.) Sometimes, when the weather was truly brutal, Mother gave me money to take Nick and Judith to the movies, considered a frivolity back home but a health necessity here. At the Sunset, on the western edge of town, nine cents apiece would admit us to watch a black-and-white movie, usually the Marx Brothers, followed by an inscrutable segment of a continuing serial full of horses and onrushing trains. These we watched over and over all afternoon while our shirts slowly dried in the pleasant, popcorn-scented dark.

Sometimes I had enough money to go to a first-run movie on the main street, in the evening, a musical starring Rita Hayworth or a war movie starring Gregory Peck, and walk home alone in the hot night that buzzed with insects and smelled stickily of jasmine.

Sometimes I was sent to the beach with Nick and Judith, on the beach bus, a rackety pre-war vehicle suffering from climate fatigue, its springs and shock absorbers long since rotted away. The best place to ride was in back, on the bench seat that ran across under the big back window. The bench was hard and lumpy, but kneeling on it you got the best long view of the new lagoons, new houses around them, small boats laying trails.

"You ought to be ashamed of yourself!"

I spun around at the voice. She was talking to me, looming over me, a stout matron in pearls and gloves.

"Don't you see those poor women standing in the aisle? Don't you know how hard they've worked all day and how tired they are? And they have to stand up because you selfish children are *in their seat.*"

I sprang up, snatching Nick and Judith with me. Yes, in the aisle stood several colored women, sagging with exhaustion, certainly cleaning women headed back toward Colored Town from their jobs in beach houses. But there were empty seats. Plenty of empty seats. I processed the thought slowly. Nobody had told me. If Mother knew, she'd been embarrassed to tell me, but she didn't ride buses and maybe hadn't heard. No sign on the back bench said "COLORED ONLY." Everyone just knew.

We scrambled into the regular seats, glared at by the matron, passing the colored women who smiled and nodded thanks.

I realized I didn't much like Florida anymore. This was no grand liberal epiphany, simply resentment. Without explaining the rules in advance, Florida had tricked me into being a mean and selfish person, and then scolded me for it. It didn't occur to me that the rules were more to blame than I was. I took it personally.

I took the relentless heat personally too.

The week before school started I rode the East Coast Champion back to Washington, standing all night long on the observation platform breathing cinders and thinking mournful, poetic thoughts, cribbed from Thomas Wolfe, about the tiny towns and lighted houses we thundered past.

Every morning two buses and a streetcar took me from Grandmother's house to school. Nobody at the school had ever seen me before. Nobody remembered me from junior high school, or knew I was a freak and an outcast. Nobody knew about Gloria, and how we'd stood together as one person and spoken with a single voice and planned a life together.

NBC sent my uncle Bob, with Peggy and my two young

cousins, to Bonn and then to Paris, and the house down the hill from Grandmother's was rented to a Japanese diplomat and his wife and rang no more with parties.

Nothing at all was left of my previous life. My whole previous self. I cut off my trademark, lifelong braids and chopped myself a normal-looking bob.

Years later I found the braids, still fastened at the ends with rotting rubber bands, in Grandmother's bureau drawer, and I was greatly taken aback. I was embarrassed. Least sentimental of women, she had saved my old hair, the hair I'd been wearing since I was five years old.

Grandmother was pragmatic. *Sensible* was her word of highest praise. Her floor-to-ceiling bookshelves were full of meaty books: I read Upton Sinclair's *The Jungle*, shuddering, but balked at *Sweden: The Middle Way*, *Das Kapital*, Adam Smith's *Wealth of Nations*, Keynes's *General Theory of Employment, Interest, and Money*, and both volumes of Spengler's *Decline of the West*.

Except for militant socialism, Grandmother had no visible neuroses, endearing quirks, petty vices, nothing to get a handle on and cherish or laugh at. By daylight, she kept busy—her sheets were ironed and folded, her white sauce was never lumpy, her garden was weeded—and in the evenings she read. I suppose my grandfather had filled all her personal spaces and after he died she was content to leave them empty in his memory. Long later, in her old age, she would call me—call me long-distance as we said then, usually reserved for emergencies and birthdays— not to complain about her troubles or ask about mine but to give pithy lectures on matters like the history of the vice presidency or the partition of Poland.

258

The braids weren't tied with a ribbon or tucked into a quilted box, but they were there in the drawer where she'd put them. Could it be that I'd meant something more to her than she'd ever hinted at? Our relationship had always been practical. She asked after my bowels, made clothes for me, and cooked my dinner. Taught me how to hemstitch and, in the absence of steam irons, how to press a wool skirt through a damp dishtowel, both of which I did badly. Scolded me and instructed me with aphorisms. I raked leaves in her yard and took out the trash and cleaned the roof gutters. Washed dishes. I thought that was our contract. Was there something I'd missed? Have I blundered through life without ever noticing that anyone noticed, or believing I ever made anyone cry?

Anyway, shorn of my past, pockets empty, I set out to invent myself from scratch.

I FAIL TO MAKE SENSE OF NORMAL LIFE
& FALL INTO CONFUSION

Without Gloria and her steady sense of purpose and pursuit of excellence, I stood on the edge of ordinary, normal life and gazed at it bewildered. What I needed to know were all the things adolescents learn from each other, in groups, watching each other and listening and trying things out. Friendless, I had to study it from a distance and read magazines, looking for some way to make my way through the ordinary days and find a new self to wear.

From the magazines I learned that women came in only the three basics: giddy blonde, serious brunette, spirited redhead. Fighting these predestined categories was not recommended; useless to try to be a studious blonde or silly brunette, because this would only confuse our prospective husbands, who liked to know at a glance who we were. Better to exaggerate our given natures, fly off the handle if red-haired, flunk math if blonder, because men, our quarry, not deep students of human nature, need to know what to expect. (My own hair lay mousily in between; how, without chemicals, to find a self at all?)

As for occupations, proper women had only the two, the second being the reward for the first. After that, our experience varied only according to our choice of a man: fur coat and washing machine for the lucky, cotton housedress and laundry tub for the rest. Securing the optimal man was job one.

Television and the Internet have pushed magazines off the stage, but in those days they were big and shiny and everywhere, handing out infallible advice. All advice was for girls and women, since men and boys didn't need it; they were the dominant species at the top of the food chain and survival for those beneath depended on adjusting to them. It was a game universally played: figure out what they want and give it to them—except, of course, sex without a written commitment, which was what they really wanted. As my vulgar grandmother put it, "If the milk's free, why buy the cow?"

Under no circumstances let a boy kiss you on a first date. It made you cheap, and the boy, even the nicest boy, would tell it all over and give you a reputation. A reputation was very nearly the worst thing you could get, second only to polio, and once acquired, nothing could expunge it except persuading your family to change its name and move to another state.

Never mention yourself on a date. Talk about him. Praise his accomplishments, however small, his ears, his haircut. Urge him to talk about himself. The male ego is huge but fragile and needs constant reinforcement, but this works to your advantage, since only a man with a well-fed ego can go forth to fight his way up in the workplace and bring home the bacon for his bride. Ask him questions about his hobbies; ask him to explain the rules of sports. Go cheerfully to basketball games with him and root for the team he roots for. Listen sweetly. Being a good talker was fatal, talking women were anathema, but being a good listener was more becoming than any cosmetic and won over the most reluctant swain.

Speaking of cosmetics, though, never let him catch sight of you without lipstick. A girl wrote to the advice column in, I think, *Seventeen*, for help getting rid of a pesky suitor who kept coming over no matter how she rebuffed him. The columnist made various suggestions, and wound up with the one that was guaranteed to work but was so radical she might hesitate to use it: the next time he comes around, go out and greet him wearing *no makeup at all*. He will leave at once and never bother you again. (This seemed to bode ill for married life, since we were also told not to sleep with our makeup on. Bad for the skin. Married, must we rise before dawn and tiptoe into the bathroom for the mascara and rouge, lest he see us all barefaced on the pillow and leave at once and never bother us again? It seemed we must.)

College was highly recommended, because, and I quote, "A college education will make you a more interesting companion for your husband and a more stimulating mother for your sons." College was also a good place to look for a mate, since you found a better class of mate there than in, say, the pool hall. The blend of swoony romance with steely pragmatism didn't seem to bother anyone; just arrange to fall madly, passionately in love with the likeliest future wage-earner.

Brush your hair a hundred strokes every night before going to bed. (I actually tried this for a while, when I remembered, but it isn't very exciting.) Wash your hair only when it desperately needs it and never more than once a week, because shampoo will strip it of its luster and cause it to break and fall out. This may have been true. The shampoo of the time was fiercely detergent, as it would need to be when used so rarely. The once-a-week rule held fast until 1949 when *South Pacific* hit Broadway and Mary Martin sang "Gonna Wash That Man Right Out of My Hair" while shampooing on stage. Eight performances a week. Naturally reporters asked her why she wasn't bald as a doorknob after a few months of this, and she said the secret was Johnson's ("No More Tears") Baby Shampoo. It was harmless. You could use it even twice a day, on matinee days. The nation's women stormed the drugstores, the shelves were stripped, and Johnson's stock went through the roof. We washed our hair.

Not while menstruating, though, as this time of the month made you more susceptible to catching colds, and wet hair, like wet shoes, caused the common cold. Never play sports while menstruating. Why not? Nobody said. Bring a note from your mother to get you out of gym class.

Much fuss was made about menstruation, perhaps because girls had so little else that was theirs. It was important to keep the whole process a secret from the males of the species, who had never heard of it and would be disgusted if they found out. Hide the box of sanitary napkins from your father and brothers. If you and your group of friends had planned to go swimming, have ready some plausible excuses to keep yourself out of the water—clear out of the water, not even dipping your feet—without confessing the real reason.

Magazines called menstruation "that time of the month," but girls and their aunts and mothers called it the Curse. This grates harsh in the ear today. The revolutions of the seventies tried to persuade us menstruation was a mark of distinction, a point of pride, almost an accomplishment. The Curse, however, was its universal name back then, and I don't remember minding. A Curse is a distinction too, with overtones of Greek tragedy that set it above mere medical matters: those on the receiving end of a Curse have been singled out for special attention.

Tampons appeared on the market, a great boon to woman-kind but not universally welcomed. What about, well, you-know-what? Suppose, just suppose, a tampon ruptured that jewel which is dearer than life and we disappointed our husbands on our wedding night? The tampon-makers did their best to persuade us there was no danger, but the delicate language of the day made it hard to get their point across and many mothers kept their daughters in sanitary napkins to be on the safe side. As in strict Islamic societies, it was the parents' responsibility to deliver a *virgo intacta* to the groom, since nothing was more exhilarating for a man than the conquering blood of the wedding night. Like shooting a rabbit, I thought.

Long later, on the very edge of the radical sixties, I knew one chaste but enlightened couple, what was called a nice Jewish boy marrying a nice Jewish girl, who decided to let a licensed physician do the deed, so the bride wouldn't blame the pain on her husband. Escorted by her mother, she went to the doctor a week before the wedding. The rest of us speculated rudely, wondering if he'd signed a verifying certificate—I think he did— and just what instrument he'd used on her: something sharp, in cold steel, or perhaps something more normal that he happened to have handy, provided by nature?

It was said you could lose your virginity horseback riding, and some felt that girls should therefore avoid horses, but I thought privately that a history of riding might give you an out, just in case you'd lost it elsewhere.

All brides were virgins. Older women claimed they could tell at a glance if a girl had had what they called an experience: something about the look in the eyes, they said. When Grandmother was young, married women were barred from teaching school because they'd learned the facts of life at first hand and the knowledge might leak out through their pores in the classroom; at the very least, their students would gaze on them and speculate improperly.

Traditionally, the night before the wedding was when the bride's mother told her what to expect the following night, but it seems some mothers funked it, or explained it too delicately, with metaphors, and the poor girl was so astonished she never recovered. Some, it was said, went stark mad and had to be put away.

Grooms weren't expected to be as ignorant. One popular handbook said, a bit wistfully, that it was sweetest when both were virgins, so they could discover the mysteries of love together, but it was generally agreed that he would have had at least one experience, the better to instruct the bride. In some societies the groom's father would arrange it with a professional, since it wouldn't be sporting to practice on somebody else's future wife.

Sex was the focal point and purpose of the wedding. It was uppermost in everyone's mind, especially the bride's. Radiant and smiling, inside she was a wreck. Often she threw up, or fainted dead away and had to be revived and supported down the aisle. Sex was the reason for the party, the food and drink, flowers and minister, and the bridesmaids escorted their comrade to be delivered on the altar like an Inca maiden on the lip of the volcano.

If she didn't panic and her husband was patient, she would, the magazines said, learn to enjoy sex. She wouldn't enjoy it too much, which would be unfeminine, and it was hinted that real enthusiasm might frighten her husband. Real enthusiasm was called being "oversexed," a rare but serious problem in women and subject of much gossip. For a man, sexuality was good and useful and powered his ambitions and led to getting rich and maybe elected president, but for a woman it could lead only to a life of shame. Safely married, she should be reluctant and shy at first but eventually learn to treasure these moments of closeness.

"Closeness" was the word the magazines used for marital sex. "Orgasm" appeared only in specialized publications of a medical nature not for sale on newsstands.

If the bride survived the dangerous waters of the honeymoon, she landed on the solid ground of housekeeper/mother and got down to the business of waxing floors, which was covered in different magazines.

How much of this was propaganda or wishful fantasy and how much reflected the real world, I had no way of knowing. I should have had a circle of female friends as a focus group, but I couldn't seem to find common ground with any. I couldn't think of anything to say to them. I couldn't start a conversation. I didn't speak the language. I was grown with children before I learned.

Grandmother made me some school clothes. We went downtown to Woodward & Lothrop and sat in the yard goods department mulling over the pattern books. I could point at anything and it would be mine, and the fabric chosen from the acres of bolts: plain or printed cotton for blouses and summer dresses, checked or plaid wools for winter skirts. She stood me on the dinner table for fittings and turned me slowly, extracting pins from her mouth one by one, tucking and shaping.

It was an era of pretty clothes. Smooth bodices, fitted waists and flared or pleated skirts, just below knee level, graceful to walk in. This was before the plumping of America, and while married women were expected to thicken up, baby by baby, the young were naturally slender. "Put some meat on your bones," the old folks would say, pinching our arms. We showed off our waists with wide belts. Grandmother was proud of mine, measuring it and nodding approval.

I remember a wool skirt in black and gray plaid, a full circle cut on the bias that swirled around my legs; and a close-fitting blouse with raglan sleeves and a heart-shaped neckline that I wore so often Grandmother finally took it apart at the seams and used it to cut out several more, a black poplin, a moss-green velveteen, a print of small pink roses on a black background. A short fall coat in bottle green corduroy, cut with a stylish flare in back, instead of my former Navy pea-jackets in a navy so dark it would never need dry-cleaning.

It seems philistine to gloat in retrospect over clothes, but they were my passport to normality in my new world. If only normality had been more appealing.

Dressed for the first time like others, I went to school.

With the lone exception of James Dean, the high-school class of 1950 is widely remembered as the dullest generation of the twentieth century, bovine in its obedience and conformity, peaceful to the point of stupor, and it's true we had no mar- ijuana, only Benzedrine for parties, though we did have suicides, pregnancies, shotgun weddings, car crashes, and the shadow of the draft over our boys: Army first, or college first? One by one they went off to boot camp and, thirteen weeks later, came home to visit, hair cropped, the weedy ones fleshed out, the plump ones slimmed down, the neurotic ones shattered to pieces, and all of them able to make a bed so tightly that a quarter dropped on it bounced. Some went on to Korea. And over us all lay the shape of the mushroom cloud.

*   *   *

Few people now remember the cloud, or want to. Historians like action and consequences, and since, after decades of waiting, it didn't happen, they've shunted it off to a siding labeled Cold War and discuss it only in political terms. At the time, though, it soaked through our lives and colored our days like a toothache.

The government issued waves of instructions, to be picked up from tables at the post office or library or studied on bulletin boards. At first, they told us to go to our basements as we had for the German bombers and put our knees over our ears; the most important thing, if we were close to ground zero, was not to look directly at the fiery ball of the explosion because it might damage our eyes, like looking at an eclipse without smoked glass. After the explosions were over, we were to climb up on the roofs of our houses and rinse them down with a garden hose, to get rid of the nuclear fallout.

If we should happen to be at work at the time, in the city, we were to go to a shelter. Black-and-yellow signs marked with a big yellow S showed the way to underground parking garages and basement stockrooms. After the all-clear, we could mosey back out and inspect the wreckage.

As the weapons got bigger, the instructions got harder. Those in the suburbs were encouraged to dig deep holes in the back yard and seal their entrances with a padlocked trap door. The government supplied construction diagrams. The holes were to be stocked with canned goods and candles and bottles of water, and lively debates sprang up all over the country as to whether it was legally and morally acceptable to shoot the neighbors if they tried to break in and share your soup; the answer was usually yes. We were to stay there until the radiation on the lawn sank to

271

an acceptable level, which we could check periodically with our home Geiger counters.

The bombs kept growing. It began to seem feasible to get away from the target cities, and the government dug retreats in the countryside where key people could be helicoptered to safety and stand ready to command and legislate among the ruins. Both my uncles were on the list to be saved, since the charred remains of the country would need print journalists and broadcast newsmen. Both my aunts and their combined five children would stay in town and get fried, but patriotism calls for sacrifice.

The pundits issued sonorous statements, the same statements over and over. Everyone said, "It isn't a question of whether there will be nuclear war with Russia, it's only a question of when." Like an abscess ready to burst, it wouldn't need any particular trigger; a minor diplomatic incident or a clumsy hand on a switch would serve. It was patriotic to look forward to it and subversive to hope to dodge it. Nuclear bombs would provide the essential cleansing. Peace could only be a cringing compromise with the forces of evil.

It wouldn't be easy. Another favorite phrase was, "The living will envy the dead." All over the country, every man who knew how to drive a bulldozer or could get his hands on one was signed into a national network and told to remain on standby, since the primary postwar task would be to shovel earth over the sprawling mounds of bodies before they spread a plague.

The next wave of instructions told us to make sure the gas tanks in our cars never went below three-quarters full, because the new word was to flee. All dwellers in major cities and their near suburbs were, at the first alert, to leap into their cars and drive as far away as they could go on a tankful of gas, and then, wherever they found themselves, get out of their cars and . . . well, nobody seemed quite sure what happened next. Perhaps the kind farmers out there in the countryside would be happy to feed and house millions of refugees. If they weren't, force would be justified.

A key point in this government-issue scenario was that all those who fled were to stop first at their neighborhood post office and fill out a forwarding-address form. Nobody explained what addresses we should use, heading into the unknown like that, or why the postal employees were lingering on the job instead of joining us in flight, but forwarding addresses must be filed.

Even the most gullible of citizens began to feel there were flaws in the plan. Finally even the government noticed. It admitted that for those of us in and around the target cities, the jig was pretty much up and the best thing was to be standing squarely at ground zero, to die immediately rather than slowly. This wasn't like watching for occasional terrorists, crossing your fingers and trusting to luck: luck wasn't a factor. None of us Washington children would live to grow up, but that was beside the point. The new point was "survivability." This didn't mean us, but it did mean a handful of people down in lead mines in Utah or up in caves in the Rocky Mountains. If it turned out that, say, several hundred Americans survived and only a few dozen Russians, then we would have won. Democracy would have triumphed over Communism. Popular books and movies followed the adventures of the little bands of survivors as they reinvented fire, love, and civics.

Nobody asked how many Brazilians or Swedes or Algerians

would survive. Perhaps they would all slowly succumb to the sweeping clouds of poison, but in any case they didn't matter. The struggle was between Americans, the good people, and Russians, the bad people, and surely, surely, good would prevail, whatever the cost.

Then it began to seem that not even Patagonians and Aleuts would still be standing, perhaps not even cockroaches. The new phrase from the scientists, uttered in deep, self-important voices, was "The end of all life on earth."

This sounded fairly grim, but here and there an optimistic scientist would perk up and point to a brighter future. A certain strain of lichen that grew on rocks up inside the Arctic Circle would almost certainly stick it out, and live on through the nuclear winter. Over the millennia, it might evolve, grow extra cells, invent mobility, and the whole glorious process begin all over again.

Some of us thought privately that, having seen what happened in this evolution business, the lichen might choose to stay on its rocks.

My aunt Lois told me that she was trapped in Washington; she had to stay because her husband was a mainstay of the *Washington Post*, but she was always afraid, and why on earth did I stay in the primary target when I could flee to remote Fort Lauderdale with Mother and Carl? I winced and looked away, embarrassed for her. Only a grownup could be so craven. Mother and Carl were in Florida because of the Lauderdale Arms, not the bomb. They would have scorned to flee.

My generation may have been boring, but we were brave. If most of my contemporaries were conformists and behaved themselves, perhaps they hoped that if they were normal, desperately normal, the world might relent and stay normal

274

too. Or perhaps nobody needs to dance far out on society's edge when survival's edge is sharp enough.

The rebels among us escape historical notice because we were lonely rebels, with no agenda except rebellion itself. The children of Woodstock had the confidence born of a vast communal movement; sheer numbers convinced them of their rightness and they congratulated themselves and each other on being more enlightened than the generations before. They instructed their elders on matters of peace, sex, drugs, and civil rights, and their elders, cowed, had to listen.

My rebels were outcasts. We were so few that we barely ruffled the surface beyond our own families, and James Dean was fascinating simply because he went out there alone. And even he wore normal haircuts and normal clothes.

The new school had its bright spots. My English teacher, Mrs. Randolph, had a face like a muffin, a hairnet full of orange hair, and a North Carolinian mountain twang that peeled paint. The subject of the year, aside from *Macbeth*, was American literature. In the first week, she stood before the opened textbook and announced, "Stephen Vincent Benét is Amurrca's greatest livin' poit."

The "poit" irritated me. I was at an irritable age. I raised my hand, and when called on said, "He did write some great stuff but he's been dead since 1943."

She drew her little orange eyebrows together and snapped back, "It says in our text, he is 'Amurrca's greatest livin' poit.' "

"Yes, but what's the copyright date?"

"That's *enough*," she said, and started again from scratch, "Stephen Vincent Benét . . ."

Blood in my eye, I went home to my bookcase. I'd scavenged some volumes from Carl's aunt Mary, who had finicky habits and had blessedly taped a newspaper obituary into Benét's *Western Star*, which I winkled out and brought to class.

"Mrs. Randolph, I thought the class would be interested in Benét's death." I brandished the clipping. "He worked himself to death during the war, writing propaganda, and had a heart . . ."

"The class is *not innersted*. Sit down and be quite."

She was wrong. The class was interested, scenting a feud, and sat on its hands for the rest of the school year, ceding me the floor while I danced rings around our hapless teacher. I did a prodigious amount of work. Where the textbook gave only excerpts, I'd read the whole book; where the text ventured opinions, I dug out and quoted dissenting opinions. I burrowed into biographies and came up with unsavory tidbits on the authors' private lives. This can't have left much time for my other classes and I'm not sure I even remember what they were.

We plowed into *Macbeth*. The Shakespeare succession was carved in stone: ninth grade, *Romeo and Juliet*; tenth, *Julius Caesar*; eleventh, *Macbeth*; twelfth, *Hamlet*. Furrowing my brow in faux puzzlement, I raised my hand. "Mrs. Randolph, I'm confused . . ."

She beamed. I was rarely confused.

"There's a piece missing here, it must be a mistake, they've left something out of our text. You know, in the second act, where the porter's talking about drink and lechery, and says 'it provokes the desire, but it takes away the . . .'"

"*Be quite!*" she barked.

A muted rustle of satisfaction through the classroom.

In the spring, I scored a crippling victory. I won the National

276

Scholastic annual poetry competition, the first high-school junior in its long history to win, and my works were printed in its newsletter, which was read, under duress, in schools all over the country. The Washington newspapers sent photographers out to Grandmother's house and ran stories. The superintendent of schools and the head of the English Department came to our classroom to congratulate me in person.

They congratulated Mrs. Randolph, too, for having nurtured my talent so well. Our eyes met. Her face was clenched with hatred and glistened with the sweat of suppressed fury. "Yes," she was forced to say, showing her little teeth, "we're all very proud of Barbara," and I gazed calmly back at her, master of all I surveyed.

But what of the rest of my world, the other parts, my real life? With my newly normal clothes and hair, I was turning out to be rather pretty, and while girls remained a mystery, it was easier to meet boys; they took the initiative. I found myself part of a roving pack of friends, the only female member. They were older, none of them schoolmates, some who had fought in the war and come home unsettled; they were smart, funny, lazy, restless, irreverent, unteachable, and I loved them, I can see now, because none of them had the slightest chance of growing into a proper adult male like Carl, even supposing they grew up at all.

Being male, they were a novelty in my life and a new field of study. It was a narrow window, these few sub-adult years when the male and female could visit across the border and argue with each other; once we'd evolved into Mothers and Fathers we would never again have anything in common or anything to say to each other.

I was called a good sport, high compliment, meaning I enjoyed arguing more than gossip, I didn't whine or sulk when the car broke down, and I'd discovered a startling capacity for beer: "She can drink *me* under the table," they said proudly.

With no door into the girls' life of Cokes and prom dresses, I'd stepped into the boys' life of cars and beer, out where cars and beer converged on the dark two-lane blacktops of Virginia and Maryland, in roadhouses with names like the Bucket o' Blood, colored Christmas lights twinkling under the eaves all year round and fist-fights in the parking lot. Inside, in their men's rooms, vending machines on the wall sold condoms for a quarter apiece, the machine and the condom packets clearly marked SOLD FOR THE PREVENTION OF DISEASE ONLY: by law, it was right and necessary to protect rutting boys from the clap, but morally and legally wrong to protect their girls from the righteous wrath of pregnancy.

Beer was sold by the pitcher. The jukeboxes sang plangent country songs of loss, trains, and cold, cold hearts.

Mostly we came safely home, but sometimes not. I remember being pulled out of a car that had rolled over on the Colesville Pike and lay on its back with its wheels still turning. I wasn't hurt, and under the streetlights I saw that I was covered, hair and coat and all, with sparkling little scraps of broken glass and glittered like a Christmas tree.

I remember precinct stations, kindly cops, and friends waked up by phone to come and rescue us.

I remember waiting in cars that had broken down—those fragile, rickety pre-war cars broke down often—late at night, on the edge of a field, and one of the boys trudging away up the dark road in search of help, and knowing how late it was and how much later it would be when I got home to Grandmother, sitting by the phone in her wrapper wondering whether to call the police first or to start with the hospitals.

Later generations would give their families even more worries to wait up for, but that didn't help my guilt at the time.

Nowadays it would be taken for granted that I was sleeping with—or, as we say now, having sex with, or hooking up with—all the young men in my group, either serially or simultaneously, but those were different times.

Sex was serious then. Beer was frivolous. In these more enlightened times young people drinking beer are criminals subject to a jail sentence, while their eclectic sex lives are taken for granted. Back then, beer was one of the happier elements of youth, mainstay of campus life, table-setting for philosophical discussion, subject of merry songs and jokes. Driving around in cars, we sang

> Drink drink drink drink
> Drank drank drank drank
> Drunk drunk drunk drunk
> Drunk last night,
> Drunk the night before,
> Gonna get drunk tonight
> Like I never got drunk before!
> Singing glorious, glorious!
> One case of beer for the four of us!
> And glory be to God
> That there are no more of us
> Because one of us could drink it all alone!

No sex, though. Casual sex was worse than just wicked, it was sleazy, and practiced only by the dimmest of girls, straggle-haired slatterns from the wrong side of the tracks who'd spent three years in tenth grade. Nobody even took them to a movie in exchange for their services.

Being in love was the prerequisite for sex, and sex with a nice girl was tantamount to a formal engagement. Thousands of my generation took this seriously and married for no other reason than those grapplings in the back seats of cars parked in the dark bushes, breath steaming the windows. Some were pregnant, of course, but others simply bowed to the social imperative.

My particular lad had yellow hair, navy-blue eyes, and bitten fingernails. He played the trumpet. Storm-tossed, we clung to each other like orphan refugees. I'd never planned to hang on to my virginity, passport to marriage and floor wax, but I put up a long struggle just the same. He was baffled, and even I didn't understand my reluctance, but I suppose it had to do with feeling bullied and conquered. The bloodied rabbit of the wedding night. When I did finally give in, I remember the occasion spoiled a pretty dress, but I remember nothing else, not where or when or how.

Not surprisingly, I hated it at first. Much as I loved the lad, I loved him as an abstract poetical concept rather than flesh, and the act of love still felt bullying. My flesh saw it as a surrender at gunpoint.

Nor could I see sex as a prelude to normal life. It seemed to have nothing whatsoever to do with marriage, with domestic life, with babies, or indeed with anything at all except itself. I remained deeply confused.

MY TRAVELS ON THE BOTTOM OF THE LAKE

The years in memory start to darken here and splinter into gaps and smudges.

I wrote to Gloria describing my new life. I tried to make it sound like an adventure, perhaps not the equivalent of Samarkand but wild and high-spirited, real life, grist for the writer's mill. She wrote back chiding me gently. Yes, she could see how my nomadic companions must be sweet, but surely the life was "febrile and distracting."

"Febrile and distracting." It was. I knew it was. But where else could I go? I knew I was living the wrong life, somebody else's life, and I was ashamed but I had to be somewhere, live somehow, and I couldn't find another way.

I think I never wrote back, and she never wrote again. For twenty years I searched the gallery openings in the *New Yorker* for her name but I never found it. She'd written that she was taking instruction to join the Catholic Church; she'd never had any interest in religion before, but her Catholic friend Marianna was her only companion now, and this was back when the church still had its lure, its secrets and spine-tingling Latin.

Perhaps she joined a cloistered order and offered up her art to God. I'm sure she didn't marry and turn into a Mother. Perhaps she simply died. People died of complications from rheumatic fever, back then.

Years later, Mother caught sight of Gloria's mother in the supermarket, pushing her cart down the aisle, and abandoned her own cart, ducked, and slipped out the door. If they'd come face to face among the canned goods, she would have had to ask, and she was afraid of the answer. She'd liked Gloria. Gloria was one of us. She spoke the language, she had talent, she had good bones.

Wherever she went, I knew she'd gone with her eyes still fixed on pure, white purpose. Somewhere I'd lost my own, and now I was falling like Lucifer, or maybe only like Icarus, arms and legs cartwheeling slowly down the sky and out of the light.

The time silts over with shame and only a few memories stick their snouts up from the murk.

I do remember the abortion. I remember it, but forget how I got there, how I told Grandmother, how she arranged it. How does a retired schoolteacher get hold of the secret number and know what to say? What did it cost, how did she pay, did she tell Mother? Did she have to take up a secret family collection? I think I remember carrying an envelope thick with cash. I suppose I must have; it was hardly a matter for personal checks.

I do remember standing late at night in the doorway of a closed sporting-goods store on a scruffy downtown street for a couple of hours, but nobody came. So I walked and walked until I found a phone booth with a pool of piss still warm on its floor and called my boyfriend and he drove downtown to pick me up. Then, the following week, another phone call, another appointment, a different doorway. This time a dark car pulled up and a yellow-haired woman, nervous and cross, hustled me into it among some other girls already huddled inside, and briskly blindfolded me.

I hadn't worn a blindfold since the birthday parties of childhood. It's a peculiar experience, almost comforting in a way, absolving you of responsibility. I felt it a matter of pride to figure out where we were going—or maybe I thought I might need to know in order to find my way back, like Hansel and Gretel—but after we crossed what I was sure was a bridge to Virginia I was lost. It was a long journey of many turns, and then a garage door opened briefly on light and closed again, and we took off our blindfolds.

We were in a modest suburban ranch house among other suburban houses, furnished as a proper home. I seem to remember there were even toys scattered around on the living room carpet, though memory may be adding this ghoulish touch on its own. Certainly any nosy neighbor could peer in a window and be satisfied by its innocence, except for the six or eight frightened girls perched around on the couch and chairs.

We were all under twenty except for a brisk woman in her forties who introduced herself as Mrs. Cohen and tried to cheer us up, and offered to play card games. She seemed to have been here before. She told dirty jokes, and we smiled politely. From time to time a matron came in to tell us to be quiet, and took a couple of us into the bedroom. When they came back out again, two more went in.

The bedroom held a pair of bureaus and a double bed made up with flounces and pillow shams, and another girl and I undressed, put on paper gowns, and sat stiffly on the bedspread. We were handed small red pills in paper cups. Painkillers, we were told. I've always been bad with painkillers, and threw it up almost at once. Cross, the matron gave me another. I threw that up too, and the doctor, or whatever he was, lost patience and decided to do me without it. All the staff seemed tense and edgy; perhaps they'd had rumors of a raid and were frantic to get us out of the house as fast as possible, or perhaps they were always tense.

Off the bedroom, in a smaller room with a blacked-out window, was a proper operating table, with stirrups. I lay down, and the bleached blonde from the pickup car, now dressed in white, stood at my head with her arms tensed, ready to muffle me if I screamed. A radio played loudly. The doctor, out of sight beyond my knees, did whatever it was. I don't think I screamed. I'm sure I didn't. The blonde looked as if strangling me might well be an option.

I thanked the matron for the sanitary napkin, put on my clothes, and went back to the living room. My stomach quivered with lingering nausea.

When we'd all been done, we were blindfolded again and loaded back into cars. I heard the garage door slam quickly behind us as we drove away. Blinded and rocking in the backseat, I felt the first stirrings of carsickness join the nausea. I clenched my teeth against it, but it kept gaining on me, and finally I bleated, "I have to be sick!"

"No, you don't," snarled the driver. "Can't stop."

"Please! I'm going to throw up!"

"Pull over, you jerk!" cried one of my companions. "Come on, asshole, let her get out!" said another.

Cursing under his breath, the driver pulled off the road and I clawed off the blindfold and staggered out of the car.

"Nobody else gets out! Can't have you all standing out there, middle of the night, cops going by. Anyone sees you . . ."

The girls told him to stuff it in his ear and poured out to stand by me in a protective shield. Someone held my shoulders. I heaved and heaved until I could heave no more, and then one of my nameless angelic comrades handed me a Kleenex. When I straightened up, I saw we were on a grassy bank beside an empty highway. On the other side of it, beyond a fringe of leafless trees, lay the river, and beyond the river, Washington shining in a long low streak of light. The Washington Monument rose up from it like a magic wand, serenely white in its spotlights, with the two small red lights at the top for warning planes. It was a Hollywood vision of heaven, all peace and brightness, far away on the other side of the cold black river.

I'd soaked through the sanitary napkin and a trickle of blood slipped down my leg.

School took up less and less of my time. It was my last year, and I was tired of it. I went there in the mornings, and then feckless lads would drive by at lunchtime and collect me and we'd drive around.

The class after lunch was Sociology—it was considered a science, and I needed another science credit—and I never went to it. The first week, I'd taken the textbook home and read it. Earnestly it instructed us to wash ourselves before going for job interviews, and dress neatly. When choosing a career, we should try for one that required a uniform, because of the respect we'd inspire in the neighbors as we strutted off to work dressed as policemen or nurses' aides. When choosing a mate, boys should look for girls with good dispositions and sound health habits. Girls should look for boys with "mature attitudes about money," meaning they wouldn't drink up the paycheck before they got home, and sound health habits. I think health habits was code for bathing, or maybe sobriety. The book was lavishly illustrated with line drawings; I remember one scene of a family,

Mother, Father, Junior, Sister, gathered at the kitchen table discussing how to spend the week's pay, a recommended ritual. How all this advice came to be classified as science remained a mystery and I never went back to the class until the final exam. The teacher must have wondered who I was. I got an A.

I remember a blue four-door convertible, a massive pre-war boat of a car that ate fuel pumps as if they were peanuts. Its canvas top weighed a ton and took several people to launch, at great risk of losing their fingers in the iron joints, so mostly it was left down, rain or shine. Gas was cheap. Honky-tonk blared from the radio, which was sometimes the car's only working element. We pushed it a lot, to get it started. It was heavy.

I tried to get back to school for the day's last class, English with Mrs. Hutchinson. She and I got along splendidly until we hit the Lake Poets, when it turned out she had a misguided taste for Wordsworth. I memorized a lot of his worst drivel and recited it in class; she retaliated with the "Ode on Intimations of Immortality"; I countered with some rousing Coleridge; the curriculum bogged down while we shouted at each other. The Lake Poets used up so much class time that we really had to hustle to get through *Hamlet*.

I won the National Scholastic poetry competition again, the first ever to hit it twice. First I won it locally, in the local branch of the contest sponsored by Washington's afternoon paper, the *Evening Star*, and someone in the family must have torn out a couple of clippings, because here they are, with a picture of me heavily lipsticked and looking like a B-movie starlet, or perhaps C-movie, the girl tied to the tracks in a Western. The clipping says I won the local contest with "a nine-line poem entitled 'To Those Who Are Not Quite Great.'" Memory has let it slip.

The national contest was judged on a group of poems about which I also can't remember a word. Of all the poems I ever read, only the ones I wrote myself have slipped away. I don't think they were terrible. Perhaps, like Mother, I was so ambitious I was waiting for something worthier.

While wandering aimlessly in later years, I kept all my papers in a cardboard box at Grandmother's house, and after she died a cleaning committee of aunts threw everything out, her pedal sewing machine, the pretty little desk where she paid her bills, the painting of a barn over the fireplace, my moldy papers.

John Updike and I were in public school during the same years. He's always written great verse. Surely he would have entered the contest, and if so, then I whupped him, not once but twice, though never again.

Poet and critic Randall Jarrell, one of the national judges, wrote, "Miss Holland's poetry is written in the style and manner of Edna St. Vincent Millay." Decades later I found out that Jarrell was famous for one-line put-downs that devastated old, established poets and drove them to drink, but that didn't help at the time. I was stung, deflated, furious. It was true. I knew it was true, but I didn't know how to expunge her. How to strike out on my own. Yes, I could write like Millay, probably like Sandburg or Archibald MacLeish, but I'd discovered Ezra Pound and I knew these people were the wave of the past and I couldn't possibly write like Pound or even learn from him. Or come up with some totally original form of my own devising.

For all their reputation for dullness, those years were a time of seismic upheaval in the arts, and newness was more important than craft; newness was everything. I didn't know how to be new.

My chosen calling broke apart at the seams and collapsed inward on itself. Old habits die hard and I went on writing poetry for years, but it was no longer my future or my guiding light. I had no guiding light and Gloria was gone.

From here on I lose my grip on the passage of time. I remember standing for hours or months or maybe years in Grandmother's living room—in my mind the place was always Grandmother's, never home—staring out a black window into the night. I remember I couldn't eat, and Grandmother baked me egg custards in little Pyrex cups because they slipped down without chewing. I suppose I was deep in clinical depression, but at the time "depression" still meant what had happened in the 1930s; people merely strangling in their own passivity and gloom were told to snap out of it. Guilt chewed ceaselessly at the back of my mind like a mouse in a cupboard.

Grandmother sent me to a psychiatrist. She must have been desperate; in my family, psychiatry was the ultimate in self-indulgence, an excuse for vain and idle people to lie around complaining instead of finding some work to do.

The psychiatrist's treatment consisted of silence. I sat on a straight chair facing his desk and said nothing. He sat behind his desk and said nothing. There are various ways of bullying, and it's possible to be silent and motionless and still be a bully. I felt bullied, and refused to speak first. After fifty minutes, he'd usher me out.

I hated it that my poor grandmother, with her schoolteacher's pension, was paying for this, and finally, after half a dozen visits, I stood up, still silent, and whacked a lamp off his desk with my pocketbook. "*Now* we're making some progress," he crowed, but I stalked out and never went back.

Mother had always assumed that I'd go to Swarthmore, a double legacy of my brilliant parents. No options had ever been mentioned. Dutifully, mutely, I took a train up to Pennsylvania for the interview. January gripped the campus and it seems in memory to be the middle of the night, with all the buildings dark, and I kept getting lost. Of course it must have been daytime, but darkness lies over that time in my life like a layer of dirt. Why were no students around? Maybe it was winter break, maybe I simply couldn't see them. I remember a steep icy path on the campus where I fell and bruised my knee and tore my stockings. I remember nothing at all about the interview or the journey back to Grandmother's.

I was accepted, with reservations, and instructions came in the mail. I sat down and read the list of what I was supposed to bring with me, and realized that all these things would have to be bought, bought and paid for. I'd been living in a stupor and it was only then that it broke over me: someone would have to pay the tuition. The days were gone when a girl could work as a summer car-hop to pay for college. Scholarship help could be had by the children of the poor, but I could hardly pretend Carl was poor.

Had anyone thought to mention it to Carl, Carl who'd hated having to pay for my sneakers? Carl, with children of his own to educate? Mother's small earnings from children's stories wouldn't go far. Who would pay? Would I get there, and unpack, and then some embarrassed official come and tell me nobody had paid, and I'd have to leave? And Mother, who so flatly refused to think about money, had tuition even occurred to her? I couldn't very well ask. You couldn't ask about money.

Perhaps I didn't want to go to Swarthmore, or to college at all. Mother's happy campus stories, when she and my father were the college darlings, the prince and princess, winning all the honors and singing rowdy songs, simply didn't apply to me. There was no way I could draw myself into the picture she'd painted. For me, it would be kindergarten all over again.

On the other hand, there was no way I could tell her, or anyone, that I wasn't going.

I suppose I must, on the record, have graduated from high school, though I didn't go to the ceremony and don't remember ever seeing a diploma.

I took the only available way out and ran away.

The boyfriend and I had to marry, of course, since under the fornication laws you couldn't rent even the dingiest furnished room without certification; landladies asked to see the marriage license. The boyfriend, overwhelmed, took up serious drinking and slipped into his own separate chaos. He disappeared for long stretches. We borrowed money from Grandmother and couldn't pay it back. My old family came home from Florida and lived in the old house again, and Mother had a new baby, but Carl put his foot down and in my disgrace I wasn't allowed to visit, not among his own children.

I spent a lot of time alone, staring out of windows into perpetual darkness. I remember a rented basement room some-where off Dupont Circle, a room hardly bigger than its sagging double bed, where if you lay awake all night you could look up and see feet passing across a high-up barred window the size of your two hands. Sometimes landladies banged furiously on doors, and I hunched in silence till they gave up and went away. Twenty years later squalor might have been part of a grand, rebellious adventure, something to write songs about, to find some meaning in, but at the time it was only squalor. I remember a battered little noisy refrigerator containing nothing but a half-empty can of beer, and it was still morning, but because I was hungry, I drank it. The rest is darkness.

I lost all the pretty clothes Grandmother had made me. With no place to wash them, finally I called a laundry and dry-cleaning place, bundled them up, and gave them to the man who rang the buzzer. They disappeared. The laundry said, quite snippily, that there was nothing they could do, no way they could find them, since the man on that route no longer worked for them. Besides, I hadn't made a list.

They were gone, after all the nights Grandmother had sat up late at the sewing machine, and all I had left to my name was a pair of blue jeans, some dingy shirts, and a gray wool dress pockmarked with moth holes that hadn't been worth cleaning.

I gnawed on shame the way I used to gnaw my knuckles, morning, noon, and night; I floundered like Alice in the Pool of Tears, only without Alice's grit and anger. Anger would have helped but I had no one to be angry with. I had ruined my own self.

I hold the scroll button down hoping the words will rinse away into oblivion like a flushed toilet. There was more, there was worse, I won't look into it. Like an overdue bill I can't afford to pay, leave it to sink unopened down under the mail-order catalogs. If you don't open it, it doesn't count. It never happened. There was a baby, of course there was a baby, babies were inevitable. I struggled to cope as best I could, but my best wasn't very good and my lad's mother came and carried her off and raised her, far away. I cried for weeks, more for my failure than my loss.

I sat in various rooms, unable to leave, with no place to go if I did. Time passed. How much time? I don't know. If it's always night, how can you tell?

If only I had fallen into alcoholism or drug addiction, this would be a better story. I could tell of the demons and temptations that possessed me and how I wrestled with them, and failed, and bravely tried again until I emerged triumphant, a modern-day hero. Few character traits are so admired as casting off addiction; even the former bulimic has admirers. And if I'd been saved by religion, by *un coup de Jesus*, I would be close to American sainthood and revered by all, since I'd been singled out for divine intervention.

But I didn't have the money or even the simple mobility for drugs or drink. The swirling dark pit of helpless despair may lack drama, but it's free, and you don't need to go out and find it. It comes to find you, and there's always plenty. Its bottles are never empty.

And even if divine help had come to my rescue, I don't know that I would have recognized it or, being bullheaded as Viola said, reached out to take it.

Saint Paul remembered his revelation on the road to Damascus. All reformed sinners in political life remember how they were saved from sin by divine grace and the love of a good woman. Everyone else who has slogged through the pits remembers the turning point clearly; I alone can't remember what happened. Where did I find the energy and the hope? Perhaps exasperated angels grabbed me by the wrists and pulled, but if so, they didn't show their faces.

Memory offers only a lighted room, the first bright light in the long darkness, a room so brilliant that the walls and furniture shiver with incandescence and there aren't any shadows, even under the tables.

It was the personnel office of the Hecht Company, the big busy department store where Mother had been so happy during the war. I was wearing the moth-pocked gray dress with glimpses of skin showing through, stockings shredded with ladders, and my scuffed and shapeless penny loafers, but I hope, as instructed by the sociology textbook, I had bathed and combed my hair.

I was filling out forms, squinting against the storm of light.

IN WHICH I AM SAVED AGAIN
& LIVE HAPPILY EVER AFTER

They put me in the sign shop, an offshoot of the display department. Perhaps Mother's old cronies had spoken for me. I was surprised to see them still there—Mel, Genie, Les, Al, Sid—after what seemed like centuries. They nodded kindly at me in the hall, passing by with stepladders or with naked mannequins slung over their shoulders like the Sabine women.

My duties were simple enough. I picked up requisition forms from a cubbyhole and deciphered their scribbles, then printed neatly on a clean form the information for what would become a sign: the nature of the merchandise, its price, its former price, and a few pithy words praising its qualities. These I passed on, either to the boy who ran the bed-press for big window or departmental signs or to the three deaf-mute women who ran the Print-a-Sign machines for shelf and table signs. Their machines made satisfying thumps when they were working but often fell silent while they quarreled, since they had to quarrel with their hands and they were an irritable lot.

It was an era of lavish employment. Since then, the Personnel Department, with its echo of "personal," has been replaced by Human Resources, with its echo of iron ore, petroleum, and other profit potentials, but those were softer days. Companies kept extra people, spares, just in case, and when likely-looking kids applied for jobs, they got hired because they might come in handy later, and some sort of work would be found for them in the meantime. Incompetent employees stayed on and on, moved from one slot to another to minimize damage but never fired, because the company felt responsible for its people, as for idiot relatives that have to be fed with a spoon.

Next to Personnel was the nurses' office, where there were cots for the ill and the weary, and a free visiting doctor, and little white envelopes full of free pills when employees were feeling poorly. We would go back to our departments and take a pill or two and then, feeling better, empty the rest into the communal bowl of pills. Anyone too busy to go to the nurses' office would rummage in the bowl and make a selection at random, or simply take one of each. They seem to have been harmless. One of the men who'd been in the Army said they were called APCs, for All-Purpose Capsules.

Cynics might say that this corporate kindliness was designed to forestall the unions—which it did—but kindness is kindness and I lapped it up like a stray cat. Starting out in this generous atmosphere shaped my whole working life as a lark: jobs should be fun and bosses gentle, if not this one, then the next; plenty more where this one came from. Nobody nowadays expects to have fun at work. They want to get rich instead, but I could see from the start that the two were probably incompatible: too much pay would mean taking the work seriously. Believing it was important. The less money I needed to make, the more elbow room I'd have for fun. I held firm to this resolve through good times and bum times.

Rubber cement, with its attendant Bestine thinner, was the basic tool of life then, in advertising as well as display. A jar of rubber cement on your desk—though I didn't have an actual desk in that first job, just a shelf heaped with papers—made an amiable companion, and when deep in thought a person could roll up its dried overflow with her thumb and form it into pellets, which bounced when dropped and could double as erasers. To this day I equate rubber cement with happiness. I was very, very happy. How had Mother found the willpower to leave this haven and go home?

For perhaps the first time, I felt *visible*. People said, "Give it to Barbara, that's the new little girl in the sign shop." I was *there*. I was me.

And amazingly, almost as if angels had indeed been involved, I was competent. Whatever I touched worked out just fine. I knew instinctively what "ASAP" must mean and what, if anything, to do about it. All my work was on time, never mislaid, never misspelled. We had an enormous paper-cutter, suitable for beheading anything smaller than a cow, with a massive blade you swung down with a deep, clean, scrunch that sliced a straight line through a stack of cardboard. Miss Turbett, a dithering person of unspecified duties, cut off the first joint of her thumb with it and bled all over the day's work, but I didn't.

I was praised, often with mild astonishment, as if my bosses could see back through my competence to the clumsy child stumbling around the volleyball court, to Mother's daughter who couldn't drive a nail or draw a flower.

The joy of competence! The praise of a paycheck! Well, it wasn't really a check, since Hecht's assumed that we, the lowliest employees, wouldn't know a bank from a bandicoot and paid us in cash, in a beautiful little white envelope. I can see it now. I can feel it in my fingers, forty-two dollars in bills and the lumps of two quarters, counted in the sharp light over the employees' exit by the parking lot.

Was that payday possibly the happiest day of my life? Happiest days are expected to be weddings or the birth of a first child, though if we could open the fold of Broca and inspect all our days, it might turn out that the happiest was unmarked by any event, just some day so gently ordinary that it slipped past us into oblivion. But I do remember I had to stop and lean against Hecht's wall for a minute, shaken with bliss. In a comic strip, a broad yellow streak of lightning would have touched down and turned me into Captain Marvel. Actually, I think it did.

I could take care of myself.

Almost. Even then, nobody could live for seven days on forty-two fifty, but I could make it through five or six days, then fast, and on the seventh, without the seventeen cents trolley fare, walk twenty-five blocks to work, followed after a decent interval by impecunious boyfriends hoping for lunch. One of them, out of work, moved in with me, which stretched the week's allotment of canned pork-and-beans even thinner, but secretly I was proud that I could afford him, or almost afford him. It was power, glorious power, my drunk-making first.

I put all my belongings in a pillowcase and moved out of the basement room, quietly, by night, and found an apartment in an ancient house in Foggy Bottom, on the first floor, with two big windows and access to a narrow little garden out back. I couldn't afford a telephone, so people who wanted to talk to me had to come knock on the door, and they did. Even Mother came, now that I was respectable, bundling her new baby into the car and driving downtown to see me, sometimes slipping me a little quiet money to help with the rent. Nick came; I have a snapshot here of the two of us wrestling in the little back yard.

I found a cat, a scrappy little black waif, and took her in and bought her real catfood and sheltered her from harm. Sometimes when friends came we sat up all night talking, and in the summer it was so hot we had to turn off the warm lightbulbs and talk by the light of the street lamp outside. And every morning I woke up and absorbed once again in all its glory the thought of my job, my pay. My future, because a person with a job can get other jobs, stride from city to city and job to job, free as a bird and brave as a lion.

I could take care of myself. The knowledge trickled backward in time and consoled the five-year-old insomniac and the nine-year-old who'd gnawed her knuckles to the bone. Maybe I wasn't Winnie and Izzy walking out of occupied China, but at least I was me, walking out of my past. As if I had drowned in a lake and then risen up again from the dark, weedy bottoms to climb the bank, dripping and squinting into the sun.

Virginia Woolf, speaking from a different world, said what we needed, what women needed, was "a room of one's own" and a modest allowance so we wouldn't be distracted by money worries. But under what guarantee? What happens when our benefactor whimsically cancels the lease on our room and cuts off our funds? No, Mrs. Woolf. A job, Mrs. Woolf.

I know people, women, who have grown up and grown old serene in the knowledge that someone else would always take care of them, as was only right and proper; women who have never seen a paycheck, or wanted to. I suppose their lives may have been enviable, but I can't envy them.

My personal life continued muddled, as I fell in and out of love with weak men, men completely unlike Carl, funny, unlucky, unemployable men—"feckless" was Grandmother's word—but whatever goblins pursued me by night, in the mornings I went to work. Work, where I knew what I was doing and did it easily and well, and got paid. Where I found friends, and made them laugh. Where I could take care of myself.

And so I lived happily ever after.

THAT'S ALL?

A voice halfway between Saint Peter and Portnoy's psychiatrist says, *That was it? That's all?*

It isn't enough?

After all that, after reading clear through The Education of Henry Adams, *you got an entry-level job in a department store?*

What did you expect? The Prince of Wales?

We were waiting for you to be a famous writer.

But I am a writer. Not a famous writer, just a plain writer. I've managed to earn a living writing, one thing or another, all my life. That's what I wanted.

We don't see you on television panels, discussing some major award you've won. We don't read essays about you in the New York Review of Books. *You aren't even poet in residence at some nice little college, with students sitting at your feet.*

Hey. Some people like what I write. People call me late at night from places like San Diego and Salt Lake City to say they're loving something I wrote. Once I had a letter from a man dying in a hospital and he said he only hoped he'd live long enough to read my next book. What more do you want? In dreams, though, I find myself back in those offices, in some scroungy little ad agency, clowning around and cracking up the layout artists. Or maybe in a sound studio, coaching an actor in a radio spot for something dumb, like kitchen cupboards, and he has to keep doing it over because we can't stop giggling. The scruffy world of small-time advertising where the creatives, inadequately restrained by the suits, relive their grade-school

307

days as they should have been and throw erasers and stick up silly signs. And get paid for it, however modestly, so they never have to ask Carl for a nickel or shoplift paperbacks.

But you never even made money in advertising. Actual money. Never even got to New York, to the big time.

My career goal was to stay unimportant. Underpaid. Fancy-free. If you're seriously badly paid, you never get fired and you can get away with murder. And I had children, and husbands, and the writing I always did late at night when the children were in bed and the dishes washed. Made brazen by my job, I wrote stories and essays for magazines, and then tackled whole books. A competitive job, a New York job, that was the last thing I needed. I have a T-shirt that says WILL WRITE FOR FOOD. That's me. Rich isn't me. Frankly—not that I'd know—rich sounds boring.

Might you have been a famous writer if you'd gone to college?

Maybe. Famous writers usually go. You read the interviews, they all went to college with other famous writers, people who could write blurbs for them later, and they had professors who sent them along to writing schools, where they met people with contacts in publishing, and so forth and so on. I suppose I could have had novels published instead of rotting in boxes in the basement. You need clout to get novels published. I never knew anyone important. I still don't. It doesn't matter. I've had fun always.

Well. Moving along. What would you call the high point of your career? Not to infer that the—

Imply.

Pardon?

Imply. Not infer.

Not to say that the high point of your career isn't yet to come, of course, but so far. That first short story you sold to McCall's *when you were twenty-three? The play that finally got produced? First book contract?*

I already told you. That first pay envelope from the Hecht Company, when I was eighteen.

Rather an anticlimax, wouldn't you say?

Anticlimax? Safety and freedom in a single envelope? Ticket to travel? Wings on my shoulders, roof over my head, and Carl shriveling in the past like a troll in the sunlight?

Leave me there in the sign shop, cleaning the rubber-cement jar with my thumb. Writing copy for signs selling socks and refrigerators and baby clothes and lamps. Cardboard cup of coffee at my elbow. Free and safe.

And always receding but never quite gone, all those voices, wherever old voices hang around in the back corners of the universe. The patrol boys crying "Off!" and "Off!" from street-corner to street-corner, and two little girls turning a long jump-rope and a third girl jumping, maybe trying for double-Dutch, and all three chanting

> Do you ever think as the years go by
> That some day you will have to die?
> They'll carry you out in a big black box
> And cover you over with dirt and rocks.
> The worms crawl in, the worms crawl out,
> The worms play pinochle on your snout.

And another child, me or someone else, bouncing a tennis ball between her feet over and over and over and singing (we were always singing something)

Who eats up all of his own peanuts
And giveth his neighbor none,
He can't have any of *my* peanuts
When his peanuts are gone.

Very interesting, I'm sure, but I'm afraid we're running out of time.

A NOTE ON THE AUTHOR

Barbara Holland is the author of fourteen books, including *Hail to the Chiefs, They Went Whistling,* and most recently *Gentlemen's Blood.* She lives in Virginia's Blue Ridge Mountains.

A NOTE ON THE TYPE

The text of this book is set in Linotype Sabon, named after the type founder Jacques Sabon. It was designed by Jan Tschichold and jointly developed by Linotype, Monotype, and Stempel, in response to a need for a typeface to be available in identical form for mechanical hot metal composition and hand composition using foundry type.

Tschichold based his design for Sabon roman on a font engraved by Garamond, and Sabon italic on a font by Granjon. It was first used in 1966 and has proved an enduring modern classic.